BETWEEN WORLDS

Pergamon Titles of Related Interest

Christian: BLACK FEMINIST CRITICISM: Perspectives on Black Women Writers

Related Journals

(Free sample copies available upon request.)

ISSUES IN REPRODUCTIVE AND GENETIC
  ENGINEERING: Journal of International Feminist Analysis
WOMEN'S STUDIES INTERNATIONAL FORUM

The ATHENE Series

An International Collection of Feminist Books

General Editors
Gloria Bowles
Renate Klein
Janice Raymond

Consulting Editor
Dale Spender

The Athene Series assumes that all those who are concerned with formulating explanations of the way the world works need to know and appreciate the significance of basic feminist principles.

The growth of feminist research has challenged almost all aspects of social organization in our culture. The Athene Series focuses on the construction of knowledge and the exclusion of women from the process—both as theorists and subjects of study—and offers innovative studies that challenge established theories and research.

On Athene—When Metis, goddess of wisdom who presided over all knowledge was pregnant with Athene, she was swallowed up by Zeus who then gave birth to Athene from his head. The original Athene is thus the parthenogenetic daughter of a strong mother and as the feminist myth goes, at the "third birth" of Athene she stops being Zeus' obedient mouthpiece and returns to her real source: the science and wisdom of womankind.

BETWEEN WORLDS

*Women Writers of
Chinese Ancestry*

Amy Ling

Rockefeller Fellow
Queen's College
City University of New York

PERGAMON PRESS
Member of Maxwell Macmillan Pergamon Publishing Corporation
New York   Oxford   Beijing   Frankfurt   São Paulo   Sydney   Tokyo   Toronto

Pergamon Press Offices:

U.S.A.	Pergamon Press, Inc., Maxwell House, Fairview Park, Elmsford, New York 10523, U.S.A.
U.K.	Pergamon Press plc, Headington Hill Hall, Oxford OX3 0BW, England
PEOPLE'S REPUBLIC OF CHINA	Pergamon Press, 0909 China World Tower, No. 1 Jian Guo Men Wai Avenue, Beijing 100004, People's Republic of China
FEDERAL REPUBLIC OF GERMANY	Pergamon Press GmbH, Hammerweg 6, D-6242 Kronberg, Federal Republic of Germany
BRAZIL	Pergamon Editoria Ltda, Rua Eca de QUEIROS, 346, CEP04011, Pariaiso, São Paulo, Brazil
AUSTRALIA	Pergamon Press Australia Pty Ltd., P.O. Box 544, Potts Point N.S.W. 2011, Australia
JAPAN	Pergamon Press, 8th Floor, Matsuoka Central Building, 1-7-1 Nishishinjuku, Shinjuku-ku, Tokyo 160, Japan
CANADA	Pergamon Press Canada Ltd., Suite 271, 253 College Street, Toronto, Ontario, Canada M5T 1R5

Library of Congress Cataloging in Publication Data

Ling, Amy.
   Between worlds : women writers of Chinese ancestry / by Amy Ling.
— 1st ed.
      p.   cm. — (The Athene series)
   Includes bibliographical references.
   ISBN 0-08-037464-6 (alk. paper) :   — ISBN 0-08-037463-8
(pbk. : alk. paper) :
      1. American literature—Chinese American authors—History and
criticism.   2. American literature—Women authors—History and
criticism.   3. Chinese American women—Intellectual life.
4. Chinese American women in literature.   5. Women and literature—
United States.   6. Chinese Americans in literature.   7. China in
literature.   I. Title.   II. Series.
   PS153.C45L56   1990
   810.9'9287—dc20   89-70968
                                                                      CIP
   Printing: 1 2 3 4 5 6 7 8 9   Year: 0 1 2 3 4 5 6 7 8 9
Printed in the United States of America

The paper used in this publication meets the minimum requirements of American
National Standard for Information Sciences—Permanence of Paper for Printed
Library Materials, ANSI Z39.48-1984

For Mother and Father
and everyone
between worlds.

... "we're caught in between times and in between
worlds . . . There are no uncomplicated Chinese left
anymore."

—Lin Tai-yi, *The Eavesdropper*

Contents

Foreword

As a picture encompasses a universe of cognition, so should words, like stones, embody a permanency of meaning, bear witness to enduring reality. Amy Ling's book is of this quality. It is a breakthrough not only in the sphere of Western studies on the manifold aspects of China, but also a beacon light for Chinese historians. The latter have been so preoccupied with events in China itself and its many metamorphoses, matrix of a world on its own, that they have not come to terms with the *diaspora*, the overseas Chinese, 50 million of them today counting the generations, nor with their contributions both in labor of body and exertion of mind to the world at large.

It was the era of the gun and the dreadnought, of violence in the name of civilization, of that vile and reviled yet inescapable historical phenomenon called colonialism, that produced the diaspora. They left by the thousands, over two centuries, the "bitter strength," the collies, driven by the starvation and misery brought about by colonial plunder, to build the railways of America and Canada, to dig the Panama canal . . . three hundred thousand of them during World War I were required by Great Britain and France to man their man-depleted factories because so many of their own workers died in the trenches of that grotesque conflict.

There were very few women in these first migrations, not only forbidden by the powers that ruled these near-slaves, but also because the Chinese Empire did not want to export its women. But later women did come, in small numbers. And it is marvelous to discover in this book that in the mid-nineteenth century two women, two Eurasians, product of that mingling of two worlds totally opposed to each other, were the first to break the smothering silence that buries all history.

History only is if it is recorded. They wrote history. The story of the diaspora as seen by the women first aware that they were between two worlds, two cultures, women who had to survive in their souls. They were the first to make that imagination leap, discovering what it is to live in perpetual contradiction, between master and slave, the highly valued and the inferior-ized.

Eurasian. So long despised, as I know so well, I who have lived through contempt and contumely, I who continue to fight against an ingrained racism, an unconscious one. For upon those who live between two worlds was imposed a spurious and in the end ignoble choice. "You must be the one or the other." Which implied a service to be performed for one or the other representatives of a culture. I rejected this diminution of the self, this having to survive. *I shall be both.* Amy Ling's book makes me discover, to my delight, that I had predecessors, forebears, women who refused to be any-thing but their own entirety.

What perturbs me about academic studies in the West is an unconscious intellectual *apartheid*, disguised as concern, sometimes benevolent probing, or, what is worse, as objective scholarship. Perhaps this should be matter for a deeper investigation.

Amy Ling's book gives us that family of woman warriors—such a felicitous word, coined by Maxine Hong Kingston—a family to which, I found to my surprise, I too belong by the skin of my teeth.

The woman warriors of Asia are many. Action warriors, like Joan of Arc—and how many of them were burnt at the stake, right up to the nineteenth century, as witches?—and word warriors, those who became literate, and wrote, and survived, and gave us that first aperture into another state of being, another wholeness.

Woman, warring against those man-imposed images, the Suzy Wong, the Madame Butterfly, submissive and delightful sex objects to be used and discarded with hypocritical regret.

Not all the examples, the quotations, in this book are centered on the phenomenon of existing, surviving, and creating between two worlds. Some—and I do not blame them—have achieved fame by pandering to that nostalgic image of a China that never was, save for an infinitesimal number of the elite. But never mind. This is the beginning of a worthwhile exploration, all the more valuable because it shows us the lacunae, the compromises in which some of the writers cited entered, to pander to the superior culture—or so it seemed. These are the books lauded as "authentic," when they are only tasty rehash of what pleases ingrained prejudice. But so many, so many, despite this fear of saying too much too soon, have gone beyond that im-posed, seemingly impenetrable Great Wall of pompous prejudice disguised as academia.

I predict that in the future this book will stand as the first milestone in a long march to understanding our world to be, a world of Eurasians, Eurafri-cans . . . a world where culture is no longer used as a weapon to impose inferiority.

October 1989   *Han Suyin*

Preface

Like Alice Walker, but from a different cultural background, I too have felt compelled to go "in search of our mothers' gardens," and this book is the fruit of my search. Born in Beijing, brought to the United States at age six and educated here from first grade through a PhD in comparative literature, at a time when the "classic" authors were white and nearly all male, I had never encountered in all my reading any Chinese American authors or even Chinese characters, except Bret Harte's "Heathen Chinee." I can still remember the red hot humiliation I experienced as my fourth grade teacher in Mexico, Missouri, read Harte's verse aloud to the class. I remember, too, her sudden embarrassed realization that my perspective on the poem was radically different from hers; she had never had to consider the Chinese perspective before.

Thus, when I first read Maxine Hong Kingston's *A Woman Warrior* and was asked to review Nellie Wong's chapbook of poems, *Dreams From Harrison Railroad Park*, I was thunderstruck. Here were people like me creating moving and artistic literature from our shared Chinese American experience. They expressed the struggle for personal balance that is the experience of every American of dual racial and cultural heritage, but, specifically, they wrote with pride and affirmation out of our common Chinese American background. My reading of these writers followed upon discoveries in the 1960s and 1970s by African American and feminist scholars working to reclaim their literary history, unearthing such neglected masterpieces as Zora Neale Hurston's *Their Eyes Were Watching God* and Charlotte Perkins Gilman's "The Yellow Wallpaper." I wondered if other Chinese women in America had produced memorable literature, if Kingston had had forerunners. If so, who were they? What had they chosen to express of our bicultural experience, and how they had done it?

Thus, I began the journey "in search of [my] mothers' gardens." Walker spoke for me when she wrote in "Saving the Life That is Your Own," "the absence of models, in literature as in life . . . is an occupational hazard for the artist, simply because models in art, in behavior, in growth of spirit and intellect—even if rejected—enrich and enlarge one's view of existence."[1] The lack of models is an occupational as well as an emotional hazard, not only for the artist but for everyone. My search for models, however, brought together the scholarly and the personal in a way that I had never experienced before. I felt a harmony and a wholeness, for each author uncovered, not only enlarged the general field of American literature, as I saw it, but enriched and validated my existence. I learned that I am not a unique and peculiar aberration, that not every Chinese in America is an engineer or a scientist, that others have also gone the literary route. I realized that uncovering these writers and publishing this book may make the way easier for those who follow. Alice Walker has written that black women with calloused hands have appeared to her in dreams to shake her hand and to thank her for speaking for them.[2] I too have seen certain of my writers in dreams, and I have spoken with others in the flesh. As Walker says, "If we kill off the sound of our ancestors, the major portion of us . . . is lost." I hope this book will capture the sound of my ancestors and speak to others yet to come.

In one way, this book is also an answer to my father, who asked me a question that has rankled in me since it was posed, when I was 13 or so. "Why is it," he asked in an innocent tone, "that those who excel in every field, even those considered women's specialties—cooking, hairdressing, fashion design—have always been men?" Virginia Woolf, of course, has answered that question in A Room of One's Own, and others have answered it as well. That men have excelled is not because women are essentially inferior, which he was slyly implying, but that women have been denied the same opportunities as men. They have been kept out of the libraries and in the kitchen "barefoot and pregnant." So it was especially gratifying to me to discover that in this very specialized field, literature written in English by ethnic Chinese and Chinese Eurasians and published in the United States, the women not only outnumber the men but the women's books are more authentic, more numerous, quite simply—better.

It has been an exciting search, a rewarding project. And a difficult one. First, I did not have such common research tools as the card catalogue and the Library of Congress subject heading directory. In 1980, when I began my research, there was no listing for "Chinese American authors." At the Library of Congress, I asked why and was told no one had yet published a book on this subject, and if no book has been written the subject does not exist, as far as their directory is concerned. Under the heading "Asian American literature" I had better luck, for three anthologies had been published: Asian American Authors by Kai-yu Hsu (Boston: Houghton Mifflin, 1972), Aiiieeeee! by Frank Chin et al. (Washington, DC: Howard University Press,

1974), and *Asian American Heritage* by David Wand (New York: Washington Square, 1974). These pioneering collections gave me a start in identifying some authors. Wayne Miller's *Handbook of American Minorities* (New York: NYU Press, 1976) and Priscilla Oaks' *Minority Studies: An Annotated Bibliography* (Boston: G. K. Hall, 1976) were also helpful. Elaine Kim's *Asian American Literature* (Philadelphia: Temple UP, 1982) was published after most of my basic research had been completed, but Professor Kim gave me some names I had not known. A colleague at Rutgers, Marjorie Li, told me about Lin Tai-yi; another colleague, Peter Li, introduced me to Eileen Chang; and one of the authors I interviewed, Diana Chang, lent me her copy of Chuang Hua's *Crossings,* which she had purchased for one dollar at a garage sale. For a while, I combed the National Union Catalogue and scoured the shelves of secondhand bookstores looking for Chinese surnames, which, fortunately, are not numerous, and in this antediluvian manner I discovered Hazel Lin and Janet Lim.

The next problem was obtaining the books. Those with copyrights as recent as five years were already out of print and most were not available in local libraries. It was further disturbing to discover that the books my university library did own, such as Maxine Hong Kingston's *China Men,* were shelved as sociology or, as in the case of Mai-mai Sze's *Echo of a Cry* or Winnifred Eaton's *A Japanese Blossom,* as juvenile books, mainly because they dealt with Asians or were illustrated and had children in them. Again, the very idea of Chinese American *literature* seemed nonexistent to the Library of Congress catalogers who determine a volume's call number. The exception was the Wasson collection at Cornell University, which has nearly all of Winnifred Eaton's novels and from which I obtained many interlibrary loans. I was disappointed to find no listing for the "Asian American Woman's Experience" in the index to Patricia Addis' *Through a Woman's I, An Annotated Bibliography of American Women's Autobiographical Writings 1946–1976* (Metuchen: Scarecrow Press, 1983), though the index identifies "American Indian Women's Experience" and "Black Women's Experience" and though the bibliography itself includes at least five Asian American women writers.

However, the tide is turning. Not only are Asian American writers increasing in number but they are also gaining wider recognition, beginning in the early 1970s when Lawson Fusao Inada's *Before the War: Poems as They Happened* (1971) was published by William Morrow, a major New York press; and Frank Chin's two plays, *Chickencoop Chinaman* (1972) and *The Year of the Dragon* (1974), were produced at New York's American Place Theatre. In 1976, Maxine Hong Kingston's *The Woman Warrior* won the National Book Critics' Circle Award for the year's best work of nonfiction. Her second book, *China Men,* won the American Book Award in 1980. In 1981, the Obie Award for the Best New Play went to David Henry Hwang's

"*F.O.B.*" In 1982, Cathy Song won the Yale Series of Younger Poets competition with *Picture Bride*, published by Yale University Press in 1983. *Island, Poetry and History of Chinese Immigrants on Angel Island 1910–1940*, edited by Him Mark Lai, Genny Lim, and Judy Yung, published in 1980, demonstrated that the literary impulse among Chinese in America has a tradition and a history. In 1982, Elaine Kim's *Asian American Literature*, the first book-length study of the field, proved that the body of work was large and significant enough to merit serious scholarly attention. In 1985, Genny Lim's play "Island" was aired on National Public Television. In 1987, Garrett Hongo's second book of poems, *The River of Heaven*, won the Lamont Poetry Prize of the Academy of American Poets. In 1988, David Henry Hwang's "M. Butterfly" won the Tony Award for Best New Dramatic Play on Broadway. In 1989, Carolyn Lau's book of poetry, *Wode Shuofa*, and Frank Chin's collection of stories, *The Chinaman Pacific and Frisco Railroad Co.*, won the American Book Awards from the Before Columbus Foundation. Our numbers are growing, our voices swelling. We are no longer a silent minority.

I have had several purposes in writing this book. My initial impulse, to uncover literary gems, I later abandoned, for axiology itself, the study of evaluation and value judgments, is now in dispute among literary theoreticians and critics, Barbara Herrnstein Smith and Jane Tompkins among them. Barbara Herrnstein Smith's finely reasoned essay, "Contingencies of Value," among other works, brought to the open the questionable but hitherto unquestioned systems of evaluation within the academy, among critics, reviewers, publishers, and librarians governing notions of "classic," canonical, or Great Literature. She calls into question the assumptions that "objectivity" governs the evaluator and that "universality" is a gauge of "quality."[3] Jane Tompkins, in reexamining *Uncle Tom's Cabin*, asks her reader "to set aside some familiar categories for evaluating fiction—stylistic intricacy, psychological subtlety, epistemological complexity." She wants us to see the texts she examines "not as an artifice of eternity answerable to certain formal criteria . . . but as a political enterprise . . . that both codifies and attempts to mold the values of its time."[4] Tompkins' request for suspension of the "familiar categories" for evaluating texts is particularly pertinent since these conventional criteria are not always applicable to the writers of my study. Without understanding the social and historical contexts of these authors' work, full comprehension and appreciation would not be possible, and judgment without full comprehension is useless.

And yet, so often the mistaken attitude prevails: if a writer falls into oblivion it must be because s/he was unworthy, and therefore fully deserving of oblivion, for surely, if a writer is "truly outstanding," this greatness cannot help but be apparent and "will stand the test of time," as cream rises to the top. But such an attitude does not take into consideration fluctuations of taste; personal idiosyncrasies and individual purposes; political and historical conditions; perspectives and proclivities of the scholars and critics who keep an author's work in the limelight and thus in the canon. That the canon has changed may be readily seen by perusing the table of contents of literary anthologies over an extended period.

Thus, fully aware of my personal interest in the subject and equally aware that this project had never before been undertaken, yet was worthy of the undertaking, I plunged in. Setting myself a narrow focus, I have attempted, nonetheless, to be as comprehensive as possible. This book, then, is an introduction, and a history, as well as my own readings of the full-length prose narratives (autobiographies, memoirs, fictionalized memoirs, and novels) written in English and published in the United States by women of Chinese or partial Chinese ancestry. I have arranged my material roughly in chronological and thematic order to give my readers a sense of the length and breadth of the tradition. The diversity of their themes has been great, yet all the writers have obviously been conscious of their difference in a white society, a society whose attitude towards them as "other" has fluctuated depending on political circumstances. How each author has reacted to this consciousness of difference, to the between-world condition, and to the political and social environment around her is my major unifying theme.

My purpose in writing this book has been to show off the flowers in my mother's garden. I want to put these writers on the scholarly map, to give them a heading in the Library of Congress Subject Catalogue, to validate their existence and their work, to retrieve them from oblivion. With this study, I hope that other women like me will not grow up without models, in ignorance of our own history. Among these writers and their books, I hope such readers will find a source of inspiration and of communal and personal pride. Women and readers from other bi- and multicultural backgrounds will understand much in this book, for the experience of marginalization and the need for self-affirmation is common to us all. And for those who are neither Chinese American, bicultural, or female, I know that the kind of curiosity, openness, and stretching that leads such readers to investigate the experience of the Other will bring its own reward.

Acknowledgments

I want to thank all who helped in the creation of this book: Katharine Newman, who pointed me down the road of ethnic literature, read an early draft of this manuscript, and generously gave me invaluable criticism and encouragement; Eleanor Withington, my composition professor from freshman days at Queens College and a loyal friend ever since; Elaine Kim, Abena Busia, and Shirley Lim, who helped me sharpen some fuzzy thinking; Gelston Hinds, Sr., who advised me to take a less defensive tone; Hilary Hinds and Waichee Dimock, who urged me to keep writing; Linda Ching Sledge and Laura Bromley for continuous sympathy and reassurance; Paul G. Rooney, L. Charles Laferrière, and Eileen V. Lewis, descendents of the Eaton family, who generously provided me with family anecdotes, newspaper clippings, and photographs; James Doyle, who shared his research on Edith Eaton's early Canadian publications and her interactions with her brother-in-law Walter Blackburn Harte; Silvia Xavier for her careful reading and thoughtful suggestions; Han Suyin for her interest, encouragement, and generosity in writing a foreword; and my editor, Gloria Bowles, for her critical acumen and faith in the project.

My father's question: "Why are men best in everything?" challenged me to prove him wrong. My mother's life as a Chinese child adopted by an unmarried American missionary nurse to China gave me the unifying theme. Without my husband, Gelston Hinds, Jr., whose love and unfailing belief in me and in this work took the form of oceans of babysitting and seas of pep talks, and without the understanding of my children, Arthur and Catherine, that Mommy at times had to work instead of play with them, this book would never have been launched. I thank them all for their assistance and encouragement in this project, but I must lay claim myself to the blemishes that still remain.

Chapter 1

Writing As Rebellion: Historical and Contextual Backgrounds

In many ways writing is the act of saying I, of imposing oneself upon other people, of saying *listen to me, see it my way, change your mind*. It's an aggressive, even a hostile act.

—Joan Didion, "Why I Write"[1]

Ladies of the diplomatic corps do not write books. The set in which I lived considered writing an unwomanly occupation, destructive of one's moral character, like acting.

—Han Suyin, "Foreword" to *Destination Chungking*[2]

A woman without talent is a woman of virtue.
It is more profitable to raise geese than daughters.

—Traditional Chinese Proverbs

1. WOMEN IN CHINESE TRADITION AND HISTORY

For women of Chinese ancestry, perhaps even more than for Joan Didion, writing is not only an act of self-assertion but an act of defiance against the weight of historical and societal injunctions. Historically, the Chinese have assigned their women to an inferior and even expendable status, as exemplified in the two traditional Chinese proverbs cited above, in Han Suyin's remarks, and in the practices of footbinding, concubinage, female slavery, and female infanticide, to cite only a few examples. In the early dawn of history, as Julia Kristeva suggests in *About Chinese Women*, Chinese society may have been matrilineal, but by the first century B.C., using as evidence the ancient classic, *The Book of Songs*, whose datable poems range from 800

1

to 600 B.C., patriarchal power already had been long established and women were being trained from birth for an inferior place.

One poem from *The Book of Songs* presents the sharply contrasting receptions and expectations for male and female offspring beginning at birth. The poem begins with good wishes to the lord and then a description of the construction of a sturdy house for him. The lord sleeps in his house and dreams of black bears, brown bears, and of snakes, and the diviner interprets this dream:

'Black bears and brown
Mean men-children.

Snakes and serpents
Mean girl-children.'

So he bears a son,
And puts him to sleep upon a bed,
Clothes him in robes,
Gives him a jade sceptre to play with.
The child's howling is very lusty;
In red greaves shall he flare,
Be lord and king of house and home.

Then he bears a daughter,
And puts her upon the ground,
Clothes her in swaddling-clothes,
Gives her a loom-whorl to play with.
For her no decorations, no emblems;
Her only care, the wine and the food,
And how to give no trouble to father and mother.[3]

The association of boys with the powerful bear and of girls with the slithery, lowly snake sets into immediate relief their relative values in the society as well as describing, metaphorically, what the author takes as their fundamental natures. The preferential treatment for the boy and the infinitely higher expectations for his lordly future compared to the humble treatment and low expectations for girls ensure that the latter will know and be conditioned from birth to their inferior place.

A second poem from *The Book of Songs*, part of a general lament, makes a very pointed complaint about adult female behavior:

A clever man builds a city
A clever woman lays one low;
With all her qualifications, that clever woman
Is but an ill-omened bird.
A woman with a long tongue
Is a flight of steps leading to calamity;
For disorder does not come from heaven,
But is brought about by women.
Among those who cannot be trained or taught

Are women and eunuchs.

Given the sexual discrimination advocated by the first poem, the second poem would be its natural outcome; if women could not be a respected part of the social structure, it was hardly in their interests to help maintain it, especially if such maintenance was at their own expense. One might well say that the second author was only reaping the fruits of the seeds sown by the first, for a child trained to believe herself inferior could well grow into a frustrated, destructive adult.

Confucius (551–479 B.C.) wrote very little about women, but his classification of women with slaves and small humans ("hsiao ren") so clearly revealed his attitude that he has been called an "eater of women."[4] About their education, he did write, "The aim of female education is perfect submission, not cultivation and development of the mind."[5] His well-regulated, hierarchical state depended on the maintenance of three principle bonds of loyalty and subordination, that of minister to prince, son to father, and wife to husband.[6] His followers in later periods were more explicit in their insistence on the inferiority and repression of women. Here are the words of Yang Chen (d. A.D. 124):

> If women are given work that requires contact with the outside, they will sow disorder and confusion throughout the Empire . . . The Book of Documents warns us against the hen who announces the dawn in place of the rooster . . . Women must not be allowed to participate in the affairs of the government.

and Han Shu:

> When a newborn baby comes into the world, if it's a boy as strong as a wolf, his parents are still afraid that he might be too weak; whereas if it's a girl as sweet and as gentle as a little mouse, her parents still fear she might be too strong.

and Sima Guang of the Sung Dynasty:

> Give a woman an education and all you will get from her is boredom and complaints.[7]

In the first century A.D., a code governing the behavior and training of women, called the Three Obediences and Four Virtues, was promulgated by imperial decree throughout China and remained continuously effective, helping to maintain patriarchal power, until the early twentieth century.[8] The Three Obediences enjoined a woman to obey her father before marriage, her husband after marriage, and her eldest son after her husband's death. The Four Virtues decreed that she be chaste; her conversation courteous and not gossipy; her deportment graceful but not extravagant; her leisure spent in perfecting needlework and tapestry for beautifying the home. The authorship of this oppressive code has been attributed to Ban Tso (A.D. 42?–A.D. 115?), a highly educated woman about whom we shall have more to say later.

Until the practice was forbidden by imperial edict in the eighteenth century, Chinese wives were encouraged to commit suicide after their husbands' death. When a widow expressed such a desire, her family would construct a platform and invite family and friends to witness her hanging. Afterwards, the family would erect a stone arch to commemorate her heroism and to inspire other women to follow her example.[9] In 1661, when Ho Chien-min, the first Manchu emperor, died, more than 30 palace women were slain and buried with him.[10] Thus, China can boast more monuments to women than any other nation; however, the valorous acts commemorated by these monuments are not achievements in science, art, or politics but the act of suicide, for women were taught that "after their husbands died they had no right to live."[11]

And yet, though the subjugation of Chinese women has been oft proclaimed and compliant women much admired, some exceptions and rebels exist. One such exception is the elderly mother. As totally as the young woman is subjected to the will of men, so the older woman, specifically the mother of married sons, may in practice be the most powerful person in a multigenerational household. She has been described as "a complete autocrat, with almost final authority over her sons, daughters-in-law, servants, relatives, everybody except her husband, who is usually absent on his business. Her old age is a complete reversal of the restraint and discipline of her youth."[12]

Throughout China's 5,000-year history, only two exceptional women—Wu Chao (A.D. 624–705)[13] and Tzu Hsi (1835–1908)—managed to attain and, even more surprisingly, maintain the most powerful position in the land: Empress and sole ruler of China. Empress Wu ruled from 655 until her death and instituted a number of innovations, including the system of competitive examinations for civil servants, which remained in place for nearly 1,000 years, new guidelines for personal surnames, and changes in the administrative structure. She even invented 19 new written characters (Kristeva, 87). Tzu Hsi sat on China's golden dragon throne from 1875 until 1908, a time of great turmoil in China created in large part by military, political, and economic aggression from West European nations. The bravery of three legendary Chinese women of the Warring States period and the Han Dynasty is preserved in Kuo Mo-jo's play The Three Rebellious Females, and a woman's military prowess in "Magnolia Lay," the popular ballad that tells the story of Hua Mulan (420–588) (Kingston's woman warrior), who, disguised as a man, rode into battle in the place of her elderly father and fought for 12 years before returning home and resuming her woman's role.

In Chinese literature, women writers were few, but one poet stands far above the others: Li Qingzhao (1081–1141). Both classical and modern critics have placed her among the greatest Chinese writers, and Kristeva writes that she is "perhaps among the greatest, not only in China, but in the literature of the entire world" (90). Her poetry went through two phases. The first, irregular in form and personal in subject matter, was characterized by a rare musicality and metaphors from the natural world to present psychological and emotional states. The poetry of her second phase, classical in form and public in subject, dealt with national themes of serious social concern.

And, finally, ironically, the woman credited with writing the oppressive code of Three Obediences and Four Virtues did not herself follow it. Ban Tso (A.D. 42?–115?), daughter of a prominent and scholarly general, was taught to read and write, accomplishments generally considered unnecessary for a girl. Married at an early age, she was almost immediately widowed, but instead of suicide, she chose to concentrate on her studies. The fame of her erudition reaching the emperor, she was invited to the palace to tutor the empress. There, she was elevated, even above male scholars, to the highest honor. When the emperor asked her to write a code of behavior for women, she produced a book called *Nujie*, "The Precepts for Women," which has been reduced to the Three Obediences and Four Virtues noted above. The following is a portion of her original text, in translation:

> In truth, as far as knowledge goes, a woman need not be extraordinarily intelligent. As for her speech, it need not be terribly clever. As for her appearance, it need not be beautiful or elegant; and as for her talents they need only be average . . . This is why the *Nuxian* says, "If a wife is like a shadow or an echo, how can you fail to praise her?" (Kristeva, 85)

Ban Tso's tone and negative phrasing softens the impact of the ideas she expresses. "A woman need not be extraordinarily intelligent" [to get by in this patriarchal society] is quite different from the Confucian edict that "the aim of female education is perfect submission." The popular reduction of her precepts into the positively stated Three Obediences and Four Virtues is thus not quite just to Ban Tso. Nonetheless, her ideas greatly pleased the emperor and the Code was decreed throughout the land. Ban Tso continued to be honored at court. When her father died, she took over the writing of the history of China that he had left unfinished, working in the imperial library until the history was completed. She died at the age of 70.[14]

Why a woman would write precepts that could be made so oppressive to women, and why, though educated herself, she did not overtly advocate education for other women, my primary source, Helena Kuo, could not answer, though she speculated on it. Kuo mused that perhaps the emperor was the actual author of the code, but to sugarcoat the pill he put a woman's name on it. Another possibility is that Ban Tso, heaped with honors from the highest male authorities in her life, identified with the patriarchy. Since she herself had always been the exception to the rule, never bound by the customs that bound other women, she merely wrote down what had been common practice for the ordinary woman. The code for women did not originate with her; she only recorded what she saw, what had already occurred, for her great intellectual passion was history. Whatever the case, Ban Tso achieved personal distinction unusual to one of her sex even as she laid a heavy yoke on the shoulders of her sisters.

2. WINDS OF CHANGE

From the mid-nineteenth century through the mid-twentieth century, China underwent a series of monumental revolutions that shook her very foundations and, with incredible speed, overturned centuries-old feudal structures. China's contact with the West—with Christian missionaries in large numbers, with modern technology and science, with democratic and egalitarian philosophies—was a catalyst for what some scholars regard as a 100-year revolution beginning with the Taiping Rebellion, carried forward by the establishment of a Republic in 1911–1912, led by western-educated Dr. Sun Yat-sen, and culminating in the Communist victory in 1949. The displacement of the emperor in 1911, the dissolution of his absolute authority at the state level, was accompanied by a displacement of patriarchal authority on the familial level. The Confucian bonds of loyalty and obligation broke their hold, for if a man no longer had to obey his emperor or prince, a woman no longer had to obey her man (or men). For traditionalists, these were earth-shattering reversals; for modernists, the changes meant exhilarating liberation. Furthermore, the overthrow of the emperor was not only a political act but an act of ethnic pride, for the emperor was a Manchu, and the majority of Chinese people are Hans. (The Chinese regard the entire Ch'ing Dynasty (1644–1911) as a government by foreigners.) Partly as a result of Christian missionary activity and partly because the time was ripe for change, Chinese girls began to be educated outside the home and these educated women became teachers and journalists, soldiers and revolutionaries. The liberating winds of revolution and patriotism, combined with the persistent tradition of the woman rebel and warrior, inspired Chinese women of this period to go so far as to become anarchists and assassins. Women participated in the struggle to overthrow the Ch'ing Dynasty by serving in the Women's National Army, the Women's Dare-to-Die Corps, and the Women's Assassination Corps. After the establishment of the Republic in 1911, women could then turn to the solution of their own problems, and women armies became transformed into women's suffrage societies.

In 1912, representatives from various women's groups from 18 provinces met in Nanking to organize an overall coordinating body and to draft a petition to present to the First National Legislature, then about to convene to draft a constitution. The petition urged equal rights for men and women, university education for women, and reform in family customs, namely, monogamy, prohibition of commerce in women, and freely contracted marriages. However, when the Legislature's Provisional Constitution was made public on May 11, 1912, it did not include a clause guaranteeing sexual equality. The women then resubmitted the petition to the new president, Dr. Sun Yat-sen. Though sympathetic, Dr. Sun was unable to change the constitution. The women then reacted with passion: they "burst into an uproarous demonstration before the legislators." Overnight they recruited supporters and "the next day stormed the Legislature, smashing windows and trampling the military guard." According to historian Roxane Witke, this "outbreak of female violence rocked the entire nation, to say nothing of the foreign ministries . . . shaken by oriental shades of the Parliament-storming London Suffragettes."[15] Kristeva, too, was surprised by this impassioned behavior, and her tone betrays a certain condescension: "The eyes of China—and of the West as well—open wide in astonishment: no one would have expected this of Oriental suffragettes. Now their rage has made them exist in the eyes of the world. Their example is followed throughout the country and similar petitions are brought before the legislative bodies of several provinces, beginning with Jiangsu."[16]

Some concessions were obtained. In the southern province of Guangdung (Canton), women secured a limited franchise and began to build support by electing women representatives to the legislative assembly. But when Sun Yat-sen resigned from the presidency and strongman Yuan Shih-kai tried to reestablish an imperial form of government, women again joined the army, resorting once more to military means to achieve political power. Astutely, they adjusted their methods to match the methods of those in power.

Throughout the era of the liberal May Fourth Movement, from 1917–1921, Chinese feminism again crested in a second wave. In 1919, women students were admitted for the first time to the University of Beijing, and women's rights organizations swelled in numbers, often with men members in the majority; for example, men made up the membership of two-thirds of the Beijing Alliance for Women's Rights.

In 1919, the young Mao Tse-tung added his voice to the struggle for women's rights. Mao, then editor of the *Hsiang River Review*, a radical publication, wrote a series of articles denouncing the Confucian traditions that led to the suicide of a Miss Chao Feng-lin, who chose to slit her throat in her bridal chair enroute to the home of the groom rather than to marry the man selected by her parents. Though Miss Chao's situation and her solution were commonplace, Mao used her case to raise the consciousness of the public to the wrong done the young woman. Mao himself, at age 13, had fought against an arranged marriage by threatening suicide and finally running away from home before his Confucian father relented. Directly countering Confucius' classification of women as "hsiao ren" (inferior or small human beings), Mao called women "ren" (human beings): "As we are all human beings, why not grant us all suffrage? And as we are all human beings, why not allow us to mix freely with one another?"[17] Today, these remarks seem nothing more than common sense, but in China in 1919 they were revolutionary ideas that threatened the status quo, and Mao's journal was suppressed by a Hunan warlord after only five issues. Again using logic and common sense, Mao boldly attacked the patriarchal requirement of female chastity in words that today still have a radical ring even in the "enlightened West": "What sort of chastity is this, completely confined to women with shrines for female martyrs everywhere? Where are the shrines for chaste boys?" (Witke, 14). For Mao, oppressive society was evil, the individual victim good; instead of killing herself, Miss Chao should have struggled against parental tyranny and worked to reform society.

In 1920, Chinese women sent a delegation to the International Council of Suffragettes in Switzerland; in 1921, the Hunan Women's Alliance secured for women in Hunan the right to vote and be elected to office. In 1934, the Chinese Communist Party advocated marriage reforms, including what is today still a radical clause: the elimination of the distinction between legitimate and illegitimate children. And in 1951, the Congress of the Peoples' Republic of China passed a marriage law whose first article is a model of equity:

> The arbitrary and compulsory feudal marriage system, which is based on the superiority of men over women, and which ignores the interests of children, is abolished. The "New Democratic Marriage System," based on free choice of partners, on monogamy, on equal rights for both sexes and on protection of the lawful interests of women and children, shall be put into effect. (Kristeva, 130)

This 1951 Marriage Law provides for the following rights:

1. A woman may retain her maiden name after marriage;
2. Her children may take her name rather than her husband's;
3. A man cannot apply for divorce during his wife's pregnancy and then not until the child is one year old;
4. A woman may apply for divorce at any time;
5. Divorce is granted immediately when both parties consent;
6. After divorce, the mother has custody of a nursing child; if the father protests, a decision is made in the best interest of the child;
7. The wife's work in the home is equal to the husband's work outside;
8. The wife is entitled to an equal share of the family property.

But despite the high promises of this legal document, a gap remains between the law and actual practices in Communist China. Apart from the women married to prominent leaders, like Chiang Ching (Mao's third wife) and Deng Ying-chao (wife of Chou En-lai), few women have independently achieved positions of real power and influence. The most notable woman revolutionary of the 1920s, Xiang Jingyu, first head of the Women's Department, was executed by the Kuomintang in 1928. A modern-day Hua Mulan,

Kuo Chung-jing, disguised herself as a man and fought in the Peoples' Liberation Army; she rose in the ranks and was given the army's highest award, "distinguished serviceman." When wounded, her sex was discovered in the army hospital, and her explanation was that she had hidden her sex to be able to fight at the front. Upon recovery, she was assigned to a more appropriate post in the army's public health section, with other women.[18]

Soong Ching-ling (Madame Sun Yat-sen), a staunch supporter of the Communist government, in an article for the *Peking Review* (February 11, 1972), admitted that women's liberation in China still had much to accomplish:

> If we ask, however, whether the Women's Liberation Movement in China has come to its end, the answer is definitely no.

> It is true that the landlord system has been abolished for nearly twenty years, but much of the feudal patriarchal ideology still prevails among the peasants, or rather, farmers. This ideology still does yield mischievous things in the rural places and some of the small towns. Only when the feudal and patriarchal ideology is eradicated can we expect sexual equality to be fully established.[19]

Though China may have taken great leaps forward in official statutes and public pronouncements concerning women, nonetheless, in practice, backed by centuries of history and tradition, the old ways die hard. Moreover, Chinese who have immigrated to other countries, whether motivated by homesickness, alienation, or persecution, often hold tightly to what they have brought from the Old Country; thus, customs and attitudes that may have altered or disappeared in the mother country may still be continued almost unchanged in isolated enclaves abroad. And young Chinese women today—even (or perhaps particularly) those living half a globe away from China—are still haunted by the misogynist proverbs and attitudes of generations past.

3. CHINESE WOMEN IN AMERICA

Initially, Chinese women in America were a rarity; in fact, they were such an exotic curiosity that money could be made by simply putting them on display. Afong Moy was one of these "displays" and was reportedly the first Chinese woman to come to America. She "caused a sensation in New York" in 1834 by just sitting "amidst the exotic Chinese trappings in vogue at that time."[20] She was followed by others, most notably Pwan-Yekoo, age 17, whom Barnum's touring Chinese Museum billed as "the Chinese belle, with her Chinese suite of attendants, [who] is drawing all Broadway to the Chinese collection. She is so pretty, so arch, so lively, and so graceful, while her minute feet (2½ inches) are wondrous!" (Yung, 17).

In contrast to this effusive and sensationalist praise, the author of a later article in *Harper's Weekly* January 30, 1858, had quite the opposite view of

Chinese women: "I defy any but the most catholic women-worshippers to admire the women of Southern China. The taste for the baboon-like faces of Hong Kong women is, I fancy, like that for mangoes, an acquired one. I have learned to like mangoes; but my tailor's wife [who is Chinese] still excites in me only unmitigated disgust" (Yung, 17).

Apparently, in judging Chinese women, Americans were divided into two extreme camps: one cloyingly sweet, the other overly sour—both unrealistic and based on fixed concepts within the perceiver's head.

When Chinese men traveled to the States—first enticed by the discovery of gold in California in the 1850s, by western railroad construction bosses desperate for manpower in the 1860s, and by sugar planters in Hawaii from 1851–1884—they customarily left their women at home because marriage before departure was thought to ensure the traveler's return; furthermore, the wife's place was to serve her parents-in-law, and the journey was believed to be too dangerous for women. But there were two nonconformists who braved the journey and became the first Chinese women to immigrate to the United States; they present an interesting contrast, for one was a domestic servant, the other a prostitute.

The first Chinese woman immigrant was Marie Seise, who debarked in San Francisco from the *Eagle* in February 1848 with the Charles V. Gillespie household. She was one of three Chinese servants; the other two were men. At an early age, she had run away from home in Guangzhou (Canton) to avoid being sold by her family as a slave. She found work for a Portuguese family in Macao, and adopted their dress and their Roman Catholic religion. Later, she married a Portuguese sailor, who abandoned her shortly thereafter. She then found a position with an American family, who, in 1837, took her to what were then called the Sandwich Islands, now Hawaii. Six years later, she returned to China, and in 1848 recrossed the Pacific with the Gillespie family to settle in San Francisco. Her story may be found at the Trinity Episcopal Church in the records of Bishop Ingraham, who baptized her in 1854.[21]

The second Chinese woman to immigrate to the United States was Ah Choi, who arrived in San Francisco late in 1848 or early 1849. She was a prostitute, a free agent, and not only popular but enterprising. Within two years of her arrival, she was the owner of a brothel. She charged one ounce of gold (then $16) per visit and had a flourishing business.[22]

These first two Chinese women to immigrate to the United States—the servant and the prostitute—neatly fit the stereotypes of the Chinese, or Asian, woman (for distinctions among Asians by Caucasians are rare), that are widely held in the West. To stereotype, G. W. Allport in his classic study *The Nature of Prejudice* tells us, is to place a newly encountered entity into a preestablished category to save oneself the effort and time in getting to know this entity and in having to think about it. To stereotype is to shortcut thought, an economy measure we all take. However, not to allow facts to change the stereotypes we hold is to be prejudiced. Two main stereotypes persist for the Asian woman in America; they are polar extremes, roughly parallel to the whore/madonna or to the "mad woman in the attic"/"angel in the house" dichotomies for white women. At one end of the spectrum is the Dragon Lady, a female counterpart to the diabolical Fu Manchu. With her talon-like six-inch fingernails, her skin-tight satin dress slit to the thigh, she can poison a man as easily as she seductively smiles and puffs on her foot-long cigarette holder. An "Oriental" Circe, she is as desirable as she is dangerous. At the opposite end of the spectrum is the Shy Lotus Blossom or China Doll: demure, diminutive, and deferential. She is modest, tittering behind her delicate ivory hand, eyes downcast, always walking 10 steps behind her man, and, best of all, devoted body and soul to serving him.

Like all stereotypes, these contain a kernel of truth, though Japanese and Chinese cultural traits are jumbled together. The kernel is generally a visible trait—long fingernails, slit dress, smiling behind one's hand. However, these visible cultural signs have been misread. In nineteenth-century China, long fingernails were indeed the fashion, affected by the empress and ladies of high station and considered marks of beauty. As winter tans are coveted in the Western world today because they signify that one can afford to take expensive vacations in warm southern climes while everyone else is confined indoors by the winter cold, so long fingernails in nineteenth-century China indicated that one could afford to hire other peoples' hands and not need to use one's own. In reality, long fingernails, then, were no more a weapon than tans, now, indicate negroid blood. In fact, special jeweled cases were created to protect such nails because, as anyone who has tried to grow long nails knows, they break easily.

The deference to men, the modesty and shyness of the "lotus blossom," are indeed traits historically inculcated in Asian women from girlhood, as we have seen in the historical overview above and particularly persistent among traditionally reared Japanese women even today. However, laughing behind one's hands is not a sign of modesty but of politeness, akin to the Western custom of covering the mouth when coughing or sneezing. In polite society, teeth are not to be displayed; Chinese men, as well as women, still use toothpicks under cover of their hands.

Allport has stated that stereotypes are self-reflexive, telling us more about the person holding the stereotype than the one being stereotyped: "Whether favorable or unfavorable, a stereotype is an exaggerated belief associated with a category. Its function is to justify (rationalize) our conduct in relation to that category."[23] Though little research has been done on the origin of these particular stereotypes, negative images of the Chinese were sent home by Western missionaries attempting to gain support for their "civilizing" cause. However, both the dragon lady and lotus blossom stereotypes have a strongly sexual component, and would seem to point to an origin suggesting a greater intimacy. Using Allport's theory to hypothesize on the particular "self-reflexive" circumstances that spawned the "dragon lady" and "lotus blossom," we may imagine that these two stereotypes were created by Western sailors or soldiers of fortune who had sexual contacts with Chinese women in the early days of trade between Asia and Europe. The dragon lady stereotype may have been the result of a sailor's mishap with an experienced prostitute who robbed him of his entire voyage's wages. His own drunken stupidity and guilt became transferred to her treachery and wiles; therefore, she became the tawny deceiver, he the lily-white victim. The lotus blossom perhaps stemmed from an affair with a docile, even a virginal girl, whom the sailor/soldier seduced and then abandoned, à la Madame Butterfly. With time and distance, her image took on an idealized, romantic aura—particularly if she killed herself. Ah, she was everything a man could desire, but, alas, she had an Asian face, spoke no English, and could never be taken home to mother.

Whatever their origin, these stereotypes were disseminated and perpetuated through the popular media and continue to distort the way in which Asian women are portrayed and perceived in the Western world. In the 1960s, Madame Nhu, the First Lady of Vietnam, was labeled a "Dragon Lady" by the press,[24] and the "classic" dragon lady reemerged in 1985 in Nicholas Meyer's film, "Volunteers," a parody of Peace Corps volunteers and the undefined Asian people who hosted them. The 1950s films, "Teahouse of the August Moon" and "The World of Suzy Wong," combined the dragon lady and shy lotus blossom into a third variant: the prostitute with the heart of a child. As a result of these stereotypes then, Asian women, when powerful, are seen as dangerous and treacherous; and when powerless, as sexual objects and submissive servants not to be taken seriously. The stereotypes continue to serve as blinders for dominant Americans and to stand as barriers to the fullest acceptance and development of Asian American women.

Examples that belie stereotypes are considered aberrations and quickly forgotten. One of these was Sieh King King, the first voice for Chinese women's emancipation in the United States. Sieh King King (Xue Jinqin) was a 16-year-old foreign student at the University of California, called by a Chinese editor "the Joan of Arc of her people," whose impassioned speech delivered on November 2, 1902, before a theatre full of men and women, as reported in the San Francisco Chronicle the day after, "boldly condemned the slave girl system, raged at the horrors of foot-binding, and with all the vehemence of aroused youth, declared that men and women were equal and should enjoy the privileges of equals."[25] Later that evening, undoubtedly as a result of the new ideas she had expressed, women were allowed for the first time to sit down at the same tables as men at a banquet in her honor. Sieh King King's father was an enlightened Tienjing merchant who had hired foreign teachers for his daughter and had imbued her with progressive ideals. A year later, according to historian Judy Yung, she gave another "eloquent and inspiring speech" to an audience of 200 women and again "expounded on the role of Chinese women and the need to abolish outdated Chinese customs." The revolutionary feminist ideas Sieh King King had expressed became a general concern in the Chinese community in America and, as Yung put it, "what she advocated on behalf of Chinese women—unbound feet, equal rights, education, and public participation—remained at the heart of social change for Chinese women for the next three decades."[26]

A foreign student, Sieh King King most likely did not remain in the United States, for the local newspapers did not report on her activities after 1903. Furthermore, the number of immigrant women from China to the United States was extremely small until the mid-twentieth century. In 1852, for example, of the 11,794 Chinese in California only 7 were women. By the 1880s, the ratio of Chinese women to men in the United States was still no greater than 1 to 20.[27] From the late nineteenth century until the middle of the twentieth, harsh laws severely limited the immigration of Chinese, particularly Chinese women. In 1882, the Chinese Exclusion Act, renewed until 1943, prohibited entry into the United States for all Chinese except diplomats, merchants, tourists, teachers, and students. In 1924, Congress passed a special law whose effect was to prohibit all immigration of Chinese women, including wives of American-born Chinese, ostensibly to reduce the number of prostitutes, but actually to prevent proliferation of an undesirable alien race. From 1924 to 1930, when this act was revised, no Chinese women were admitted into the United States.[28] Only after 1943 could Chinese women immigrate more freely, and only after 1954 did their numbers in the United States reach parity with Chinese men.

The majority of Chinese women immigrants to the United States in the late nineteenth century were working class with neither the education nor the leisure to write books; their lives were engulfed by the duties of childbearing, childcare, and the business of earning a living. Contemporary authors have researched and recreated the daily life of these pioneers. Monfoon Leong's unfinished novel Precious Jade,[29] for example, vividly recreates the life of a nineteenth-century Chinese woman in the western United States, whose youth and energies are sapped by the grinding work of her husband's small hand laundry. Ruthann Lum McCunn's Thousand Pieces of Gold[30] is a fictionalized biography of the eventful life of Lalu Nathoy, or Polly Bemis, who as a young woman in 1872 was sold naked on the block in San Francisco to a saloon keeper from Oregon and who ended her life as a respected homesteader on the Salmon River (the River of No Return) in Idaho. Her life bore certain general similarities to that of Negro slave women, but she had neither the time nor the inclination for writing her own story as did ex-slaves Harriet Wilson and Harriet Jacobs. Lalu Nathoy's story remained untold until nearly

100 years later, when McCunn, a former librarian who is herself one-quarter Chinese, researched and reconstructed it.

Thus, through cultural and historical circumstances, the majority of authors in this study are not only foreign-born but also upper- or upper-middle class in background. Because of the immigration restrictions, many come from families in diplomatic circles, often Christian families, who educated daughters as well as sons in Western cultures and languages. The majority are first-generation immigrant women. Some, such as Edith Eaton, Mai-mai Sze, Chuang Hua, and Bette Bao Lord, immigrated as children. Others (Helena Kuo, Hazel Lin, Eileen Chang, Yuan-tsung Chen) immigrated as young adults. One (Han Suyin) maintains a residence in New York where she spends three or four months a year and the rest of the time in other parts of the world. Another (Lin Tai-yi) lived many years in the United States then lived in Hong Kong, but she continued to write in English and has recently returned to the United States. Only 5 (Jade Snow Wong, Virginia Lee, Diana Chang, Maxine Hong Kingston, and Amy Tan) of the 18 authors in this study were born in the United States. One (Winnifred Eaton) was born in Montreal.

Though some readers may consider this group unrepresentative of Chinese Americans or overly narrow in its perspective because of the preponderance of émigrés, we must remember that since racial characteristics have an immediate visual impact, race has always played a more significant role in the lives of minorities in white America than has class. Thus, the experience of an upper-class Chinese émigré in white America is closer to that of a working-class American-born Chinese American than to that of any white person. And, thus, Mai-mai Sze, daughter of Ambassador Alfred Sze, could say to an African American woman whom she had seen snubbed at a lunch counter in Wellesley, Massachusetts, in the 1940s, "We're cause people, whether we like it or not."[31]

In addition to the difficulty of writing in a second language, another handicap peculiar to women in the upper- or upper-middle class, despite their Western education, was social constraint, as expressed by Han Suyin in the foreword to *Destination Chungking;* writing was frowned upon as an activity lacking in respectability. Modesty and reticence were the ideals established for women; writing was extreme egotism, even self-exposure. Therefore, in order for a Chinese immigrant woman to write and publish a book in English, she must be something of a rebel, for writing, an act of rebellion and self-assertion, runs counter to Confucian training. Also she has to possess two basic character traits: an indomitable will and an unshakeable self-confidence. She must also be propelled by the undeniable drive to communicate with the readers and speakers of the dominant language of the society into which she has been transplanted either because of the rightness of her cause or because of the force of her need to express herself.

In addition to nationality or ethnicity, one's sex is a third factor significant to the experience of immigrant and minority groups in the United States. The women of a minority group, whether Asian, African, Indian, or Hispanic, have received a different treatment at the hands of the white majority than have the men of their race, and for this reason their writing, their record of their particular experiences, thoughts, and feelings are separate from those of the men of their ethnic group. Though their men may feel, with resentment, that "the dyad of Asian Woman and Western male [is] . . . the essence of any relationship between East and West,"[32] and though physical beauty may, in individual cases, seem to offset certain liabilities of race, beauty itself is short-lived, and the notice or status gained by it momentary and borrowed. Without doubt, the female sex itself is a liability in any patriarchy, and the ethnic minority female is triply vulnerable: as Chinese in an Euro-American world, as a woman in a Chinese man's world, as a Chinese woman in a white man's world. How these women writers responded to their between-world position and how they manifested this response in their writing will be the subject of this study. And not only do their texts tell us something about individual women of Chinese ancestry, but, as responses to living in the United States, they tell us something about Americans as well, reflecting a portion of American cultural history.

When comparing books written by men of Chinese ancestry and those written by women, I discovered three startling facts: first, women writers have been more numerous; second, women have written more books; and third, women's books have been more authentic, meaning that fewer women have fallen into what I call the alien observer trap. The Chinese as alien observer may be traced back to Oliver Goldsmith's "Letters from a Citizen of the World" (1762), which purported to be written by "Lien Chi Altangi," a Chinese traveler to England; these letters derived their humor and charm from the unexpected and unfamiliar angle of vision given to things familiar to the readers themselves. Since then, Chinese have been asked so often to write their impressions of life in the West that we may call this form a subgenre.

The rationale behind this subgenre is simple: everyone knows that the Chinese come from the other side of the globe and thus do many things in an upside down sort of way—for example, reading books from the back cover to the front, from the right to the left, and up and down on a page; beginning their dinners with a sweet and ending with soup—thus, one can assume that their initial reactions to unfamiliar customs they encounter in the West cannot help but be amusing to the Western reader. The popularity of the series of more than one dozen books published by painter/writer Chiang Yee, from *The Silent Traveler in Lakeland*, (1937) to *The Silent Traveler in San Francisco* (1964), may be attributed in part to this appeal. (Since the Chinese have lost a modicum of their strangeness, the most recent manifestation of the alien observer is now the extraterrestrial, as seen in such television shows as "My Favorite Martian" and "Mork and Mindy," and such films as "The Man Who Fell To Earth" and "Star Man.")

The other side of the "alien observer" was the "tourist guide" role, in which the alien was asked to describe how things are done in his country with the expectation that he would provide titillation by his exotic and quaint revelations. Lee Yan Phou's *When I Was A Boy in China* (Boston: Lothrop, Lee & Shepard Co., 1887), Wu Ting Fang's *America through the Spectacles of an Oriental Diplomat* (New York: Frederick Stokes, 1914), and New Il-Han's *When I Was a Boy in Korea* (Boston: Lothrop, 1928) are representative samples of this genre.

Though a few women have written books that fall into the category of "alien observer" or "tourist guide," there are fewer of this type written by women than by men. Women writers account for most of the novels and the more personal, rather than the official, autobiographies. The very first Asian American fiction writers were women: the Eurasian sisters, Edith Maud Eaton and Winnifred Eaton. Thus, to concentrate on the women writers of Chinese ancestry is not to spotlight a minority within a minority but to focus, in the areas of fiction and autobiography at least, on the most significant texts and writers.

How can we account for this greater productivity among the women and for the greater authenticity of their voices? Restrained by a traditionally oppressive background and blocked by a society holding alien and negative views of her, what would prompt a woman of Chinese ancestry in the United States to draw attention to herself by writing? The answer lies in the very oppression itself. Physicists tell us that every action has its equal and opposite reaction, and this law holds as well in the animate world, where the greater the repression, the greater the force for liberation, or, as Emily Dickinson put it, "A wounded deer leaps highest."[33] In the case of Chinese women, whose repression has been protracted and extreme, the reaction from one who has managed to break free will be strong and vocal. Such a woman is imbued with so intense a sense of her own identity and the validity of her personal experience and perspective that despite, or perhaps more accurately because of, opposition, her perspective must come forth and be expressed. Her expression may fall into one of two types, or, as in the case of poet Li Qingzhao, into a conjunction of the personal and political. Her work may have its source from her own internal and individual well-spring, or a catalyst may come from outside, from a consciousness of social wrongs and injustices to the larger group with which she identifies and from her desire to right wrongs by writing them. In either case, she must have faith in herself—that her words deserve a hearing—and faith in the power of the word, either to recreate her interior world by giving substance to the insubtantial or to move people and create social change, or both.

If it seems incredible that greater oppression can result in greater creativity and productivity, one might, as a useful analogy, think of the damming up of a stream; when one route is cut off, the water finds other channels in which to flow, for flow it must. What Julia Kristeva has noted as an unexpected result of foot-binding seems applicable in the present case as well. Kristeva writes, perhaps somewhat romantically, that along with the suffering of foot-binding comes

> the symbolic premium as well: a sort of superior knowledge, a superior maturity, because it is in her feminine world that the difficulty of the social contract is felt, in all its most painful, impossible, murderous aspects. Thus, the depreciation of woman becomes its own opposite: the refuse of society retains society's secret . . . As if the first archaic matriarchal model had avenged itself on the patriarchy by slipping in under the door and drawing certain advantages from the very oppression itself. (Kristeva, 84)

The same paradoxical principle seems to be at work in the case of these writers; the result of silencing has been stronger voices; out of humiliation and handicap has emerged beauty and strength.

Not only have women of Chinese ancestry in the United States not been entirely silent and demure, but loud and vocal warriors who, like African American women, in the words of Alexis DeVeaux, are "fighting the central oppression of all people of color as well as the oppression of women by men."[34]

This study, then, is a work of what Elaine Showalter has coined "gynocritics," or "the study of women as writers, and its subjects are the history, styles, themes, genres, and structures of writing by women."[35] It is a work of literary archeology, excavating and bringing to light the "word warriors"[36] of Chinese ancestry who have had the courage and rebelliousness to express themselves, despite silencing forces, through the written word, in English, in prose, and in the United States. My purpose in unearthing them, in gathering them together so that their light can shine collectively for the first time, is manifold: to break the old stereotypes of demure lotus blossoms and treacherous dragon ladies, to give young Asian American women much-needed models and a female literary tradition in which they may root themselves, and to contribute to feminist scholarship by retrieving the work of women.

4. CHINESE–AMERICAN
POLITICAL RELATIONS

For the woman of Chinese ancestry in the United States to write, not only must strong internal motivation be present but the external conditions, such as the political climate, must also be favorable if she is to find her voice and if this voice is to be heard. One of the major external conditions affecting the writers of Chinese ancestry in the United States is the social and political climate between the United States and China. The polar opposites displayed in the nineteenth-century statements about Chinese women quoted above from Barnum's and *Harper's Bazaar* and in the stereotypes of the lotus blossom and dragon lady may be seen as well in the relations between the two nations. Throughout America's 200-year history, the attitude of Americans toward China has vacillated dramatically between admiration and contempt; alternately, China has been embraced as an ally and friend, only to be later rejected as a dangerous enemy.

Stuart Creighton Miller, in *The Unwelcome Immigrant: The American Image of the Chinese, 1785–1882*, focuses on the sinophobia during the entire century from the first Sino–American contacts to the passage of the 1882 Chinese Exclusion Act. Miller thoroughly examines the writings by Americans who had first-hand dealings with the Chinese—traders, diplomats, and missionaries. Most of these, with no sense of anthropological relativism, had negative responses to the Chinese. However, Harold Isaacs, covering a longer period in *Scratches on our Minds: American Images of China and India*, and corroborated by another cultural historian, A. T. Steele, traces what seems to be the major characteristic of Sino–American relations: a phenomenon I call the swinging pendulum.

Isaacs calls the eighteenth century the "Age of Respect," when European esteem for things Chinese carried over to the American colonial states. The highly rationalistic philosophy of Confucius accorded well with the principles of the Age of Reason; the Confucian hierarchical social structure, for example, neatly paralleled the image of the Great Chain of Being. And Chinese domestic arts (porcelain, tea, silk) were highly prized by wealthy Europeans and Americans alike. But the next century, particularly the years 1840–1905, Isaacs has called "The Age of Contempt." During this period, Europeans discovered how weak China was and took military and economic advantage of her, forcing opium into her ports, and encroaching on her land by carving out "spheres of influence." As Steele put it, "Although we were vocally idealistic and not active in the scramble for spheres of influence, our behavior otherwise differed little from that of the British or the French or the Russians."[37] In the continental United States, Chinese "coolie" labor on the western railroads and the subsequent fear of the economic threat posed by these "yellow hordes" led to anti-Chinese agitation and legislation.

The next period, 1905–1937 (whose dates I would extend to 1949, given America's friendship toward China throughout World War II and lasting until the Communist victory), Isaacs has called "The Age of Benevolence." This was the period of greater amicability. The Open Door policy stated America's desire to "protect" Chinese territorial integrity. Journalists, businessmen, and missionaries traveled to China in increasing numbers. A Christian convert, Dr. Sun Yat-sen led the revolution that overthrew the Ching Dynasty; Chiang Kai-shek married Soong Meiling, a Wellesley graduate, and both were devout Methodists—these were positive signs from the American perspective. When

Japan invaded China, Madame Chiang made triumphant trips to the United States to appeal in person for American friendship and aid. The pervasive attitude was "The Chinese were, after all, a charming and intelligent people. Peking and Shanghai were great cities. China offered a tremendous market for American manufactures. And so forth."[38] After Pearl Harbor was bombed, in 1941, China became even more firmly an American ally.

Eight years later, however, after the Communist victory, the American government did an about-face, and from 1949 until 1972 China was regarded as an American enemy. Diplomatic relations were severed. China's seeking assistance from Russia in the 1950s only increased her threat as America went through the Cold War period and the McCarthy hearings, a period of paranoia about Communism. Throughout the 1950s and 1960s, China and the United States exchanged increasingly hostile rhetoric and fought on opposing sides of the battle lines in Korea and Viet Nam. With Richard Nixon's visit to Beijing in 1972, however, diplomatic relations between China and the United States were restored, and the pendulum swung back again.

Since then, the United States had assumed once more a positive, almost euphoric attitude: China was embraced a long-lost ally, to counterbalance the power of the USSR, and was seen once more by businessmen as an immense potential market. Chinese acupuncture, martial arts, acrobats, and cuisine have all excited a great deal of interest in the United States, and China has become a fashionable place to visit: films of their trips have been made by movie stars, musicians, fashion designers; television shows have been broadcast from the Great Wall. In 1987, an English producer, an Italian director, and Chinese American actors completed an epic film of the life of China's last emperor, Henry Puyi, a film that won numerous Academy Awards. In 1988, David Henry Hwang's "M. Butterfly" won a Tony Award for Best New Play on Broadway. For the moment at least, China is unmistakably "in." Though the violent dispersal of the student demonstrators in Tiananmen Square on June 4, 1989, has cast a shadow on US–Chinese relations, the restraint and caution of President George Bush's reactions would suggest that the shadow will pass and that, for a president who was once ambassador to China, and who represents business and economic interests, the maintenance of friendly relations between the two nations is likely to have the highest priority.

All these fluctuations on the level of international politics have obviously filtered down to and affected people on an individual level. What is written, what is published, what is read, what makes the best seller lists, what is forgotten, what is rediscovered has much to do with the political, social, and emotional climate of the day. When China and the Chinese are in general disfavor, few are the voices speaking for her. When China is in favor, the voices increase in number and volume, and more attention is paid them. Now seems a particularly propitious time to reexamine the history of writings by people of Chinese ancestry because, at the moment, people in the United States, and in the Western world in general, have the ears to hear.

It is important, also, to examine these writings because, despite the two centuries of Western love for Chinese objects, the reaction to Chinese people living in America has been and continues to be problematic and more often than not negative. To the Western mind, Chinese porcelain, carpets, paintings, antiques, jade carvings, furniture, from the eighteenth century until today, continue to symbolize wealth and elegance. Chinese people, however, are looked upon askance as potential threats, taking too many jobs, winning too many prizes or places in colleges. As Asian Americans are becoming more and more successful, academically and economically, envy and resentment against them is growing proportionally. When resources are believed to be limited, and this seems a perennial fear, the one perceived as the outsider, obviously the nonwhite, is always the resented one, the scapegoat. One may be a descendent of the Chinese laborers who built the transcontinental railroad and thus a sixth-generation American, yet because of her facial features and skin tones she will still be asked what country she is from. Or, one may hold a doctorate and be a professor in a college English department, but still he will be asked where he learned such good English. Moreover, those asking these questions, making the easy assumption that anyone with Asian features must be foreign, have not the slightest awareness of the injury they are inflicting, of the walls they are erecting, but believe, instead, that they are being friendly and hospitable.

Whether recent immigrants or American-born, Chinese in the United States find themselves caught between two worlds. Their facial features proclaim one fact—their Asian ethnicity—but by education, choice, or birth they are American. The racial features that render them immediately visible, by differentiating them from the Caucasian norm, at the same time, paradoxically, render them invisible, in the metaphoric sense that Ralph Ellison used in his novel, *The Invisible Man*. At certain times in history, the racial minority person in the United States has been a nonperson—politically, legally, and socially—and these traditions also die hard.

Racism continues to rear its ugly head, sometimes subtly, sometimes overtly. No one who lives in the United States can be unaware of the differentiation of people along color and ethnic lines. If racist incidents do not occur between whites and people of color, they occur between different minority ethnic groups. Ignorance and fear, the roots of racism, can only be dispelled by knowledge and understanding. And knowing the literature, the record of the history, culture, thoughts, and feelings of a people is a first step towards that critical understanding.

Chapter 2

Pioneers and Paradigms:
The Eaton Sisters

1. SUI SIN FAR AND ONOTO WATANNA: THE HISTORICAL BACKGROUND

The first Asian American writers of fiction were two Eurasian sisters: Edith Maud Eaton (1865–1914)[1], who wrote under the Chinese pseudonym Sui Sin Far, and Winnifred Eaton (1875–1954)[2], who published under the Japanese-sounding name Onoto Watanna. As daughters of a Chinese mother and an English father, neither woman looked particularly Asian; however, when embarking on a literary career, each sister chose to assert an Asian identity. Edith's choice was a revelation of part of her ancestry while Winnifred's was the assumption of a related but different ethnicity. The use of pseudonyms, particularly for nineteenth century women writers, has had a long tradition (such names as George Eliot; Acton, Currer and Ellis Bell; and Fanny Fern come readily to mind). Pseudonyms were generally used as cloaks in which to hide one's true identity; however, the Eaton sisters' pseudonyms were chosen not so much to cloak their English patronym but to assert and expose their Asian ancestry. Both pseudonyms were the means to imply and thus acquire an ethnic authenticity to support writing careers based in large part on ethnic themes. But why one sister so totally embraced her Chinese heritage while the other assumed a Japanese identity is as fascinating a story as the fiction each produced. To understand their choices, we must briefly review some relevant history.

Under the last rulers of the Ch'ing Dynasty, China was weakened by oppressive and venal officials who raised taxes and used public funds for private purposes. Funds allocated for the repair of dikes and dams went into private pockets with the result that more and more floods destroyed the staple rice crops in the south[3]. Monies allocated for the Chinese navy went to the building of a marble boat and other pavilions at the Empress's summer palace outside Beijing. Xenophobia led to a disdain for western technology; internal unrest and "medieval weaponry of bows, arrows, and antiquated cannon" (Chen, 8) made China an easy prey for the imperial aspirations of Western nations possessing gunboats and heavy artillery. As a result of the 1840–1842 war, provoked by Britain, China was forced to open five port cities (Canton, Amoy, Fuzchou, Ningbo, Shanghai) to foreign trade, to cede the island of Hong Kong, and to pay indemnities totaling forty million silver dollars. Britain then flooded the Chinese ports with opium, and other western nations followed England's lead in carving out spheres of influence on the Chinese continent. The Second Opium War (1856–1860) resulted in further indemnities levied on China, tax exemptions for foreigners, and severe crippling of China's economy. All these political and economic disasters in combination with natural disasters (floods and droughts) made emigration an attractive alternative even though it was forbidden by imperial decree until 1894. Since Quangzhou (Canton) was the first Chinese port opened to Western trade, a greater familiarity with foreigners made emigration especially prevalent among the Cantonese.

Thus when gold was discovered in California, and one of the early Gold Rushers, Chang De-ming, amassed a small fortune and wrote home to Quangzhou in 1849 urging his brother to join him, the news spread quickly. The story that gold could simply be picked up in American mountain streams gave the United States its Cantonese nickname *Gam San* or Gold Mountain[4], and was an irresistible attraction. In 1850, 500 Chinese were seeking their fortunes in gold mining; by 1860, of the estimated 83,000 men in the California mines, some 24,000 were Chinese. Their great numbers, high visibility and their tendency to cling to Chinese ways and customs elicited racially based protectionist tendencies among Caucasians, and soon the Chinese were only allowed to work mines that white men had given up as unprofitable. When the patient Chinese continued to extract a profit from these abandoned mines, a special tax was levied solely against them. When Chinese were robbed and even murdered for their findings, many retreated to the cities to do the only work permitted them—the "women's work" of laundry, cooking, and gardening.

Additional Chinese had been lured to the United States by gold in the form of wages when Charles Crocker, in charge of construction, convinced Leland Stanford, president of Central Pacific Railroad Company, that Chinese labor was both efficient and dependable. From 1866 to 1869, between 10,000 to 12,000 Chinese made up ninety percent of the railroad workforce. They laid 1,800 miles of track over the most difficult terrain, dynamiting through the Sierra Nevada mountains, living in tunnels when the snow piled up in 60 foot drifts during the winter of 1865–1866, building bridges over canyons, dying in rock slides and avalanches before the Central Pacific met and joined the Union Pacific on May 10, 1869 in Promontory, Utah. After this heroic work was completed, Chinese men built other railroad lines within California and worked in fishery, canning, and agriculture, reclaiming swamplands to create the fertile San Joaquin valley, successfully drying raisins to establish the raisin industry, creating vineyards, growing vegetables, grain, fruit. But on September 19, 1873, the stock market crashed, and California experienced its first economic depression. Unemployment ran high; a scapegoat was needed.

Anti-Chinese sentiment had been high nearly from the beginning of Chinese immigration, as demonstrated in a series of statutes and resolutions passed at the city and state levels, particularly in California, where most Chinese immigrants landed and remained. Some laws lumped the Chinese with all non-whites, such as the 1849 ruling forbidding any Chinese, African American, or American Indian to give testimony in court against a white man, thus enabling whites to brutalize anyone from these groups without repercussion. But many laws were specifically aimed at harrassing and restricting the Chinese, such as the 1860 law prohibiting "Mongolians" from attending public schools or gaining admission to public hospitals, the 1870 law forbidding the peddling of vegetables hung from shoulder-borne poles (a custom peculiar to the Chinese), the 1875 ordinance requiring all Chinese who were arrested to have their queues cut off, the 1879 law forbidding corporations and municipal works from hiring Chinese and permitting cities to remove Chinese from their boundaries to specified areas—to list only a fraction of these laws. During the depression of the 1870s anti-Chinese sentiment intensified, fanned by Irish agitator Dennis Kearney, who, in 1877, backed by the Anti-Chinese Union and the United Brothers of California, began a series of inflammatory speeches each beginning and ending with "The Chinese must go! They are stealing our jobs!"[5] Though Kearney was jailed when he proposed setting up gallows in vacant lots as a solution to the Chinese problem, the California State Legislature in 1882 supported him to the extent of declaring a legal holiday to facilitate public anti-Chinese demonstrations[6]. Immigration historian, Henry Pratt Fairchild, noted that "the Chinaman became the scapegoat for all the ills that afflicted the . . . community from whatever cause they really arose, and in time, an anti-Chinese declaration came to be essential for the success of any political party or candidate." A special Congressional Committee of 1876, which "came to its task committed to an anti-Chinese conclusion"[7] underscored popular opinion by reporting that the Chinese were "loathsome in their habits . . . and vile in their morals," . . . "They did not assimilate with whites and never could become an integral and homogenous part of the population."[8] (That discriminatory laws prevented Chinese from becoming an integral part of the population was not taken into account.) In 1882 Congress passed the Chinese Exclusion Act, forbidding entry to all Chinese except five classes of people who were admitted in small regulated numbers: tourists, merchants, diplomats, students, and teachers. This law officially confirmed the inferiority and undesirability of the Chinese and seemed to sanction any expressions of hatred so that, particularly in the western states, Chinese were robbed, assaulted, lynched, burned, and entire populations driven out, even murdered with impunity[9]. The voices that spoke out against this trend, like Mark Twain's in *Roughing It*, were few and far between. And China herself, too weak to prevent foreign nations from helping themselves to large portions of her own land, was powerless to protect her nationals abroad.

Japan, on the other hand, after 1854 when Admiral Perry forced open her ports to Western trade, had recognized the significance of modernization and had been rapidly importing scientific, military, and technological experts from the west. By the end of the century, she had successfully embarked on a road toward geographic expansion through military aggression and conquest. The victories of this small island nation against the large continental nations of China in 1895 (after which China ceded Korea and Taiwan to Japan) and Russia in 1905 gained her much respect and admiration throughout the world. Since domestic conditions were stable, few Japanese emigrated to the U.S. before the turn of the century. Therefore, they posed no economic threat and could be admired from a safe distance. In 1907, when Japanese immigration rose to 127,000, the U.S. signed a "Gentleman's Agreement" with Japan calling for voluntary limitation of immigration, in striking contrast to the unilateral Exclusion Act against the Chinese, who were, by clear implication, not "gentlemen." In 1924, a law was passed that has come to be known as the Japanese exclusion act, though it did not mention the Japanese by name but only stated "no alien ineligible to citizenship (naturalization) shall be admitted to the United States" (Garis, 332).

In Edith Eaton's youth and young adulthood, then, the distinction between Chinese and Japanese on the part of white Americans was extremely pronounced, as clearly demonstrated on a personal level in the following passage from her autobiographical essay, "Leaves from the Mental Portfolio of An Eurasian." Edith had just accepted a stenographer's position in an unnamed place, only identified as "a little town away off on the north shore of a big lake" in mid-western United States. She was seated at the dinner table with a number of people including her new employer and her landlady when the following conversation ensued:

> My employer shakes his rugged head. "Somehow or other," says he, "I cannot reconcile myself to the thought that the Chinese are humans like ourselves. They may have immortal souls, but their faces seem to be so utterly devoid of expression that I cannot help but doubt."

"Souls," echoes the town clerk. "Their bodies are enough for me. A Chinaman is, in my eyes, more repulsive than a nigger."

"They always give me such a creepy feeling," puts in the young girl with a laugh.

"I wouldn't have one in my house," declares my landlady.

"Now the Japanese are different altogether. There is something bright and likeable about those men," continues Mr. K.[10]

Ironically, none of these people realized that they had just accepted into their midst a woman who considered herself Chinese. Edith confesses an initial reluctance to speak out:

> a miserable cowardly feeling keeps me silent. I am in a Middle West town. If I declare what I am, every person in the place will hear about it the next day. The population is in the main made up of working folks with strong prejudices against my mother's countrymen. The prospect before me is not an enviable one—if I speak. I have no longer an ambition to die at the stake for the sake of demonstrating the greatness and nobleness of the Chinese people.

Nonetheless, when asked by her employer why she is so silent, she finds the courage to confront the prejudice around her and to reveal her identity, "Mr. K., the Chinese people may have no souls, no expression on their faces, be altogether beyond the pale of civilization, but whatever they are, I want you to understand that I am—I am a Chinese." The other dinner guests are astonished into silence and her employer apologizes for his ignorance and prejudice. For Edith, though speaking up had been an effort, keeping silent was not a viable alternative.

Winnifred, on the other hand, realizing that, though they vilified one and admired the other, most people could not distinguish Chinese from Japanese and since her sister had gone the Chinese route, decided to be the admired kind of "Oriental." Inventing a Japanese-sounding name, Onoto Watanna, she also created an appropriate history, claiming Nagasaki as her birthplace and a Japanese noblewoman for her mother.[11] For the frontispiece of her third novel, *The Wooing of Wistaria* (1902), Winnifred had herself photographed in a kimono with hair piled high in Japanese fashion, standing before a screen painted with wisteria and iris. Decorating the title page, identified as a "Fac-simile of the author's autograph in Japanese," is a reasonable imitation of cursive Japanese writing. We do not know whose idea it was to go to such lengths to authenticate a Japanese identity, but apparently the plan worked. Many readers assumed that Onoto Watanna possessed an insider's knowledge of her subject and were charmed by her novels.

Thus, the social environment into which the Eaton sisters were born presented them with a dilemma to which they reacted in opposing ways. Edith chose to resist the prevailing winds and stand tall against them, like the solid oak tree, a position of courage and integrity. But the very act of standing tall makes one more of a target by giving greater surface resistance to the wind, and if the winds are strong enough, one may be entirely uprooted. Winnifred's choice was to be accommodating and bend with the wind. Ironically, by denying her Chinese affiliation, she was like the pliant, hollow bamboo so admired in China. Bending to the ground may be a humiliating position, but it is not a permanent condition, for such flexibility enables one to rise back to vertical when one is no longer facing the full force of the wind. It is but another method of survival, as African American novelist, Kristin Hunter, noted: "I marvel at the many ways we, as black people, bend but do not break in order to survive."[12]

The separate choices made by the Eaton sisters in the very selection or creation of a pseudonym not only reflected their different personalities and determined the direction and outcome of their careers, but served as paradigms of human behavior under adverse conditions. When something that one is affiliated with is under attack, one can either admit the affiliation, face the enemy, and do battle, or one can hide that affiliation and circumvent the entire issue. One immediately assumes that being open and doing battle is the noble and honorable reaction while hiding the truth is cowardly and dishonorable. However, if the enemy is so numerous and powerful as to make resistance suicidal, how wise is it then to engage in battle? Under these circumstances, doesn't open resistance suddenly appear impractical and unrealistic? Would it not be better for one's cause to resist subversively, to use camouflage and guerilla tactics? These are the knotty questions brought to light when we examine the Eaton sisters' choice of pseudonyms and their subsequent careers. Rather than judge the morality of each sister's actions, we shall examine both their choices as alternate tactics of survival and negotiation within a hostile environment.

2. BIOGRAPHICAL BACKGROUND

The Eaton sisters' parents also had an unusual and romantic history. Their mother, Grace Trepesis (or Trefusius) (1847–1922) was Chinese, abducted from home at age three or four, presumably by circus performers, and later adopted by an English missionary couple who gave her an English education. Their father, Edward Eaton (1838–1915), was an Englishman who in his youth took frequent trips to China to further his father's business. The couple met in Shanghai and married when Grace was sixteen. They then traveled to England, living for several years at the Eaton family estate in Macclesfield, Cheshire, where six children were born, including Edith, their second child and first daughter. Because Edward's parents disapproved of his marriage, the burgeoning family emigrated to America, first living in Hudson City, New York and in 1874 settling in Montreal, Canada. There Winnifred, in 1875, their eighth child, was born. In total, the Eatons had sixteen children, fourteen of whom—five boys and nine girls—survived into adulthood.

With a large family and a small income, derived primarily from Edward's landscape paintings, the family was extremely poor. Winnifred remembered the deprivations and crowding of her childhood home: "Just think, though I was one of fourteen children (two of the original sixteen had died), I can never remember a Christmas when we had a tree! (273)" When she left home and stayed for the first time at a YWCA, she found her room, "genuinely charming," for "at home I slept in a room with four of my little brothers and sisters. . . . I was the one who had to mind the children . . . and I hated and abhorred the work" (Me, 113–4). For a school paper, she once described her concept of hell, which was also a description of her home: "a place full of howling, roaring, fighting, shouting children and babies. It is supreme torture to a sensitive soul to live in such a Bedlam" (Me, 113–4).

Though crowded and poverty-stricken, the Eaton home was hospitable to and encouraging of the development of the arts. In Marion (the biography of Sara, another sister), Winnifred wrote that their mother used to read them Tennyson's Idylls of the King, and the children would act out the characters. The children seemed unusually spirited and talented. Three of them wrote poetry, and both Edith and Winnifred as teenagers began publishing poems and articles in the local papers. One daughter, Grace, became the first Chinese American woman lawyer in Chicago; Sara and Mae became painters; George made a fortune as an inventor, and was an independent contractor for Kodak and General Electric; and Edith and Winnifred were professional writers, both beginning as journalists and then turning to fiction. Edith achieved a moderate success, publishing numerous short stories and articles but only one volume of her collected stories. She reportedly had a novel in manuscript being considered at a publisher that was lost after her death. Winnifred's rise was meteoric, with her first novel attracting wide notice and her second novel a best-seller undergoing several editions, many foreign-language translations, and an adaptation into a Broadway play[13]. Her nearly two dozen books, the majority of which were best-sellers, were published by major houses, most often Harpers, and given exquisite treatment, printed on pre-decorated paper with full-color illustrations by Japanese artists. The popularity of her work led to a position as chief scenarist for Universal Studios in Hollywood where she worked from 1924–1931.

As the eldest daughter of the family, Edith took her position very seriously, assuming many of the parental responsibilities. She is reported to have sat up at night waiting for siblings who had gone out, even her older brother, and questioning them as to their whereabouts upon their return. Sara, four years her junior, remembered Edith with some resentment: "she heartily disapproved of my choice in friends and constantly reiterated that my tastes were low . . . To [Edith], I was a frivolous, silly young thing, who needed constantly to be squelched; she undertook to do the squelching, unsparingly, herself."[14] Edith apparently worked to help to support the family from an early age, making lace and selling it and her father's paintings door-to-door. A dutiful daughter throughout her life, she regularly sent money home for the support of her parents and her many younger siblings. She was particularly close to her mother, felt personally and keenly the humiliations heaped upon the Chinese, and her "literary ambition," according to the writer of her obituary in the *Montreal Star* (April 8, 1914), was "to show the Chinese in America up in their true colors, dispel the erroneous impression that had taken such a strong hold in the American mind about their supposed failings, and lay bare the many good and noble qualities of which they are entitled to boast" (7).

As a child, Edith contracted rheumatic fever, the disease which made her semi-invalid, weakened her heart and eventually caused her death. Though physically weak and for long periods bedridden during her childhood, her imagination was strong and she often wrote poems and fairy tales with which she entertained the family. She taught herself secretarial skills and worked as a journalist first for the *Montreal Star* and later briefly for a Canadian-owned newspaper in Jamaica, West Indies. In 1888 she published her first article, "A Trip in a Horse Car," in the Montreal magazine *Dominion Illustrated*, a journal to which she thereafter contributed many occasional pieces and brief stories. The first use of her pseudonym, initially spelled Sui Seen Far, appeared around 1896 in her stories published in *Fly Leaf* and the *Lotus*, edited by her brother-in-law Walter Blackburn Harte[15]. In 1898, on the advice of her doctor she went west, working for two years as a typist for the Canadian Pacific Railway based in San Francisco, and in 1900 moved to Seattle, where she lived and worked approximately ten years[16]. With a letter of introduction from the Montreal Chinese community, she was accepted into the Seattle Chinese community, which, in 1900, numbered 438, barely one percent of the city's total population. She worked at a Baptist mission in Chinatown, teaching English to Chinese immigrants in the evenings and gathering materials for her stories[17], which she published in such major journals of the day as the *Independent, Century, Hampton's, Out West, Ladies Home Journal, Good Housekeeping, Gentlewoman, New York Evening Post, New England, Overland, Sunset,* and *Western*. Thirty of these stories were collected in one volume and published by A. C. McClurg of Chicago two years before her death.

The last article Edith wrote, a year before her death, "The Chinese Workmen in America," continued the battle to which her life's work was devoted, the battle against classism and racism. It is a plea for acceptance not only of diplomats and prominent visitors from China but of the ordinary Chinese Americans living and working in this land. Almost as an answer to the Congressional Special Committee of 1876, Edith, in 1913, was still asserting that many former laundrymen become college graduates and influential people; others were actually artists and poets, sons of good families. The children of these people had become assimilated, for half the class in a

Sunday school she visited in San Francisco wore American clothes while in Eastern public schools all the Chinese children "wear only the American dress."[18] If her arguments seem meager and insignificant, they only reflect the meagerness of the arguments brought up against the Chinese. Ironically, on the day of her death, April 7, 1914, the Montreal Gazette printed an article on the proposed segregation of "Oriental schoolchildren" in the public schools of Vancouver in the wake of the murder of a white woman by her Chinese servant. Apparently, the anti-Chinese winds, against which Edith had stood for nearly two decades, continued unabated while she herself, at age forty-nine, was swept away.

Winnifred was the middle child of the family. Though she later claimed 1879 as her birthyear, in order perhaps not to be older than her second husband, recent research by family descendents into official records disclose that she was born August 21, 1875 and christened Lillie Winnifred.[19] Though her family's poverty precluded a great deal of education, Winnifred was a born storyteller and had chosen the vocation of writer at an early age. According to her autobiography Me, at age seventeen Winnifred sailed away from home to take the same position Edith held as reporter for the Canadian-owned newspaper in Jamaica, West Indies and to make her way in the world.

Finding Jamaica an unsatisfactory place, she went to Chicago, where she worked as a typist for the stockyards and wrote her first book, Miss Numè of Japan (Chicago: Rand, McNally, 1899), which has the distinction of being the first piece of imaginative literature in a broadly defined Asian American field. Winnifred was then attracted to New York, where she wrote nearly all of her "Japanese" novels and had her greatest success. In 1901, she married Bertrand W. Babcock, whom she met when they were both reporters on the Brooklyn Eagle. After bearing four children, Winnifred divorced the alcoholic Babcock. Thereafter, she supported herself and her children entirely by her pen, publishing, with one exception, a book a year from 1901 through 1916. All but three of her novels were written in New York City. Her books were so successful that "in many cases she received as much as $15,000 advance royalty before publication, with 50% over-riding royalty after publication." In New York City, she moved in a distinguished circle including such luminaries as Edith Wharton, Anita Loos, Jean Webster, David Belasco, Mark Twain, and Lew Wallace.

Edith never married and referred to herself even when young as a "very serious and sober-minded spinster." That she boldly embraced this pejorative term was comparable to her insistence on asserting her Chinese identity. In both cases, she rejected the negative connotation and employed both terms with pride. In "Leaves," Edith Eaton writes in the third person, but with such intimate detail that it must be her own story, of a Chinese Eurasian who, after refusing a man nine times, agreed to an engagement because she "had a married mother and married sisters, who were always picking at her and gossiping over her independent manner of living" and, as she recorded in her diary, "because the world is so cruel and sneering to a single woman— and for no other reason" (131). One day, her fiancé made an irreparable mistake by asking her, "Wouldn't it be just a little pleasanter for us if, after we are married, we allowed it to be presumed that you were—er—Japanese? So many of my friends have inquired of me if that is not your nationality. They would be so charmed to meet a little Japanese lady." To this insult, she snapped back, "Hadn't you better oblige them by finding one?", returned his ring, and wrote with relief in her diary: "Joy, oh, joy! I'm free once more. Never again shall I be untrue to my own heart. Never again will I allow any one to 'hound' or 'sneer' me into matrimony" (132). Edith was the only one among the nine daughters of Grace and Edward Eaton who never married, and she may be compared to the heroine of Sara Parton's novel *Ruth Hall*, as described by Nina Baym, "the liberated woman was sexually liberated, not in the modern sense, but in the sense of being liberated from sex" (Baym, 255), for she found her happiness not in a husband and family circle but in the satisfactions of a successful writing career. So for Edith Eaton, integrity in the question of her ethnicity and her personal independence took precedence over everything else in life, including the roles of wife and mother to which women are generally conditioned to give the highest priority.

In 1917 Winnifred married Francis Fournier Reeve, who was then in the tugboat business, and abruptly changed her life by following her husband to Calgary, Alberta, to farm and ranch. He later sold the ranches and became a prominent figure in the oil business. Doris Rooney, Winnifred Eaton's daughter, remembered one episode from the ranch that demonstrates well her mother's strong will and ingenuity, character traits found in Onoto Watanna's heroines:

> I remember when we first moved to our "Bow View Ranch" forty miles west of Calgary, on what is now number 1A highway. Mama was determined that the house should be repainted. She had already restored the interior and made it into a charming home. She ordered the paint for the outside, but when it arrived my Dad told her he could not call the men away from their work with the cattle—I believe it was branding time—and the paint would have to be returned. In order to prevent this, my mother drove nails into the tops of the cans making a hole in each. She then started to paint the house herself, from the bottom up! At this my Dad gave up, called in the men and the house was painted, the job taking a couple of days.

From 1925 to 1932, Winnifred Eaton Reeve worked in Hollywood, editing and writing film scripts for Universal and MGM Studios, rising to chief scenarist. She adapted many of her own novels into screenplays, wrote original scripts and edited still others including *The Mississippi Gambler, The Road to Honor, Movie Madness, Belle of the Bowery, What Men Want, Five Thousand Dollars Reward!, The Hold Up, Barbary Coast, Ropes, Shanghai*

Lady, Showboat, and Phantom of the Opera. She died suddenly on April 8, 1954 in Butte, Montana enroute to Calgary from a winter vacation in Phoenix, Arizona, and is buried in Queen's Park Cemetery in Calgary. Her papers, formerly held by the Glenbow Foundation, are now at the library of the University of Calgary.[20]

As a writer, Winnifred clearly had her finger on the pulse of her time, gave the public what it wanted, and attained the pinnacles of popular success: best-sellers, Broadway, and Hollywood. But in 1915, after Edith's death, while recuperating in the hospital after surgery, Winnifred had second thoughts about the career route she had taken and the persona she had assumed to support this career:

> What then I ardently believed to be the divine sparks of genius, I now perceived to be nothing but a mediocre talent that could never carry me far. My success was founded upon a cheap and popular device, and that jumble of sentimental moonshine that they called my play seemed to me the pathetic stamp of my inefficiency. Oh, I had sold my birthright for a mess of potage. [sic] (Me, p. 153–154)

Identifying with Esau, the unfavored child, she acknowledged that she had betrayed her heritage. Perhaps the obituary she wrote for Edith, described below, was weighing heavily on her conscience. However, she was still business-conscious enough not to reveal everything. Only those already knowledgeable would understand what she was alluding to when she wrote of selling her birthright.

Further on, she explicitly writes about Edith and seems conscience-stricken:

> I thought of other sisters . . . the eldest, a girl with more real talent than I—who had been a pitiful invalid all her days. She is dead now, that dear big sister of mine, and a monument marks her grave in commemoration of work she did for my mother's country.
> It seemed our heritage had been all struggle. None of us had yet attained what the world calls success . . .
> It seemed a great pity that I was not, after all, to be the savior of my family, and that my dreams of the fame and fortune that not alone should lift me up, but all my people, were built upon a substance as shifting as sand and as shadowy as mist. (194)

The "dreams of the fame and fortune that not alone should lift me up, but all my people," may have been an afterthought inspired by the memory of Edith, by an unflattering comparison between the motivation behind her sister's work and her own, perhaps by a sense of envy for Edith's memorial from the Chinese community and guilt for her own disavowal of her ancestry. It is difficult to understand how Winnifred could have thought she would "lift up" the Chinese by pretending to be Japanese.

The Chinese, even during her lifetime, recognized Edith's efforts on their behalf, as she was pleased to note in "Leaves:"

> My heart leaps for joy when I read one day an article signed by a New York Chinese in which he declares 'The Chinese in America owe an everlasting debt of gratitude to Sui Sin Far for the bold stand she has taken in their defense. (128)

To memorialize their gratitude after her death, the "Chinese community of Montreal and Boston" placed on her tomb in the Protestant cemetery in Montreal, a special headstone inscribed with these characters: "Yi bu wong hua" ("The righteous or loyal one does not forget China.") [My translation]

Despite her own righteous stand, Edith herself did not condemn the route her sister had taken. Instead, she recognized Winnifred's choice of persona as a strategy for survival in a hostile social environment, and placed the blame squarely where it belonged—on the society creating such an environment. In "Leaves," she devotes a paragraph to the phenomenon of Chinese Eurasians "thinking to advance themselves, both in a social and business sense, [who] pass as Japanese" because the Americans have "for many years manifested a much higher regard for the Japanese than for the Chinese." Though she does not advocate such deception, she asks a pointed question that inverts the blame and reveals her big-sisterly loyalty: "Are not those who compel them to thus cringe more to be blamed than they?"

3. AUTOBIOGRAPHICAL WRITING

The fact that two sisters both wrote autobiographies would seem an unusual opportunity to arrive at verifiable reality; however, this is possible only to a limited extent. Edith, whose veracity is more reliable, wrote only one essay of seven-and-one-half pages, "Leaves from the Mental Portfolio of an Eurasian" (1909), which ranges over her entire life from age 4 to 40. Winnifred wrote a 346-page book, *Me, A Book of Remembrance* (1915), devoted entirely to her first year away from home. Her biography of their sister Sara, *Marion, the Story of an Artist's Model* (1916) gives some revealing glimpses into their childhood. However, Winnifred's talent for fiction was so pervasive that the boundary between fact and fiction is not at all clear.

Despite its flowery title, reminiscent of Sara Willis Parton's popular book *Fern Leaves from Fanny's Portfolio* (1853), Edith's "Leaves from the Mental Portfolio of an Eurasian" is sincere and earnest, straightforward, and purposeful. In this essay, as in all her writing, her mission was to right wrongs by writing them, and the wrong she focused on here was one with which she was personally most familiar: bigotry, which, as a Eurasian, she had experienced from Asians as well as Caucasians. *Me*, by contrast, is novelistic in style, filled with dialogue and vivid, at times improbable, details, and artistically organized to produce a sense of rising tension and wholeness. The

Tombstone Erected for Edith Eaton by the Chinese Community of Montreal and Boston, circa 1915

narrator calls herself "the ugly duckling of an otherwise astonishingly good looking family," and portrays herself as a bold, lively seventeen-year-old setting forth to conquer the world with a sheaf of poems and 10 dollars in her purse. Naïve and unworldly, she is armed with self-confidence, her dreams of success, an active imagination, and a charming personality that draws to her many friends and numerous marriage proposals. *Me* begins with her departure from the parental nest and ends with her entrance into adulthood: the publication of her first novel and the disillusioning realization that she has been toyed with by the man to whom she had proffered her first love, a playboy millionaire.

"Self-identity ('I' looking at 'me') is constituted not only by our looking at ourselves, but also by our looking at others looking at us and our reconstitution of and alteration of these views of others about us,"[21] as R. D. Laing has pointed out. Both Eaton sisters' autobiographies reveal the consciousness of the gaze and judgment of others while their lives testify to their attempts to reconstitute or alter these views. Though Winnifred occasionally mentions the curiosity about her ethnicity in the gaze of others—noting in *Me* that people look at her "as if I interested them or they were puzzled to know my nationality. I would have given anything to look less foreign. My darkness marked and crushed me, I who loved blondness like the sun" (p. 166)—she focuses instead, on her sexuality. The narrator of *Me* is much concerned with and aware of the gaze of the opposite sex. Though only "interesting" rather than "beautiful," Nora Ascough, the heroine of *Me*, tells the story of how she managed to become engaged to three different men simultaneously.

Though *Me* devotes a great deal of time and space to Nora's romantic involvements, it does include one paragraph revealing the indignities suffered by an unprotected girl seeking a living in the world of men:

> I have known what it is to be pitied, chafed, insulted, "jollied"; I have had coarse or delicate compliments paid me; I have been cursed at and ordered to "clear out"—Oh, all the crucifying experiences that only a girl who looks hard for work knows! I've had a fat broker tell me that a girl like me didn't need to work; I've had a pious-looking hypocrite chuck me under the chin out of sight of the clerks in the outer offices. I've had a man make me a cold business proposition of $10 a week for my services as a stenographer and typewriter, and $10 a week for my services as something else. I've had men brutally touch me, and when I have resented it, I have seen them spit across the room in my direction. . . . (124)

Such a protesting note is rare, however, for Winnifred Eaton's intent in this book is not polemical; she does not seek to right sexist or racist wrongs. Instead, she seeks to involve the reader, to appeal to his or her sense of compassion by presenting her protagonist (herself) as a credulous, untutored country lass, making her way through the nets of a corrupt world. She also wishes to justify herself; for at the book's end, though disillusioned in love, the heroine is successfully launched in a writing career. This text may well be considered part of a genre made popular in the previous century, which Nina Baym has called "woman's fiction": the story of a "heroine beset by hardships [who] finds within herself the qualities of intelligence, will, resourcefulness and courage sufficient to overcome them."[22]

Edith's autobiography, on the other hand, has an altogether different emphasis. She touches only briefly on sexuality, for her demeanor of a "very serious and sober-minded spinster," puts off would-be suitors. Instead, "Leaves" focuses almost exclusively on ethnicity, chronicling the suffering Edith has endured from age four until forty simply for being Eurasian. At the same time, it is the story of her reaction to racism: the development of her racial consciousness and pride. Though her own initial reaction to the first Chinese she saw (apart from her mother) was "to recoil with a sense of shock," when taunted by other children and called "yellow-face, pig-tail, rat-eater," her fighting spirit is roused and she retorts, "I'd rather be Chinese than anything else in the world." Nonetheless, being Chinese exacts a tremendous cost. In dancing class one young man says "that he would rather marry a pig than a girl with Chinese blood in her veins." Later, she attributes her lifelong physical frailty to the social burden of being a Eurasian and does not think it an overstatement to parallel her suffering with that of Jesus: "I am prostrated at times with attacks of nervous sickness . . . in the light of the present I know that the cross of the Eurasian bore too heavily upon my childish shoulders."

The same commitment and sense of responsibility that she had for her immediate family, Edith extended to her mother's people, taking personally all insults to the Chinese and assuming the role of a warrior defending a just cause: an unjustly maligned race. That she saw her mission in this light is clear in her frequent use of *battle* in her autobiographical essay, initially in a literal sense and later figuratively. After she shouts back at her childish taunters that she'd rather be Chinese than anything else, a fight ensues:

> They pull my hair, they tear my clothes, they scratch my face, and all but lame my brother; but the white blood in our veins fights valiantly for the Chinese half of us. When it is all over, exhausted and bedraggled, we crawl home, and report to our mother that we have "won the battle." ("Leaves," 126)

Despite her assertion of Chinese pride, Edith slips unwittingly into the assumption that her "white blood" is the stronger, more martial half. Nonetheless, she writes further of her girlhood in Montreal, "There are many pitched battles, of course, and we seldom leave the house without being armed for conflict." Later, as an adult, a writer, "I meet many Chinese persons, and am often called upon to fight their battles in the papers. This I enjoy." Edith Eaton lays out the scene of the battle: racial prejudice among the English, the Canadians, and the Americans, among children, adolescents, and adults. Prejudice seems universal, ubiquitous. She describes her preparation for battle: researching and reading about China to increase her knowledge and to develop her pride. Her method of fighting: writing articles to correct misconceptions, to right wrongs, to fight injustice by defending the Chinese. Her style is direct, her purpose focused and clear.

In contrast, *Me*, like its author, is curious and indirect. Purporting to belong to the self-revelatory genre of autobiography, it was, however, published anonymously. The author wanted to tell her life story, to explain herself, and yet, paradoxically, she did not want to reveal her identity. *Me* is written in the first person, but the author gives herself yet another pseudonym, Nora Ascough. She plainly reveals that her father was a poor painter and "an English-Irishman" but is deliberately vague about her mother, saying only: "she was a native of a far-distant land, and I do not think she ever got over the feeling of being a stranger in Canada." If names are changed and facts are not forthcoming, how can the reader be certain that this is indeed an autobiography and not a novel? As if anticipating such doubts, the book begins with an introduction by a personal friend, who has "known her [the author] for a number of years." The introducer, herself a popular writer, Jean Webster, author of *Daddy Longlegs*, and Mark Twain's niece, affirms that "the main outline of everything she says is true, though the names of people and places have *necessarily* [emphasis added] been changed in order to hide their identity." After reading the book, one realizes that Jean Webster did not know the author during the time of the narrative; thus, the word of the guarantor is no guarantee. And why was it necessary to hide peoples' identities, including the author's? Webster replies: "The author has written a number of books that have had wide circulation." Thus, because Onoto Watanna's novels are so well-known, Winnifred Eaton cannot tell the truth about herself.

The real reason for Winnifred's reluctance to reveal all was that she had already supplied no less august a publication than *Who's Who* with a fabricated biography to support her pseudonym. *Who Was Who in America*, Volume VI still publishes the following misinformation for Winnifred Eaton Babcock: born Nagasaki, Japan (when in fact it was Montreal, Canada) in 1879 (when it was 1875). For Edith's obituary in the April 9, 1914 issue of *The New York Times*, Winnifred romanticized further by calling their mother "a Japanese noblewoman who had been adopted by Sir Hugh Matheson as a child and educated in England." This obituary is another peculiar text, unbalanced in its emphasis. It only notes at the beginning that Edith Eaton was the "Author of Chinese Stories Under the name of Sui Sin Far," also known as the "Chinese Lily." Then it devotes eight sentences to the vicissitudes of the life and career of their father, who began as an "intimate friend of General Gordon . . . the English soldier killed at Khartoum in 1885," and the article ends with Winnifred herself: "One of Miss Eaton's sisters, Mrs. Bertram W. Babcock of New York, is an author writing under the pen name of Onoto Watanna." By embellishing their parental history, Winnifred heightened the romance of their ancestry and by claiming a Japanese mother, she neatly made herself the legitimate daughter and Edith the aberration. Perhaps it was the continuation of her deception even into the obituary of her older sister that weighed heavily on Winnifred's conscience and accounted for the notes of regret in an otherwise cheerful *Me*.

Me fits well into what Jean Starobinski has called the "picaresque" tradition of autobiography, one in which the author, having "arrived at a certain stage of ease and 'respectability' . . . retraces, through an adventurous past, his humble beginnings at the fringes of society." Then, unworldly though not unclever, "he got by as best he could . . . encountering on the way all the abuse, all the oppressive power, all the insolence of those above him."[23] Indeed, about the poverty of their parents, both sisters' autobiographies agree. "Leaves" tells of Edith's "tramping around and sell[ing] my father's pictures and also some lace which I make myself . . . a dangerous life for a very young girl" (128). And in *Me*, Winnifred waxes effusive over a colored lampshade in the room she rents at the YMCA, remembering that in her parent's home such an item was unknown:

> Our home in Quebec had been bare of all these charming accessories, and although my father was an artist, poor fellow, I remember he used to paint in the kitchen with us children all about him, because that was the only warm room in the house. In our poor home the rooms were primitive and bare. Papa used to say that bare rooms were more tolerable than rooms littered with "trash" and since we could not afford good things, it was better to have nothing in place but things that had an actual utility . . . there were no pictures at all on our walls. . . . (112–114)

Winnifred describes their parents as overwhelmed by the immense family they had brought into being. "I thought of papa, absent-minded, impractical dreamer . . . I was one of many, and my father and mother were in a way even more helpless than their children. It was almost pathetic the way in which they looked to us, as we grew up, to take care of ourselves and them" (90). For Winnifred, ethnicity was not to be blamed for her cramped and deprived childhood, poverty was the cause. Poverty was the reason their family lacked social standing and material comforts, to say nothing of luxuries and extended education for all the children. She lays the blame for a certain moral laxity or blindness at the doors of poverty as well. Partly through youthful inexperience but more because of their need for money, she advised her sister Sara to take a job as an artist's model, and Sara, in turn, urged Winnifred to go to Richmond to be secretary to a doctor whom she had just met. Both positions turned out disastrously, for the "employers" were more interested in obtaining mistresses than employees. In *Me*, Winnifred reflects on this incident and its causes:

> It is curious how natural it is for poor girls to slip along the path of least resistance. We wanted to help each other, and yet, each advised the other to do

something that upon more mature thought might have been inadvisable; for both courses held pitfalls of which neither of us was aware. However, we seized what was nearest to our hand. (60)

Her childhood experience of poverty led her to choose the route that would bring her the greatest economic success. Since storytelling was her talent, and "nearest to hand," she made full use of this gift, and was both surprised and delighted when her talents were recognized and rewarded. Houston Baker's observation about Ralph Ellison holds true also for Winnifred Eaton: "The folk artist may even have to don a mask that distorts what he knows is his genuine self in order to make his product commensurate with a capitalistic market-place."[24] If inventing stories about her own life would help to sell the fictions on which she depended for her living, she would not balk at such niceties.

Though little attention is given in *Me* to the issue of ethnicity, there are, nonetheless, passages that reveal a painful consciousness of the subject. Winnifred confesses that as a child, she was "dark and foreign-looking like my mother," while it was "the blond type I adored. In all my most fanciful imaginings and dreams I had always been golden-haired and blue-eyed."(40) Like Toni Morrison's Pecola Breedlove, and millions of non-white girls in the western world, Winnifred Eaton had also imbibed Caucasian standards of beauty and believed these traits—blondness and blue eyes—to be the only desirable traits. Any deviance from this absolute standard could not help but be deplored, and if one was so unfortunate as to be born "dark and foreign-looking," one was doomed to carry for life an incurable and highly visible wound. One had to compensate for this wound by developing other personality traits with which to distract others from such obvious inferiority.

The trait that Winnifred Eaton developed above all and that she demonstrates well in *Me* is a skill as a storyteller. "I had not had an Irish grandmother for nothing," she writes. Late in the book, angered and jealous of the other woman with whom her admirer is involved, Nora Ascough declares:

No, no, she was not better than I. Strip her of her glittering clothes, put her in rags over a wash-tub, and she would have been transformed into a common thing. But I? If you put me over a wash-tub, I tell you *I* would have woven a romance, aye, from the very suds. God had planted in *me* the fairy germs; that I knew. (*Me*, 350)

And of her life, Winnifred did weave a romance, seeing herself akin to the heroines of the romances of her fiction, but with a difference, for though her novels all end happily, *Me* has a mixed ending: joy at having found her calling and sadness at her disillusionment in love.

On a symbolic level, the playboy millionaire who breaks Nora Ascough's heart, Roger Hamilton, symbolizes the sexual and economic power of the world with which the young, inexperienced Nora must learn to deal. During their initial encounter on a train, she charms him and is in turn charmed and fascinated. Like Blanche Dubois, she depends on the kindness of strangers and accepts a loan from him to make her start in life. But by the end of the book, when she makes the two discoveries, closely following each other, that he is an immoral man and that she has powers within her—namely, her imagination and writing ability—enabling her to make her way in the world without assistance, she is freed of his corrupting influence and of her economic dependence on him.

The autobiographies of the Eaton sisters illustrate from an Asian American perspective what Roger Rosenblatt in writing of Black autobiography called "a special reality."

> Minority autobiography and minority fiction deserve their minority status not because of comparative numbers but because of the presence of a special reality, one provided for the minority by the majority, within which each member of the minority tries to reach an understanding both of himself and the reality into which he has been placed.[25]

The special reality for Chinese Eurasians was initial rejection from both sides. Edith, for example, reveals that the Chinese did not always identify her as one of their own. In San Francisco when a newspaper hired her to obtain subscriptions in Chinatown, she discovered to her chagrin that . . . "save for a few phrases, I am unacquainted with my mother tongue. How, then, can I expect these people to accept me as their own countrywoman? The Americanized Chinamen actually laugh in my face when I tell them that I am of their race . . . " ("Leaves," 131) But laughter from the Chinese was a mild reaction compared to the extreme hostility from the whites, as revealed in several of her stories.

What Rosenblatt noted as true of African-Americans, like Malcolm X, also held true for Asian Americans, like Winnifred Eaton:

> Recognizing an elusive and unpredictable situation, they adapt to it for survival, becoming masters of both physical and psychological disguise, in part to avoid their hunters. (175)

Edith's response to racism was a frontal assault, direct and confrontational. Winnifred's response, in contrast, was indirect, covert, and subversive—like the Trojan Horse, an ambush from within the walls. Well aware of the prejudices and stereotypes both about Asians and about women, she exploited all these popularly held notions in her novels and in her personal dealings with the wielders of power—rich men and publishers. If they preferred Japanese, she would play the Japanese; if they enjoyed being charmed and seduced, she would be charming and seductive. Though their methods diverged, ultimately, both sisters worked together, for what Edith in her writing asserted— the Chinese are human and assimilable—Winnifred, in her life and successful career, demonstrated.

4. THE FICTION OF SUI SIN FAR

The personal story of what life was like for the Chinese and Eurasians in America at the turn of the century is Sui Sin Far's special contribution to American letters, for she was the first person of any Chinese ancestry to take up this subject. And she took up the subject as a woman warrior takes up her sword: to right/write wrongs and to uplift the downtrodden. Her major purpose in writing was to right wrongs done the Chinese in America, but her minor themes were to give credit due to working class women and to acknowledge the strength of the bond between women.

Edith Maud Eaton (Sui Sin Far)

Sui Sin Far, translated literally, is "water fragrant flower," or narcissus; also called Chinese lily. A story that appeared in the September 19, 1891 issue of the *Dominion Illustrated* may be the origin of Edith's choice of a pseudonym. The legend of the Chinese lily appeared in an article, "Episodes of Chinese Life in British Columbia," by James P. MacIntyre.

> It is said a farmer left half each of his estate to two sons, the eldest receiving good land in which he planted tea, and prospered; the younger son having only land of a swampy character, nothing would grow in it, and he was sorely moved to grief. But a white elephant presented him with a bulbous root which he placed in water and the result was, through time, grief changed to joy and a paradise of flowers. Through the outcome of this incident which brought him great wealth, he became a mandarin, and attained to the third degree of state in the kingdom, the Emperor planting the yellow flag with golden dragon on his horse. (279)

Certainly, the transformation of grief into joy, handicap into glory, failure into success would have appealed to Edith Eaton, who, "carried the burden of the Eurasian" upon her slight shoulders throughout her life. Great, too, was the appeal of the humble beauty of these small bulbs that needed only a shallow bowl of water and rewarded little effort with a cluster of highly perfumed, modest white flowers, becoming in the dead of winter a symbol of the persistence of life and beauty, and a particular favorite in Chinese homes.

Mrs. Spring Fragrance, her collected stories, is an attractive book. Its vermillion cover is embossed in gold letters and decorated with lotus flowers, a dragonfly and the moon. Like Winnifred's novels, which had appeared before this, the physical appearance of the book attests to the publisher's attempt to promote sales by appealing to a particular notion of things "oriental" as exotic, delicate, and lovely. The book is printed on decorated paper, each page imprinted in a pastel "oriental" design: a crested bird on branches of plum blossoms and bamboo with the Chinese characters for Happiness, Prosperity, and Longevity vertically descending along the right margin. Some of Sui Sin Far's stories are appropriately delicate, charming, and lovely; however, the more serious ones strike ironic, tragic, and even somewhat bitter notes very much at odds with their physical presentation. The medium and the message thus engage in a tug of war.

The reviews for *Mrs. Spring Fragrance* were generally favorable, with the progressive New York *Independent* praising the book thus:

> The conflict between occidental and oriental ideals and the hardships of American immigration laws furnish the theme for most of the tales and the reader is not only interested but has his mind widened by becoming acquainted with novel points of view.[26]

Though *The New York Times* recognized that "Miss Eaton has struck a new note in American fiction," its reviewer did not think that she had "struck it very surely, or with surpassing skill." But he did recognize that "it has taken courage to strike it at all." This reviewer goes on to elucidate her purpose and makes a puzzling judgment on her task:

> The thing she has tried to do is to portray for readers of the white race the lives, feelings, sentiments of the Americanized Chinese on the Pacific coast, of those who have intermarried with them, and of the children who have sprung from such unions. It is a task whose adequate doing would require well-nigh superhuman insight and the subtlest of methods.

Why should it be a "superhuman" task to render the Chinese understandably human to white readers? Is it because the Chinese are so far from being human or that white readers are so far from being willing to accept them as such?

> In some of the stories . . . she has seen far and deep, and has made her account keenly interesting. Especially is this true of the analysis she makes occasionally of the character of an Americanized Chinese, of the glimpses of the Chinese women who refuse to be anything but intensely Chinese, and into the characters of the half-breed children.[27]

In style and tone, Sui Sin Far's stories, like her characters, are unpretentious, gentle, sometimes sentimental. Like other late nineteenth century American women writers, she also wrote stories for children, which make up nearly half of this collection. Through basic human themes—love of men and women, parents and children, brothers and sisters, she draws forth the reader's empathy. What sets her stories apart is her sympathetic portrayal of the Chinese characters living in the United States. Bret Harte had used Chinese characters in his Western stories, but he always presented them from the white man's perspective. Sui Sin Far gave to American letters the Chinese perspective on racial prejudice, economic harassment, and discriminatory immigration regulations. A strident or militant tone was hardly necessary, for she had only to show the situation as it was for the injustice to be apparent; instead, she employed irony.

One of the best examples of Sui Sin Far's ironic tone may be found in the title story of the collection. Lively, unconventional Mrs. Spring Fragrance, while visiting in San Francisco, writes a letter home to her husband in Seattle after attending a "magniloquent lecture" entitled "America the Protector of China" to which a white friend had taken her:

> It was most exhilarating, and the effect of so much expression of benevolence leads me to beg of you to forget to remember that the barber charges you one dollar for a shave while he humbly submits to the American man a bill of fifteen cents. And murmur no more because your honored elder brother, on a visit to this country, is detained under the roof-tree of this great Government instead of under your own humble roof. Console him with the reflection that he is protected under the wing of the Eagle, the Emblem of Liberty. What is the loss of ten hundred years or ten thousand times ten dollars compared with the happiness of knowing oneself so securely sheltered? All of this I have learned

from Mrs. Samuel Smith, who is as brilliant and great of mind as one of your own superior sex. (8–9)

Mrs. Spring Fragrance first reaches out a sympathetic hand to her husband, who would immediately understand the emptiness of the patriotic rhetoric, given the prejudicial treatment he has received from his barber and the indignities his brother has suffered at the hands of immigration officials. Then she uses this opportunity to her own advantage by drawing a parallel between her well-meaning but misguided friend, who thought she would find this lecture edifying, and her self-righteous husband, who is always critical of her actions. In other words, racism and sexism are rooted in the same error: the belief that one is innately superior to another. As a Chinese American woman, Mrs. Spring Fragrance must endure the superior attitudes of both white people and of Chinese American men. Though thinly veiled in apparent good humor, the ironic force of this passage, with its double-pronged attack, is strong and uncompromising, and the barb at the end unexpected.

Humor is another of Sui Sin Far's weapons, as in the following exclamations by Mrs. Spring Fragrance to her husband, when their Caucasian neighbor's lovelorn son fails to give them his usual greeting: "Ah, these Americans! These mysterious, inscrutable, incomprehensible Americans! Had I the divine right of learning I would put them into an immortal book!" (30). Sui Sin Far is obviously taking delight in the inversion of her Chinese character's appropriating the adjectives commonly used to describe "Orientals" and applying them to whites. The author is also commenting subtly on the supposed superiority—"the divine right of learning"—of those who pass such judgments on other people; the implication here is that the Chinese are not "inscrutable" because of qualities inherent in themselves but because of blind spots in those doing the scrutinizing. Furthermore, Sui Sin Far is taking delight in inverting the character/reader relationship, for a character, who has been made most scrutable, is expressing a desire to write a book about the "inscrutable" white Americans, the reader. We are all comprehensible, of course, to ourselves; it is only the other who is incomprehensible.

Sui Sin Far attempted to reproduce the speech rhythms and patterns of ordinary Chinese Americans in her stories. But her use of literal translations from the Chinese—as in proper names, honorific titles, and axioms—results in a flowery, exotic language somewhat at odds with her purpose of rendering the Chinese familiar to whites, as in the title of the book and in this letter from Mrs. Spring Fragrance to her protégée:

My Precious Laura,—May the bamboo ever wave. Next week I accompany Ah Oi to the beauteous town of San Jose. There we will be met by the son of the Illustrious Teacher, and, in a little Mission, presided over by the benevolent American priest, the little Ah Oi and the son of the Illustrious Teacher will be joined together in love and harmony—two pieces of music made to complete each other. (7)

At other times, the syntax more realistically reproduces Chinese English, as when Lae Choo urges the white lawyer to go to Washington to procure the papers releasing her toddler son from immigration authorities in "In the Land of the Free":

> "Then you go get paper. If Hom Hing not can give you five hundred dollars—I give you perhaps what more that much." (175)

Though Edith Eaton's linguistic portraits may seem at times quaint or strained, her purpose is unfailing: to dramatize the humanness of the Chinese, to draw the reader into their lives, their tragedies, their triumphs. As critic Florence Howe recently noted in a different context, "their view is generic not individualistic; their ideology is explicit";[28] so is Sui Sin Far's work also the "literature of social documentary—and unabashedly partisan." (Howe, p. 190) Her fiction is comparable to the early stories by Black women, which Carole McAlpine Watson described as "purpose fiction . . . [employing] moral suasion . . . as a conscious strategy of racial self-defense."[29]

Watson's description of the fiction of late nineteenth century Black American women writers, in fact, can very easily be applied to the fiction and purpose of Sui Sin Far:

> . . . black women novelists, beginning in the 1890s, produced works of social protest and racial appeal based upon Christian and democratic principles. During the final decade of the nineteenth century, their stories challenged the social order then being established in portrayals that refuted the black stereotype, exposed injustice in both the North and South, and, in curious tales about tragic mulattoes, focused attention on the irony and irrationality of the color line. (Watson, 3)

Sui Sin Far faced with the same irrational color line also wrote stories about mulattoes or Eurasians, who were not only victims of racial discrimination but were figures "with whom white readers could identify" (Watson, 12). In such stories as "Its Wavering Image," in which a Eurasian, living in Chinatown with her Chinese father, finds her trust betrayed by a white newspaper reporter, and "The Story of a White Woman Who Married a Chinese" and "Her Chinese Husband." Sui Sin Far is highly successful in personifying and personalizing her cause by embodying it in characters caught in the between-world condition. These characters may be Eurasians wavering between the cultures and peoples of their parents; whites adopted by or married to Chinese; or Chinese who have assimilated Western ways but still are tied by Old World bonds.

In "The Wisdom of the New," tragedy results when an Americanized Chinese immigrant, Wou Sankwei, does not realize the extent of his Chinese wife's fear of American ways. Pau Lin, the wife, a Chinese villager suddenly brought to America by a husband she has not seen in seven years, is unhinged by jealousy and culture shock and comes to believe, literally, that the Americanization of their son is a fate worse than death. The night before the boy is to start American school, the mother kills him to save him from impending doom. To his credit, the husband, Wou Sankwei, shows great solicitation for his deranged wife and takes her back to China. Sui Sin Far maintains a balanced perspective in the narration of this story, neither condemning the husband for insensitivity nor the wife for rigidity. Instead, her purpose is to show the tragedy of being between worlds. As Wou Sankwei's American friends observe,

> "Yes, I admit Sankwei has some puzzles to solve. Naturally, when he tries to live two lives—that of a Chinese and that of an American."
> "Is it not what we teach these Chinese boys—to become Americans? And yet, they are Chinese, and must, in a sense, remain so." (71)

Nor can the blame of the tragedy be laid at the feet of these kind white women who helped a Chinese student adjust to American life. The fault lies in the situation itself, in the clash between cultures and the fragility of the people caught in this clash.

In "Pat and Pan," a white orphan boy, reared by a Chinese family until the intervention of a white missionary, learns, after spending some time with whites, to be contemptuous of his Chinese family. In the "Story of One White Woman Who Married a Chinese" and its sequel, "Her Chinese Husband," Eaton writes a moving tale of an interracial marriage from the perspective of a white woman. Abandoned by her first husband, a Caucasian, who found her too unsophisticated in politics and, ironically, too ignorant of women's rights to hold his interest, a white woman eventually marries the Chinese man who rescued her from an attempted suicide and gave her a means of employment. For herself, she does not mind the contempt of other whites, but she does worry about the future of their little son in a racially biased world:

> . . . as he stands between his father and myself, like yet unlike us both, so will he stand in after years between his father's and his mother's people. And if there is no kindliness nor understanding between them, what will my boy's fate be? (*Mrs. Spring Fragrance*, 132)

Undoubtedly, Edith Eaton is here writing out of a deeply felt personal experience. She expressed the same anxiety in her autobiographical essay by concluding it with these words:

> After all I have no nationality and am not anxious to claim any. Individuality is more than nationality. . . . I give my right hand to the Occidentals and my left to the Orientals, hoping that between them they will not utterly destroy the insignificant "connecting link." ("Leaves," 132)

In "Her Chinese Husband," the white wife gives a fuller picture of her Chinese husband and of the life she led with him. On finding her weeping over the future of their child, her husband asks her pointedly:

> What is there to weep about? The child is beautiful: the feeling heart, the understanding mind is his. And we will bring him up to be proud that he is of Chinese blood; he will fear none and, after him, the name of half-breed will no longer be one of contempt. (141)

But the father with these idealistic visions is brought home one night with a bullet through his head and, in his pockets are the presents his children had requested: two red rubber balls, an image with undeniable sexual implications. Since race was the only motivation for the murder, the story would seem to indicate a despair at society's ever arriving at a time when different races can live in mutual respect. However, the very writing of the story itself moves us in that direction.

In addition to her major cause—rendering the Chinese human—Sui Sin Far's stories plead two additional causes: acceptance of the working class woman and of friendship between women. In "The Inferior Woman" her sympathy lies with the hard-working, self-made woman as opposed to the wealthy, privileged suffragette. Alice Winthrop, who began working at the age of 14 as an "office boy" in a law office and is now private secretary to the most influential man in Washington, is at first rejected by the mother of the man she loves and called the "inferior woman" because of her family's poverty. She is given her rightful due, however, when her more privileged but generous friend says of her:

> It is women such as Alice Winthrop who, in spite of every drawback, have raised themselves to the level of those who have had every advantage, who are the pride and glory of America. There are thousands of them, all over this land: women who have been of service to others all their years and who have graduated from the university of life with honor. Women such as I, who are called the Superior Women of America, are after all nothing but schoolgirls in comparison.[30]

This story courageously criticizes the Suffragettes for class discrimination, and praises the self-made working-class woman.

Of friendship between women, Sui Sin Far wrote explicitly in several stories in *Mrs. Spring Fragrance*. In "The Inferior Woman," it is the "superior woman," the well-educated, upper-class Ethel Evebrook, who recognizes the actual superiority of the so-called "inferior woman," as demonstrated in the quote above. In a story called "The Chinese Lily," a character transparently named Sin Far sacrifices her life for another woman, a cripple. The cripple, Mermei, had been used to evening visits from her brother. When he fails to come one evening, Sin Far, her neighbor, pays her a visit which both enjoy immensely. Comparing this visit to those from her brother, Mermei concludes, "Lin John is dear, but one can't talk to a man, even if he is a brother, as one can to one the same as oneself." To which Sin Far replies, "Yes, indeed. The woman must be the friend of the woman, and the man the friend of the man" (180–1). One night a fire breaks out in the rooming house; the brother arrives in time to save only one person. Though he has fallen in love with Sin Far, at her request, Lin John saves his sister, and Sin Far perishes in the flames.

Here we find not only the woman-bonding theme, but the ideal of self-sacrifice, or martyrdom, as the ultimate expression of love. Using the transparent non-artifice of her own name, Sui Sin Far declares her willingness to make the ultimate sacrifice for others. In "Leaves" she had revealed a childhood Joan-of-Arc fantasy that foreshadows the theme of this story: "I dream dreams of being great and noble . . . I glory in the idea of dying at the stake and a great genie arising from the flames and declaring to those who have scorned us: 'Behold, how great and glorious and noble are the Chinese people!' (128)[31]. On another level, since Edith Eaton herself had a limp (See "Leaves," 130) and was sickly throughout her life, the two characters may be a doubling of herself, with Sin Far, her active assertive self, coming to the rescue of *Mermei*, (little sister in Chinese) her weak victimized self. What is sacrificed, then, is sexual love embodied in the person of Lin John.

"The Heart's Desire" is a parable about a Chinese princess surrounded by all that wealth and tender care can provide her but who is nonetheless unhappy. Her attendants attempt to cheer her by bringing her successively a father, a mother, and a brother, but all fail to make her happy. The princess then takes the matter into her own hands and sends a note to a poor girl who lives outside the palace walls. When this girl arrives, the princess announces to all the palace: "Behold, I have found my heart's desire—a little sister." And the two girls "forever after . . . lived happily together in a glad, beautiful old palace, surrounded by a glad, beautiful old garden, on a charming little island in the middle of a lake." The tale has a symmetrical shape since the ending is identical to a sentence in the opening paragraph, with the exception of one significant change, the replacement of the word *sad* by *glad*. However, the language of the conventional fairy tale ending is so little changed as to draw attention to the bold inversion of this tale's ending. This princess does not ride off to live happily ever after with a handsome prince, but finds her "heart's desire" and life-long happiness in a relationship with "another like herself."

In an early essay, "Spring Impressions: A Medley of Poetry and Prose" in the June 7, 1890 issue of *Dominion Illustrated*, Edith Eaton announced her chosen career, for "the comunicativeness of our nature will no longer be repressed" and set forth her causes as a writer:

We can suffer with those who have suffered wrongs, we can weep for those whose hearts unnoticed broke amidst this world's great traffic; we can mourn for those whom the grave hath robbed of all that was dear to them, and can sympathize with those remorse-tortured ones, who, gifted with utmost divine wisdom, yet wilfully turned from the guiding light and with eyes that saw all the horror and shame before them walked into the arms of sin.

Her Christian upbringing is apparent in the rhetoric: "divine wisdom," "guiding light," "arms of sin." She would be the great empathizer, and she did indeed make it her life's work to "suffer with those who have suffered wrongs." But perhaps part of her empathy and melancholy had roots in a deep sense of guilt over what she may have perceived as her own sexual deviance. It is pure speculation on my part, but "Heart's Desire" and "The Chinese Lily" are suggestive of a lesbian sensibility, which the author herself would not have approved and would have striven to repress.

Sui Sin Far's major theme, of course, was the plight of the Chinese in America. The full extent of her accomplishment in this area stands out when contrasted to contemporaneous works about the Chinese in the so-called Chinatown fiction written by Caucasian authors, examined ably and thoroughly by William Wu in *The Yellow Peril: Chinese Americans in American Fiction 1850–1940* (Hamden, Connecticut: Archon Books, 1982). That so many negative images of the Chinese appeared in white American writing of the late nineteenth and early twentieth centuries, Wu traces to the European memory of Mongol invasions and the subsequent fear of history repeating itself in the New World. This fear gave rise to the stereotypes of Chinese as opium addicts, prostitutes, cheaters, cleaver wielders, and clever villains. Even the sympathetic white writer "envisions the Chinese as subhuman pets incapable of morality until they are converted into the Christianity of the West" (Wu, 29).

Such missionary zeal is much in evidence in Helen Clark's *The Lady of the Lily Feet and Other Tales of Chinatown* (Philadelphia: Griffth and Rowland Press under the imprint of the American Baptist Publication Society, 1900). Published a dozen years before *Mrs. Spring Fragrance*, Clark's book was a collection of short stories focused entirely on the atrocities of foot-binding, wife beating and selling, the literal enslavement of Chinese women by their men, showing the Chinese to be in desperate need of Christian salvation. The characters are flat, the plots repetitious, the author's perspective outside of and obviously superior to the Chinese community. Christian zeal so overrides artistry that finally only the rare photographs of nineteenth century Chinese women and children in their elaborate Manchu clothing and formal poses remain as the most interesting aspect of the book.

Though the plight of some Chinese women was a cause comparable to Negro slavery, an entire book focused exclusively on the peculiar, horrifying aspects of Chinese culture would give readers additional proof of the "heathenness" of the Chinese, serving to increase the rift between the two races. By contrast, Sui Sin Far, with her stories of ordinary family life, of love triumphing over or thwarted by obstacles, of characters with three-dimensional depth, did much more to bridge the gap between Chinese and whites.

Finally, Edith Eaton fully recognized the pioneer quality of her work and accepted the fact that as a bridge between two worlds, she had to expect to be stepped on. Martyrdom, as she expressed in her stories "A Chinese Lily" and "The Smuggling of Tie Co," and as Jane Tompkins explained in her analysis of *Uncle Tom's Cabin*, is a strategy of the powerless. The major purpose of both Sui Sin Far's life and her writing may be summed up in this passage from "Leaves":

> Only when the whole world becomes as one family will human beings be able to see clearly and hear distinctly. I believe that some day a great part of the world will be Eurasian. I cheer myself with the thought that I am but a pioneer. A pioneer should glory in suffering. (129)

5. THE FICTION OF ONOTO WATANNA

Like folk and fairy tales[32], Onoto Watanna's "Japanese" novels all have the same narrative structure and form: they are invariably short works that can be read easily; they are escapist in plot and exotic in setting, they prolong the separation and estrangement between two potential lovers; and they end happily. Following the meeting of girl and boy there is an initial obstacle to love: a difference in class, a previous engagement, opposing families, parties, or religions. The initial obstacle overcome, love develops only to be met by another obstacle: war, meddling third parties, misunderstanding, duty elsewhere. This second obstacle is followed by prolonged separation during which both lovers suffer either mental anguish or physical hardship and illness. Finally, with the aid of mutual friends, with the passage of time, by chance and by fate, the lovers are reunited at the novel's end.

In middle age, when she published her anonymous autobiography, *Me*, Winnifred Eaton frankly acknowledged the limitations of her novels, confessing that her success was "founded upon a cheap and popular device" (153–4) and she wrote admiringly of Edith, "the eldest, a girl with more real talent than I" (*Me*, 194). But, in fact, though her personal integrity did not measure up to Edith's, Winnifred's own literary talents were considerable, and the "cheap and popular device," known as the romance novel, was the total support for herself and her four children for sixteen years.

Romances today continue to sell by the hundreds of millions, and since the buyers and consumers are primarily women, feminist scholars have been examining this popular genre. In her reader-response analysis *Reading the*

Winnifred Eaton (Onoto Watanna), circa 1914

Romance, Janice Radway came to somewhat contradictory conclusions. On the one hand, the reading of romances is an act of "mild protest" for the housewife whose sole function is to nurture others while her own desires for nurturing remain unmet. It is her way of saying "This is my time, my space. Now leave me alone[33]." On the other hand, it is a conservative act of maintaining the patriarchal status quo, for "romance reading supplements the avenues traditionally open to women for emotional gratification by supplying them vicariously with the attention and nurturance they do not get enough of in the round of day-to-day existence" (212), attention and nurturance, of course, in heterosexual love. And yet,

> the story opposes the female values of love and personal interaction to the male values of competition and public achievement and, at least in ideal romances, demonstrates the triumph of the former over the latter. Romance reading and writing might be seen therefore as a collectively elaborated female ritual through which women explore the consequences of their common social condition as the appendages of men and attempt to imagine a more perfect state where all the needs they so intensely feel and accept as given would be adequately addressed. (Radway, 212)

Though Radway's study was based on interviews and questionnaires conducted in 1980 and 1981, while Onoto Watanna's novels were published from 1899 through the 1920s, Radway's conclusions are applicable to Onoto Watanna's work, for the romance as a genre and its appeal seem very stable. The wide popular appeal of the novels of Onoto Watanna may be accounted for by the features that Radway noted as constituting the appeal of contemporary romances, with an additional feature: their oriental settings and heroines. Since the two historical settings most often employed to give additional interest to the romance have been Regency England and American Civil War, one can readily see that Onoto Watanna's novels set in far-away Japan would have the appeal of novelty.

Onoto Watanna's novels exploited Western stereotypes of the "Orient," being filled with birdlike young women in colorful kimonos, showers of cherry blossom petals, nightingale songs in bamboo groves, moonlit assignations in Japanese gardens. But she was also alert to the sensitive issue of miscegnation; though laws against miscegnation were on the books in many states during this time, Onoto Watanna's interracial romances seemed acceptable as long as they took place in Japan and as long as the couple was white male/Japanese female. Though her first novel, *Miss Numè of Japan*, portrays a possible romance between a Harvard-educated Japanese man and a white American woman, their relationship is a secondary plot in the novel and the relationship is terminated when the wavering American coquette finally rejects her would-be Japanese lover and he commits suicide (a male version of Madame Butterfly.) The primary romantic relationship in this novel is between a Japanese woman and a white man. Seven Onoto Watanna novels couple American men or Englishmen with Japanese or Japanese Eurasian women, while only one, *A Japanese Blossom*, depicts the reverse. However, it is not technically a romance since the husband is a widower with children and the wife a widow with children; instead, it is the story of an internationally blended family and how the composite halves learn to adapt to each others' ways. Unlike the stories of Sui Sin Far, Onoto Watanna's novels do not so much challenge social myths as reinforce them.

Though Onoto Watanna's heroines are ostensibly Japanese or Japanese-Eurasians, they are in fact "bohemians" (her word) unbound by any culture's conventions and possessing strong individual wills: they are uninhibited and high-spirited. Economically and socially, these heroines always begin in disadvantaged positions—orphans (*Sunny San* and *The Heart of Hyacinth*), an unwanted stepdaughter (*Love of Azalea*), a teahouse dancer or geisha in bondage (*A Japanese Nightingale*, and *The Honorable Miss Moonlight*), and a social outcast (*Tama* and *The Wooing of Wisteria*). The heroes, on the other hand, are invariably in positions of responsibility and established power: a diplomat (*Miss Numè of Japan*), a professor (*Tama*), a minister or missionary (*Love of Azalea*), an architect (*Sunny-San*), a prince (*The Daughters of Nijo* and *Wooing of Wisteria*). With this lack of empowerment, Onoto Watanna acknowledges the patriarchal status quo. Eighteen-year old Miss Nume not only recognizes the injustice of the preferential treatment given to boys but complains about it, in not very accurately rendered Japanese-English, during her first meeting with Arthur Sinclair:

> Japanese boy go long way from home—see all the big world; but liddle Japanese girl stay at home with fadder and mudder, an' vaery, vaery good, but parents luf always the boy. Sometimes Japanese girl is vaery sad. Then on account she stay at home too much, but she not show that she is vaery sad. She laugh and talk so that parents do not see she is vaery sad. (87)

Despite their seemingly inferior positions, the heroines manage in modest ways to invert the power structure, for it is the blind wood-sprite-outcast Tama who teaches the American professor how to survive in the woods; Azalea joins Reverend Varley's church choir for the money choirmembers are paid; Yuki, the Japanese Nightingale, wrangles money out of her American husband to pay secretly for her brother's foreign educational expenses and passage home. Thus, Onoto Watanna's heroines are a far cry from the demure, deferential, totally self-negating, stereotypical Asian woman. They are, like their creator herself, sturdy survivors who use whatever means are nearest to hand—their ingenuity, beauty, resourcefulness—to achieve their own ends. At the same time, however, by employing generally covert means of subversion, they may still be seen as acknowledging their lack of power, for their methods of survival do not challenge the established power structure but work within it, at the fringes or in the interstices.

In her novels as in her autobiography, Onoto Watanna focusses on sexuality, or seductiveness, rather than ethnicity; however, racial references do emerge, and when they do, though they are expressions of the between-world condition, the Caucasian perspective is nearly always maintained. A number of Eurasian heroines with red hair and biologically improbable blue eyes are scorned by the ignorant Japanese they live with. For example, here is how the owner of the teahouse where she dances describes Yuki, the Eurasian heroine of *The Japanese Nightingale*:

> a cheap girl of Tokyo, with the blue glass eye of the barbarian, the yellow skin of the lower Japanese, the hair of mixed color, black and red . . . alien at this country, alien at your honorable country, augustly despicable—a half caste! (15)

Since the teahouse owner is speaking to the American man who has fallen in love with Yuki, his scorn is misplaced and reveals his own ignorance and prejudice.

In *The Heart of Hyacinth*, Onoto Watanna devises a curious story in which an English orphan girl, reared by a Japanese family, grows up with Japanese standards of beauty. When the girl first realizes that she has the blue eyes of the "barbarian," whom she has learned to fear, she recoils in shock. Though the Japanese ideal of beauty seems on the surface to have the author's approval, the quotation marks around the word "barbarian" indicate her ironic tone and reveal her subtext—that the fear of blue eyes is a foolish Japanese prejudice. The temporary inversion of the notion of beauty is but another method of reinforcing Western standards.

In her last novel, *His Royal Nibs*, set in western Canada, the Englishman, Cheerio, finds the Indians a "never-failing source of inspiration" for his paintings. The canvases in his cave studio are filled with

> Tragic faces of half-breeds, pawns of an undesired fate. Something of wildness, something of sadness, something of intense longing and wistfulness looked from the strange eyes of the breeds, legally white and permitted the "privilege" of the franchise, subject to conscription and taxation, yet doomed to live among their red kindred.
>
> Beauty peered from the half-lifted ragged magenta shawl of an Indian Madonna, upon whose back the tiny blond head of a blue-eyed papoose told a story more eloquent than words. (245–6)

Again, since blue eyes and blond hair are recessive genes, we find a genetic improbability and very ambivalent tone. As a Eurasian, she obviously sympathizes with the Indian half-breed's ambiguous position, but despite the quotation marks around *privilege*, making the franchise, conscription, and taxation dubious advantages, the author's perspective is ultimately white. The word *doomed* expresses her opinion of life with the Indians, and she pities the blond, blue-eyed papoose whose white beauty is wasted in the Indian village.

Many factors accounted for the success of Onoto Watanna's novels. Some of these we have discussed above: admiration for the military and political strength of Japan; the novelty of her Japanese setting and characters; her skill in weaving stories filled with variety and incident; her talent in depicting protractedly unconsummated, tremulous first love; and her strong, lovable heroines. As notable a literary figure as William Dean Howells praised *A Japanese Nightingale*, writing about it in the *North American Review*: "There is a quite indescribable freshness like no other art except in the simplicity which is native to the best art everywhere." He further noted that "The charm, the delight, the supreme interest is in the personality of Yuki [the heroine]."[34]

Another factor worked to favor Onoto Watanna's success: general ignorance about Japan. "Me? I lig' you. You are big—and thad you nod lig' poor liddle Japanese womans—still I lig' you just same" says 19-year-old Miss Numè at her first meeting with American diplomat Arthur Sinclair. This is not the English spoken by a real Japanese, who would pronounce her l's as r's. This is English spoken by someone with a stuffy nose, but such a detail would not occur to those who had never met a real Japanese. Furthermore, her Japanese-sounding name blinded reviewers who assumed the name reflected authentic ethnic origins and therefore the author could be expected to produce authentic Japanese writing. The *New York Times* reviewer of *Tama*, for example, found the novel "charmingly Japanese in form as well as in atmosphere . . . it holds the very spirit of Japan, a spirit fragrant, dainty, elusive."[35]

How did the Japanese themselves regard her writing? In a small publication *Essays on Japanese Literature* by Thomas E. Swann and Katsuhiko Takeda, printed in Japan, Onoto Watanna's work is described as "artistically of the second order" but worthy of study alongside the work of Lafcadio Hearn and Pierre Loti because it plays an "important role in introducing things Japanese to the American public." "As a consequence of Onoto Watanna's work, Japanese customs and manners were properly introduced to the West."[36] Swann and Takeda concede that "generally speaking, her novels reflect the feelings and sentiments of a visitor to Japan"; however, in one area she is judged superior to Hearn and Loti, for "her descriptions of human feelings are more delicate than those of both famous writers" (58). They quote Kafu Nagai, a Japanese who studied at Princeton and Rutgers Universities between 1871 and 1873, who wrote in his diary about *The Heart of Hyacinth*:

> This novel is hardly to be counted among the best literary works, but the style is exquisite and its pretty sentiment is well displayed. Since she described things Japanese, I became so interested in her work that I finished the bulky book of more than two hundred pages in a single day. (67)

Though the Japanese themselves recognize that she is a "visitor" rather than a native, they nonetheless acknowledge that her books "properly introduce" Japanese customs and manners to the West. Winnifred Eaton must, therefore, have done her homework sufficiently well. That Japanese themselves grant her this much significantly increases her credibility and her accomplishment.

In mid-career, tiring of the Japanese theme, Winnifred Eaton tried her hand at another ethnic disguise with greater linguistic fidelity. *The Diary of Delia: Being a Veracious Chronicle of the Kitchen with Some Side-lights on the Parlour* purports to be the diary of an uneducated Irish-American maid, filled with contrived "illiterate" orthography, similar in colloquial style and feisty tone to the popular Samantha series by "Josiah Allen's Wife" (Marietta Holley, 1836–1926). Like Samantha and Huckleberry Finn, Delia takes the outsider's perspective in observing middle- and upper-middle-class foibles. Eaton's Irish English is greatly superior to her Japanese English, as may be seen in these examples:

"Indade," ses I. "Then I'll set here till the 24th, but divil a bit of work will I be doing . . ."
    "Its an onest gurl I am . . . and its ashamed I'd be to mix mesilf in any such mess as that."[36]

Delia, with her Irish accent, is nonetheless a typical Winnifred Eaton heroine: consigned to a lower socio-economic class but lively, outspoken, resourceful. The story abounds in humorous episodes, surprising turns of plot, and a happy ending with a double wedding, upstairs and down. (For the first time in literary history, we have the anomaly of an Irish-American novel written by a Chinese-Anglo-Canadian published under a Japanese name.)

With her last two novels, *Cattle* and *His Royal Nibs*, Winnifred Eaton abandoned her Japanese pseudonym and exotic romances. *Cattle*, in particular, is a radical departure from her other books, replacing the exoticism and romanticism with realistic, even naturalistic elements[37]. Set in the Albertan cattle country where Winnifred Eaton was then living, *Cattle* is the story of a young woman purchased at auction by a cattle baron and raped by him, who finds companionship and help in an older woman. Together, the two women foil the efforts of the cattle baron to bankrupt them. A feminist intent seems very strong in this novel—the protest against abusive male power, the sisterly bond between the older independent woman and the younger victimized one—but Winnifred Eaton did not follow this path to its logical conclusion. Instead, she took the more familiar road and gave her novel a conventional happy ending in yet another double wedding.

Finally, we have in Winnifred Eaton not a challenger or protester, not a word-warrior, but a woman with her finger squarely on the pulse of her time. Her novels reflect the taste of her day; the popular prejudices and values; the social, sexual and racial myths dear to the hearts of her readers. She made herself a dazzling career by catering to and expressing these myths which she understood so well because she herself, at a fundamental level, also believed in them.

Chapter 3

Focus on China: Stances Patriotic, Critical, and Nostalgic

1. THE WORLD WAR II PERIOD

On December 7, 1941, with the Japanese bombing of the American naval base at Pearl Harbor, Americans made an about-face in their opinions of China and Japan. The favored position enjoyed by the Japanese and the hostility shown the Chinese in the nineteenth century were totally reversed, and now the Chinese became America's long-suffering ally while the Japanese were seen as the hated enemy. What the turn-of-the-century Americans regarded as a noble samurai tradition, when Japan won wars against China and Russia, became bald military aggression when it was directed against the United States. Admiration for the Japanese had been gradually eroded by the increased numbers of Japanese immigrants to the United States throughout the early decades of the twentieth century and by increased Japanese occupation of Chinese territory throughout the 1930s. Pearl Buck's Nobel-Prize-winning novel *The Good Earth* (1938) played a large part in boosting popular sympathy for the Chinese, but the attack on Pearl Harbor was clearly the demarcation line in the complete reversal in American opinions of the relative merits of the Chinese and the Japanese. The Chinese, once regarded as subhuman, were now fellow sufferers from Japanese aggression; the Japanese, once seen as charming and noble, were now regarded as treacherous and despicable. For Edith Eaton, assertion of her Chinese ancestry had meant fighting against the current; for the writers of the 1940s, however, to focus on China and their Chinese ancestry was, so to speak, to go very much with the flow.

The problem for white America after Pearl Harbor, however, was how to differentiate between allies and enemies who looked so much alike. Attempting to solve this problem, *Life* magazine, on December 22, 1941, in an issue devoted to the war, published an article entitled, "How to Tell the Japs From the Chinese." The Chinese were described as "smooth-skinned, tall, aristocratic and slender," while the Japanese were "hairy and squat." Displaying two photographs—"Chinese public servant, Ong Wen-hao" and "Japanese Warrior—General Hideki Tojo"—*Life* attempted to point out different facial traits in anthropological terms. But the physical traits they noted—"parchment yellow complexion" (Chinese), and "earthy yellow complexion" (Japanese); and "more frequent epicanthic fold" (Chinese) and "less frequent epicanthic fold" (Japanese); "higher bridge" (Chinese) and "flatter nose" (Japanese)—were hairsplitting distinctions, not of much practical help, particularly in the photos exhibited, which were black and white. Admitting the weakness of these physical distinctions, *Life* concluded with cultural mystification: "An often sounder clue is facial expression, shaped by cultural, not anthropological, factors. Chinese wear rational calm of tolerant realists. Japs, like General Tojo, show humorless intensity of ruthless mystics." How one was to recognize such a contradiction in terms as a "ruthless mystic," the author apparently thought self-evident and wisely did not attempt to clarify.[1] That *Life* Magazine was not only a reliable indicator of contemporary concerns, but very likely even a setter of trends, is borne out by its rapid growth. It began in 1936 with a run of 466,000 copies and gained nearly instant popularity; within one year the circulation had risen to one million. In the first quarter of 1939, *Life* had a circulation of 2,408,466 and an audience of over eighteen million. Two years after the end of World War II, *Life* had almost one-fifth of every magazine advertising dollar in the United States and its readership was estimated at 21% of the entire population over 10 years of age.[2]

In the same issue of *Life* is further striking evidence of the magazine's interest in promoting pro-Chinese sentiment while simultaneously satisfying a seasonal requirement. The Art section was devoted to "The Story of Christ in Chinese Art. Scholars at Peking University Make Christmas Portfolio for *Life*." Eight full-color scrolls, presented, in Chinese style, scenes of the life of a Christ with Chinese features. The effect of the paintings is one of charm and novelty, delicacy and exotic elegance. The text is openly political and partisan:

> In time of war there might seem to be no time for art. But the wise Chinese have decided differently. On the next pages are eight recent Chinese scrolls . . . They were painted at the Catholic University in Peking, now occupied by the Japanese. They are a touching affirmation that China, even in the midst of battle, holds to the spiritual and cultural values which America and China alike are now fighting to preserve. (40)

Since the need of Americans to distinguish enemy from ally was great, the climate was right and a veritable spate of books by Chinese in America appeared throughout the decade of the 1940s. Among these were half a dozen memoirs and novels about China at war, written, for the most part, by newly arrived immigrants. Also published around this time were the first autobiographies by American-born Chinese American writers: Pardee Lowe's *Father and Glorious Descendent* (1943) and Jade Snow Wong's *Fifth Chinese Daughter* (1945). Because *Fifth Chinese Daughter*, about growing up in America, fits more closely into the subject of the next chapter, we will reserve discussion of it until then. In this chapter, we shall concentrate on the books that focused on China.

A brief historical review will help to set these books into their context and provide an additional explanation as to why so many came to be written and published during this period.

In the late nineteenth and early decades of the twentieth century, Japan, technologically abreast of the times, embarked on a military crusade to enlarge her territories, a large part of which she intended to carve out of China, which she rightly judged to be a giant sleeping unguardedly on ancient laurels, militarily and technologically backward. Winning a war against China in 1895, Japan wrested Taiwan, Korea, and the peninsula of Liaotung from Chinese control. In 1915, Japan forced China to agree to Twenty-One Demands, "virtually imposing Japanese sovereignty" on the continent. Among these demands, "Japan was to control Shantung, to extend her influence in Manchuria, to have special rights in Fukien, and . . . mining and railway concessions elsewhere; China was to purchase most of her munitions from Japan, give Japan partial control of the Chinese police, and appoint Japanese political advisers."[3] In 1931, Japan seized southern Manchuria, and by 1939 she controlled all of Manchuria, half of Inner Mongolia, the capital of Beijing, all of the major seaports—Tientsin, Nanjing, Shanghai, Amoy, and Guandong, as well as the valleys of the Yellow River and the Yangtze River. The Japanese army had a well-deserved reputation for extreme brutality. "War itself is an atrocity. But the Japanese make war even more horrible than it usually is," noted contemporary observer journalist John Gunther in *Inside Asia*.[4] During what is now called the Nanking Massacre, which the poet W. H. Auden compared to Dachau, Japanese soldiers reigned in terror and in six weeks killed 300,000 Chinese, many of them civilians; raped several thousand women; and created sixteen million refugees.[5] The Chinese retreated to the west, walking thousands of miles inland to escape the Japanese invaders, taking with them entire universities and factories, even disassembling machinery, and reassembling everything in the interior of China, near Chungking, the mountain-ringed wartime capital (Gunther, 248). The Japanese then pursued the naturally fortified Chinese by air, dropping bombs on Chungking and its environs each sunny day and each moonlit night.

The intense emotions evoked by the prolonged humiliations and horrors of war produced an outpouring of books by writers anxious to express their outrage, frustrated idealism, and intensified patriotism. The few able to travel to the United States, because of expense and immigration restrictions (not lifted until 1943), were, as we have noted before, journalists or daughters of diplomats and scholars. Though English was not their mother tongue, Helena Kuo, Adet Lin, Lin Tai-yi (Anor Lin)[6] and Mai-mai Sze nonetheless expressed their thoughts and communicated their experiences to the West. I include Han Suyin among this group, though she did not immigrate to the United States, because her first novel fits into the genre of patriotic outcries stimulated by World War II written in English and published in the West. All five women were, of course, highly educated and had been exposed to Western culture and thus well prepared to be unofficial diplomats and bridges between East and West. Seizing advantage of the opportunity of their physical presence in the West and fueled by patriotic ardor, they felt impelled to make friends for China through the vivid stories of suffering and heroism they each had to tell.[7]

In the decade of the 1940s alone, this group of five women published a total of 10 books, including one translation, four autobiographies, and five novels. The translation, *Girl Rebel. The Autobiography of Hsieh Pingying with Extracts from her New War Diaries* (1940), by the youthful sisters Adet (age 16) and Anor (age 13) Lin is significant since it is the first introduction that Western readers were given to the phenomenon of the Chinese woman warrior that Maxine Hong Kingston would make well known 36 years later. The woman warrior is such a rare phenomenon in the West that the figure of Joan of Arc stands preeminent. In China, however, despite or because of the long tradition of female suppression, women who bore arms and engaged in battle, while not common, were certainly not unique. Hua (or Fa) Mulan, the legendary woman warrior who donned masculine garb and took her father's place in battle, lived during the Liang Dynasty, about A.D. 500, and thus the precedent was set early. Hsieh Pingying was but a modern example, and Kuo Ch'ung-ch'ing of the People's Liberation Army, whom we mentioned in the introduction, yet another. Thirty women left the Kiangsi Soviet in 1934 on the Long March (6,000 miles) to Yenan, including K'ang K'e-ching, the wife of General Chu Teh, and more joined the march in Szechuan.[8] Thus, the woman warrior willing to give up the shelter and comforts of home to endure the hardships of battle and to risk death was a model available to Chinese girls, and one that Dr. Lin Yutang, Adet and Anor's famous writer father, evidently encouraged. Hsieh Pingying was a social and political rebel whose life encompassed the extremes of a bound-feet girlhood to a gun-bearing adulthood, from strict Confucian parents to free marriage and divorce. She was a courageous young woman of strong will and determination, who lived untrammeled by worn-out conventions; who was unafraid of public censure, poverty, imprisonment, and hardship; who firmly believed in the common man and woman and gave herself unstintingly for her country.

Translating the diaries of this woman warrior, Adet was deeply moved, and her patriotism fueled:

> And then suddenly all the things around me no longer had any meaning . . . Only where Miss Hsieh was seemed to mean anything. It meant everything. It was real life over there, to suffer for a common cause. I felt that I belonged over there, over there in China . . . And when I gave myself to that thought, nothing else seemed real.[9]

For Adet Lin, living in security and comfort with her family on New York's upper East Side was a frustrating and ignoble unreality; to suffer in the defense of one's own country, however, was to her an infinitely more heroic and noble life. Shortly after the publication of this book, Adet Lin was able to immerse herself in this "real life" when her father took his entire family on a six-month visit to China. Out of this experience came *Dawn Over Chungking* (1941) by the three Lin sisters: Adet (age 17), Anor (age 14), and Meimei (10).

Like Anne Frank's *Diary of a Young Girl*, *Dawn Over Chungking* is also the work of intelligent, sensitive young girls in extreme times when life is pared to its essentials and nightmares are everyday realities. Both books describe life on the knife's edge but also radiate idealism and hope. They are testimonies to physical and spiritual strength all the more touching because of the tender ages of their authors. Both are wrenching when we consider the kind of world we have created in which a 14-year old has such thoughts as these:

> Often I wondered what would I choose; for a Japanese plane to be shot down and crash on me, or let it fly away. $150,000 was what a bomber cost in American money, and I was not sure I was worth that much. Yet I wanted to live. I never dared decide, and never did have to . . . Still, I did want to know which would profit the people more. (159)

The Lin family chose to set up housekeeping in Peipei, a quiet village that had never been bombed, 50 miles from Chungking. Three days later, Peipei was attacked by Japanese planes, and a bomb fell 100 yards from their house. During the second air attack, a bomb fell 20 feet away. The third bomb directly hit their home. The family was in the air raid shelter. Despite the horrifying sights of rotting corpses, incendiary bombs, burning buildings, cratered streets, and daily fearing for their lives, the Lin sisters kept up their spirits. Anor could even be humorous. She wrote that one side effect of the destruction of their house was the recovery of the checkers that the rats had stolen from her and hidden in the attic. Impishly, she concluded: "the Japs were not only trying to gain our love by bombing us, but trying very hard to help us kill rats too!" Adet could write eloquently about the air raids as having a socially leveling and community-strengthening effect, in a passage that would presage her war novel, *Flame from the Rock*:

It was the air raids that made me forget the rich, the poor, the faults of people near me and around me. It was the air raids that made me feel that I was truly a citizen of China. It was the air raids that made me feel the pulse of war. It was the air raids that made me think everyone, even the worst, should live. And I like to see a group of people feel truly and universally about something . . . I liked to see something that touched every heart, and an air raid was universally felt. (108)

To celebrate an air raid as a socially levelling and community-bonding event is a reversal of expected values and, to a certain extent, a romanticization of war, but the phenomenon does exist, however briefly.

1.1. Brief Biographies of the Five World War II Writers

Biographical information on the authors in this group will provide a useful background to their work. Of the group, Han Suyin and Helena Kuo have been most forthcoming about the details of their lives, having agreed to personal interviews and written autobiographies (Han Suyin's is four volumes long). The others have written about limited periods of their lives, specifically childhood and the war period, but have been reticent about later years, not answering written letters of inquiry nor agreeing to interviews. Thus, of necessity, the quantity of information on these five women will be somewhat unbalanced.

All the women in this group have had prominent Western-educated fathers and less prominent but imaginative or patient and tolerant mothers. Han Suyin's father, Chou Yentung, was a railroad engineer educated in Belgium and her mother, Marguerite Denis, a Belgian woman entranced by a storybook notion of China, who had a rude awakening when she followed her husband to his Chengtu home in 1913, to a family and a nation wracked by political and economic crises. Her parents' fairy tale courtship and disintegrating marriage are powerfully evoked from multiple perspectives in the brilliant first volume of Han Suyin's autobiography, *The Crippled Tree* (1965). Helena Kuo's father was a hard-working, successful contractor in Macao, a progressive and unconventional man who married for love and believed in educating his two daughters as well as his six sons. Her mother, whom she described as "a person of quiet dignified beauty" (*I've Come a Long Way*, 22) was a traditional woman with bound feet and gold ornaments in her hair; she was a devout Buddhist who daily rose at 4:30 or 5 in the morning to wash and say prayers. Mai-mai Sze's father, Alfred Sze, studied in the United States from 1893 to 1902, receiving an M.A. degree from Cornell University in 1902. He was China's ambassador to England in 1914 and in the 1920s ambassador to the United States.[10]

Adet and Anor Lin (who prefers to be known as Lin Tai-yi) have the most famous father, Dr. Lin Yutang, the most prominent and prolific Chinese writer in the United States in the 1930s and 1940s. The son of a Presbyterian minister, Lin Yutang (1895–1976) married Liao Tsuifeng in 1919, earned an M.A. from Harvard in 1920, and a doctorate in philology in 1923 from the University of Leipzig. Returning to China, he taught at the National Peking University from 1923–1936, was a professor of English and Dean of the College of Arts at National Amoy University from 1926–1927, and founded and edited several radical literary journals including *Analects Fortnightly, Cosmic Wind*, and *This Human World*. In 1927, he worked for the Ministry of Foreign Affairs in Wuhan, China; in 1936, he emigrated to the United States with his wife and three young daughters. His first prominent English book, *My Country and My People* (1935), established his reputation as a spokesperson for China in the West. Apart from three breaks—a few years in Paris, London, and Singapore—Lin Yutang lived in New York City for 30 years before retiring to Taiwan in 1966; he died in Hong Kong on March 26, 1976. His literary output was prodigious and varied, numbering more than 50 books, including collections of philosophical and political essays, novels, translations, and biographies.

Not surprisingly, he encouraged writing in his three daughters, who are the youngest in this group of five writers, and his second daughter, Tai-yi, is one of the most prolific and talented of this group. The first book by the Lin sisters, a collaborative effort, is a collection of diary entries by Adet, age 16, and Anor, age 13, with comments by Meimei, age 8, entitled *Our Family* (1939). With humor and charm (and misspelled words), they describe their lives as the daughters of a famous writer, their first impressions of America, their trip to France, and their memories of China. Their characters shine through their prose. Adet is the most serious, the most romantic, the most idealistic and patriotically Chinese. Anor is the most imaginative, the liveliest, the most original. Meimei is a tough realist not terribly interested in writing. (She would later make science her career.)

Adet was born in Amoy, China, on May 6, 1923. She was 13 when her family came to the United States but, despite many years in this country, always retained her sense of belonging to and identifying with China. After studying at Columbia University from 1941 to 1943, she did some secretarial and publicity work before finding a position more to her liking at the Chinese Blood Bank, a unit trained and sponsored by the American Bureau for Medical Aid to China. From 1943–1946, she served with this unit in Kunming, China as a part of the Chinese Army Medical Service. This experience gave her background material for her novel *Flame from the Rock*, in which a blood transfusion provides the link between a peasant soldier and a professor's niece. Back in the United States, Adet Lin worked for the U.S.I.S. and the Voice of America as a stringer correspondent in the Amoy dialect. Eighteen years after *Flame From the Rock*, she published *The Milky Way and*

Other Chinese Folk Tales (Harcourt, 1961) and nine years later *Flower Shadows: Forty Poems from the T'ang Dynasty* (1970). She died in 1971.

Lin Tai-yi was born April 1, 1926, in Beijing, China. Following in her sister's footsteps, she too attended Columbia University (1946–1949) and for one year taught Chinese at Yale University. In 1949, she married R. Ming Lai, chief information officer for the Hong Kong government. She has one daughter, Chih-wen, and one son, Chih-yi. She has contributed to *Punch, U.N. World, Tienfeng Monthly*, and from 1964 until 1988 she was the editor-in-chief of Chinese edition of *Reader's Digest* in Hong Kong. She now resides in Washington, DC. Her literary precocity was astonishing, for by age 20 she had already published two very accomplished novels: *War Tide* (1943), when she was 17, and *The Golden Coin* (1946), at age 20. Her third novel, *The Eavesdropper*, discussed in the last chapter, appeared in 1958 (the hiatus of 12 years may be explained by the demands of motherhood), followed shortly by two additional novels, *The Lilacs Overgrow* (1960) and *Kampoon Street* (1964). In 1965, she published *Flowers in the Mirror*, her translation of an eccentric early nineteenth-century Chinese novel by Li Ju-chen, which is the source for the opening episode about the man in the Country of Women in Maxine Hong Kingston's *China Men*.

Of this group of five authors who focused on China during the war, Helena Kuo (Kuo Ching-ch'iu) is the eldest. Born in 1911 on the island of Macao, she was the fourth of eight children. To her father's liberality and to the international and artistic atmosphere of Macao, which she called the "Monte Carlo of the Far East," Kuo attributes her sense of adventure and love of literature. As a child, Kuo studied Portuguese and Catholicism in a Portuguese Convent school in Macao while private tutors at home taught her Mandarin Chinese, English, mathematics, bookkeeping, shorthand, and typing. Later, she was one of two young women to attend the middle school of the missionary-sponsored Lingnan University in Canton, "one of the most expensive colleges in China . . . (and) consequently the most aristocratic." (55) At Shanghai University, she first had to master the Shanghai dialect before she could pursue studies in industrial chemistry and Chinese and European literature. When China gave away her northern provinces of Kirin, Feng-tien, and Helung-Kiang, Kuo demonstrated with outraged students all over China against the policy of appeasement and became a volunteer in the Red Cross hospitals. But when Japanese troops opened fire on Shanghai civilians in 1932, her father called her home. Anxious to be part of the war effort, however, she returned to Shanghai the following year, gave up her university studies, which now seemed irrelevant, and found a position on the *China Times*. She published articles both in Chinese and English and soon was made editor of the women's page of the *China Evening News*, an affiliate paper.

Her life then became a chain of fortuitous events that eventually led her to the United States. A chance meeting with an American businessman, who had made a fortune in China and wanted some way to repay the Chinese, provided her with travel funds to Europe and the United States. In London, a three-minute broadcast she did on the BBC about the Chinese New Year celebration brought her an invitation from the *London Daily Mail* to write a column. On the strength of the column, Methuen gave her a contract to write a book, the result of which was *Peach Path*, which she completed in Vence in southern France. With Europe on the brink of war, she wrote a letter to First Lady Eleanor Roosevelt, telling of her desire to visit the United States. Mrs. Roosevelt secured a visa for the young writer and sent her a personal invitation to visit the White House.

A slender, beautiful, young woman with the First Lady's personal invitation in hand, Helena Kuo created a mild sensation on her arrival in New York in 1939. Her picture and story appeared in many newspapers and magazines, among them *Newsweek* and the *Christian Science Monitor*. She had a half-hour interview with Mrs. Roosevelt in the White House, followed by an appearance on the Martha Deane radio program and invitations to many parties and dinners, where she met such Chinese luminaries as Dr. Lin Yutang and Dr. Hu Shih, China's official ambassador, himself a literary man and a philosopher. She received advice on writing from Pearl Buck. On a lecture tour around the United States, she was given a personal tour of his modern art collection by director Joseph von Sternberg and was offered a screen test by a Hollywood talent agent but warned to stick to her writing by Chinese American cameraman, Jimmy Wong Howe.

Her literary work encompasses essays, autobiography, fiction, and translations. In 1940, she published *Peach Path*, a collection of essays with a strongly feminist tone. In 1942, she completed an autobiography, *I've Come a Long Way*. In 1944, she published a novel, *Westward to Chungking*, and a second collection of essays, *Giants of China*, an introduction to 11 Chinese heroes and heroines. She then turned her hand to translations of two novels of Lao Shaw, one of China's foremost contemporary novelists noted for his biting satire. In 1948, she completed Lao Shaw's *The Quest for Love of Lao Lee* and in 1952, his novel, *The Drum Singers*. She edited a Chinese-American dictionary for use by the armed forces, wrote occasional articles for American magazines, and had her own program on the Voice of America. In 1956, she married the Chinese American painter Dong Kingman, whom she had interviewed on her radio show several years before. They now make their home in New York City, and she has subordinated her career to his, traveling a great deal around the world with his exhibitions, helping him with large murals, such as the one in the Lincoln Savings Bank in New York's Chinatown, and writing the text of a book about his work, *Dong Kingman's Watercolors* (New York: Guptil and Watson, 1980). She has taken very seriously her own words in an early article she wrote contrasting American and Chinese women: "When we Chinese women marry, we want to believe that we have moulded our lives into another life. We feel it as an act of creation. We believe that 'woman is made of water and man of clay.'"[11] Alluding to but diverging from the creation of Adam and Eve in Genesis, she implies that woman was not formed as a separate entity from a rib of the man but that she becomes one with him, as water is necessary to clay if it is to be shaped and made useful. Occasionally, she is invited to write an article on Chinese food or Chinese kites, subjects very remote from what she chose for herself in earlier days.

Kuo's writing career began with an outspoken, confident, at times deliberately provocative, stance, particularly notable in her first book, *Peach Path*, which we shall discuss in a later chapter, but it seems to be ending in a quiet way, subdued by masculine and Western dominance. The subduing process began early in her contact with the West. In England, she wanted to write like an English person, but her editors wanted her to conform to the style they expected of a Chinese—to write in "unconsciously funny ways," in other words, to play the amusing alien observer role. "So I gave it up," she confesses in her autobiography, "and wrote what they expected."[12] Her first book, *Peach Path*, is her most personal, most authentically herself. Her latest work, an article on Chinese kites for the *New York Times*, about which she had to do research at the library, seems a capitulation to writing "what they expected."

The author about whom we have the fewest facts is Mai-mai Sze. In her autobiography *Echo of a Cry* (1945), she writes engagingly of her early childhood in Beijing, schooldays in England, holidays in Scotland, high school in Washington, DC, college at Wellesley, and a year of art training in France, but gives no dates. Instead, Sze's autobiography is particularly introspective and thoughtful. At the same time, it is spiced by the author's wit and humor and by her own lively drawings. Since *Echo of a Cry* discusses the between-world condition in a thorough and poignant way, we shall reserve discussion of it until a later chapter. In 1946, Sze published a two-volume book, *The Tao of Painting. A Study of the Ritual Disposition of Chinese Painting*, and in 1948 a strange and haunting novel about the effects of war, called *Silent Children*. She lives in New York City but does not answer letters from strangers nor grant interviews.

The most prolific and protean in this group is Han Suyin, whose comprehensiveness, diversity of subject matter, and form, quantity, and quality make her a major writer. Author of nearly two dozen books including a four-volume autobiography, fictionalized autobiographies, a biography, travel books, and numerous novels, Han Suyin is a woman of indefatigable energy and resources, who has taken active advantage of her position between worlds. Daughter of a Belgian and a Chinese, she is in herself a bridge between East and West. Widow of a Kuomintang army officer and biographer of Mao Tse-tung, she has bridged political parties. Trained in England to be a doctor and practicing medicine until 1963, when she left medicine to devote herself full time to writing, she has bridged the worlds of science and literature. Interweaving history, biography, and fiction within a single text (see especially *The Crippled Tree*), her work bridges genres. Married three times—first to a Chinese, then an Englishman, and finally to a black-skinned Indian—she has bridged racial and social barriers. Dividing her time between homes in China, India, Switzerland, and the United States, she is truly an international figure defying any simple national categorization.

Han Suyin was born in China in 1917, one of eight children, and christened a long string of names which she shortened to Rosalie Chou, though her former son-in-law calls her Elizabeth. As a Eurasian growing up in China, she was made to feel inferior by both Europeans and Chinese, and has felt this negative self-image to be the biggest handicap in her life. On the other hand, it has also propelled her into unceasing effort and consequently significant achievement. After a Catholic convent education, she worked several years as a typist at Peking Union Medical College, starting at $35 a month and rising to $175 when she left, while an English woman was paid $350 and a Chinese man, father of six, earned $35 and would never get more. This early experience of racial discrimination left a lasting mark on her character, developing in her a sympathy for the underdog. From 1933–1935, she attended Yenjing University in Beijing, admitted as an overseas Chinese because she did not pass the entrance examination in Chinese. In 1935, she took the Trans-Siberian train to Belgium, attended the Université Libre of Brussels, and basked in her maternal grandfather's affection. Between 1936 and 1938, she studied in England, passed her Bachelor of Science exam with highest distinction, and fell in love with the English language, "that rich and inexhaustible treasure of moods and music, feeling and thought, endless ambrosia, a firm enchantment, lifelong."[13] But with China in the throes of war, she returned home, arguing with herself:

> . . . maybe you are only a Eurasian, a dirty half-caste, as some people say, but you cannot live without (it.) China . . . Like that famous Greek giant Antaeus, who had to touch the Earth his mother, you can't do without China. Here you've been three years in Europe and have had everything you wanted and all you feel like is a stinking pool of dead water. You've got to go. (411)

Aboard ship, enroute to China, she met Tang Paohuang, a Kuomintang officer, who became her first husband. The courtship and early years of that marriage, the hardships of life in the beseiged capital, and her belief in Chiang Kai-shek's ability to rid China of the Japanese are recorded in her first book, *Destination Chungking*.

1.2. World War II Novels and Autobiographies: The Patriotic Stance

1.2.1. Han Suyin's *Destination Chungking*

All the wartime books written by this group of five women stress the courage, ingenuity, and even humor of the Chinese people amidst the horror that is war, and all except the last, Mai-mai Sze's *Silent Children*, were written from first-hand knowledge of both horror and courage. The earliest of these books is Han Suyin's somewhat fictionalized autobiography *Destination Chungking*. In the Foreword to the second edition of *Destination Chungking*, Han Suyin captures the youthful optimism that characterizes the psychological mood of nearly all these writers:

> Casting back mind and body to eleven years ago, to myself when young in Chungking at war, I recall the world as it then was, a solid one; words of assured meaning; ends self-evident, right and honourable; doubt a grievous offence against oneself and others; virtue, and faith, carrying one through hunger, pain and trouble. One was sure to laugh again, to enjoy life in spite of present trouble and the ever-recurring theme of bombing which accompanied each sunny day; everything was surely going to come right in the end.

Destination Chungking had a very interesting genesis. The book would not have been written without the encouragement and assistance of an American missionary doctor, Marian Manley, who was in charge of the midwifery hospital in Chengtu where Han Suyin worked. It was Manley who suggested creating a book out of the letters and jottings Han Suyin had written "to friends in England who wanted to know how things were going in China." Han Suyin herself lacked confidence: "I was frightened. My English learnt in Peking when I was only ten years old, and mostly acquired through reading, not conversation, would never be sufficient to write a book." But the book was written, despite separation from Manley, despite the war, in the interstices between her work as a doctor and her duties as wife and mother: "in the evening by oil light in what was left of the room after the day's bombing; in the afternoon returning from a night- and morning-long case; in intervals of respite between cooking, cleaning, a peering at the sky for more enemy airplanes. Wedged in with the family cooking pot and my daughter I carried to the shelter of the hill dugout the manuscript of *Destination Chungking*." Finally the book was finished to the satisfaction of both author and editor, and a publisher, Jonathan Cape in England, was found. But, "for an odd reason," at the time Han Suyin could not acknowledge authorship:

> I had become, if only temporarily, through my husband, a member of my country's diplomatic corps. Ladies of the diplomatic corps do not write books. The set in which I lived considered writing an unwomanly occupation, destructive of one's moral character, like acting.

She took up a pseudonym and published her book under the name Han Suyin. Needless to say, Han Suyin did not give up writing but gave up, instead, that particular social set.

Destination Chungking intertwines personal history with the history of China in the style that would later characterize Han Suyin's best work. It tells the story of her courtship and marriage to Tang Pao-huang, an officer in the Kuomintang army, against the vivid background of China at war. Though her autobiography would later reveal the profound unhappiness of this marriage, the intolerant, "feudalistic" tyranny of the husband who was not above beating his wife and who died in his first battle, *Destination Chungking* was written in the first flush of love and loyalty, in ignorance of the tragic sequel, and in an attempt to smooth over the rough spots. The first paragraph, however, reveals the ambivalence of their relationship right at the start:

> Ever since the day Pao pulled off the red strings wound tight around my three stiff little pigtails, and sent me howling to my mother, we have not been able to do without each other. Most of the time there lay an unfinished quarrel between us and, neither willing to let it rest, we stubbornly sought each other for a chance to renew it. Now in our life together the contrary pull of our will and thought continues still, to spice with excitement the deep accord of our marriage.

Even without the benefit of hindsight, this is a problematic relationship. How sound can it be to base a marriage on an unfinished quarrel? With the benefit of hindsight, the paragraph clearly reveals an awareness of the relationship's inherent conflict even though this variance is clothed initially in seemingly innocent, childish play—Pao's pulling off her red ribbons. It quickly moves to conflict on a more abstract, adult level—"unfinished quarrel"—and then bravely attempts to pull together what is clearly tending to fall apart, to brush away the conflict by claiming, simply by asserting it, "the deep accord" of their marriage.

A fictionalized autobiography, *Destination Chungking* tells the story of Han Suyin's stormy relationship with Tang Pao-huang with great novelistic skill, with irony, and paradox. The author vividly recreates the details of their shared childhood on the same quiet street in Peking; Pao's adamant refusal of three marriages his parents tried to arrange for him (the third candidate, ironically, was Han Suyin but he would hear nothing about her, not even her name); their meeting in London when she was an absolute pacifist and he a military student; their decision to return to China together to be part of the resistance against Japanese aggression and to marry. His traditional, patriarchal ways and her fierce, defiant independence led to repeatd clashes. In the final analysis, what drew and kept them together was a deep love for China; her passion for this patriotic man was but an extension of her own passionate patriotism. When they were both students in a foreign country half way around the globe seeing newsreels of their people's suffering at the hands of the Japanese, both were moved to return home, to give their all for the cause of Chinese liberation. Thus, though the book sets out to be the story of love and marriage between a man and a woman in a wartime setting, it is actually the story of the love of one's country. What the author called "the deep accord of their marriage" is really the fervent patriotism they shared, as evidenced in this paragraph:

> We have lost proud and stately cities. The earth drinks the blood of our dead. The smoke of our burning homes is black and tawny against the sky, But history is not determined by captured cities, burning towns, farm lands laid waste. China is not lost when territory is lost. Where there is an indomitable heart, there is China, unconquerable. (94)

The descriptions of their travels across China, of Chinese resistance, of narrow brushes with death in the daily bombings of Chungking and the long hours in air raid shelters, of the war's casualties and tragedies, of woman warriors, opium dens, Communist idealists, fat and cynical Kuomintang officials—all are recreated in vivid detail and together form a portrait of China during a period of life-and-death struggle. Thus, it is fitting that the book ends with an apostrophe to the Chinese coolie. A name spoken of disparagingly throughout the world is one Han Suyin would make "a name of honour before the world" for they are "builders and carriers, the peasant farmers, the workers of China" (251). Although *Destination Chungking* records great youthful admiration for the Kuomintang leader, Chiang Kai-shek, it ends on a note prophetic of the outcome of the Chinese civil war, for in praising the common coolie and the peasant farmer Han Suyin demonstrated that she was in tune even then with the Communist cause, and her later books, particularly her two-volume biography of Mao Dze-dung, would further demonstrate this.

1.2.2. Tan Yun's *Flame From the Rock*

The most romantic of the books in this World War II group is *Flame From the Rock*, Adet Lin's first and only novel, published under her pen name, Tan Yun. It combines all the patriotic ardor and youthful idealism she expressed in *Dawn Over Chungking* (the Anne Frank-type book she wrote with her sisters discussed above) with a tender, tragic love story. The appeal of this novel is attested to by a Canadian edition published in 1944 and a French translation in 1946. Richie Maybon in the *Saturday Review of Literature* praised the book's unusual blend of romance and realism:

> Because of the simplicity of its telling, and the tenderness of the love episodes, this little story has something of the remote and haunting quality of medieval love stories. And this despite the fact that the Chinese characters—the scholar uncle, the nagging wife, the wise old peasant woman, the modern hospital staff—are all vividly portrayed and undoubtedly wholly "modern."[14]

Drawing on her experience with the Mobile Blood Unit, Adet Lin uses a simple but very effective device to bring together her ill-matched lovers: a blood transfusion. Twenty-year-old Kuanpo Shen, a volunteer nurse, is badly wounded in an air raid and a blood transfusion from the taciturn soldier, Wang Tsai, who happens by, saves her life. With this literal blood tie between them, and despite her uncle's strong disapproval and the large differences in class, education, and temperament, the young couple fall passionately in love. But Wang Tsai is eventually killed in battle, his body blown into such fragments that there is nothing left to bury. And Kuanpo, taken away from the scene of her heartbreak by her family, falls ill and dies.

Flame From the Rock may be read as an allegory of Adet Lin's love for the land of her birth; backward and stolid though it may be, the blood bond is there in her veins and it is ineradicable. The rock in the title is symbolic both of China's spirit of resistance and of Wang Tsai, one physical manifestation of this resistance. Though the nation is rock-like in its massiveness as Wang Tsai is initially rock-like in relation to Kuanpo's lighthearted advances, sparks and even flames—patriotism, heroism, passionate ardor—may be struck from both.

The novel also may be a criticism of her famous father's safe, civilized distance from China during her bloody struggle. One scene is particularly telling in this regard, highlighting the differences between the professor and the soldier and, by implication, finding the professor wanting. Wang Tsai is having dinner with the Shen family when the conversation turns to Lo-Yang, a city that both host and guest have visited. Professor Shen recalls his delight in seeing "some of the already vanishing traces of an ancient city, the grandeur and gaiety of it," particularly the famous White Horse Temple, the oldest in China. He asks if Wang Tsai recalls this temple, assuming that everyone knows it, and reprimands the young man when the answer is negative: "It is a crime to pass through Lo-Yang and not visit it"(142). Wang Tsai then tells of his visit to Lo-Yang. After three days and nights of hard marching, his company camped outside the city walls, lying sick on the ground and slowly recovering from the starvation diet of the front. And now he is rebuked for being ignorant of a temple.

For Adet Lin, the professor's antiquarian, bookish, even touristic interests are irrelevant and useless in this time of crisis when all Chinese should be working together to rid their land of foreign invaders. The very survival of the cultured, "civilized" world of the more privileged class depends on the strength of the simple, unpretentious soldier; as Han Suyin's coolie is the builder of the world, so Tan Yun's soldier is its protector and defender. The professor, however, does not realize this and refers to Wang Tsai as a "common soldier" and, worse, as the "scum" of the earth.

Not only is this attitude wrong for a man so proud of his education and culture, it is uncivilized. In a China struggling to wrest itself from foreign strangulation, such snobbery and narrowmindedness have no place. Thus, *Flame from the Rock*, drawn from the experiences recorded in *Dawn Over Chungking* and from the autobiography of Hsieh Pingying, may be read as Adet Lin's repudiation of her father's decision to return to and remain in the United States, far from the fray.

1.2.3. Lin Tai-yi's *War Tide*

War Tide, also published in 1943, is Lin Tai-yi's contribution to China's war cause, and a powerful, extraordinary book it is. Drawing also from the same sources as her sister, namely *Dawn Over Chungking* and the autobiography of Hsieh Pingying, Lin Tai-yi added her own originality, a strong expressionistic style and a fuller canvas of characters and incidents than her sister's *Flame from the Rock; War Tide* is less autobiographical and less focused on one intense relationship. The plot centers on an 18-year-old girl, Lo-Yin Tai, whose resourcefulness, intelligence, and courage keep the Tai family together through the turmoil and horrors of war. Her family is a large, multi-generational group comprising her emotionally remote father, owner of a silk shop in Hangzhou; her ineffectual mother, who is wasting away from tuberculosis; her older brother Fa-An, a pilot at the front, who brings home and leaves a pretty but totally useless young wife, Royal Pearl; a 7-year-old brother, Little Bean; Third Aunt, her father's sister, a fat, pleasant widow who does the housekeeping and cooking for the family; and the Old Lady, her paternal grandmother, a typical matriarchal tyrant unrelenting in her meddling in the lives of all the members of the family and in her insistence on her need for a great-grandson. War erupts, and the family's life is totally shattered: Royal Pearl is nearly raped by a Japanese soldier; the family must abandon shop and home and join the hordes of refugees fleeing westward. Mr. Tai is killed enroute, and the family's welfare and living devolves upon Lo-Yin, whose young shoulders bear the burden with courage and competence. In addition to the members of the immediate family, *War Tide* is peopled with a host of interesting characters. Among them are Tsa Tse, a traumatized 12-year-old boy (a forerunner of Mai-mai Sze's *Silent Children*) whose mother has been raped and murdered before his eyes, and Dragon Eyes, a former schoolmate of Lo-yin's who, unencumbered by family responsibilities, becomes a woman soldier and captures a Japanese prisoner.

The episodes of *War Tide* are propelled by the principle of yin and yang, a circular whole that is formed from wavering halves of darkness and light. Throughout the book, opposite emotions are continually juxtaposed and counterbalanced, for they are what make up life; there is no final fixed resolution, only a continual flow between extremes. The novel begins with Lo-Yin's sudden awakening one night in a nameless terror; then she hears, in the rain, gay laughter which is transmuted into weeping and sobbing. In the midst of rumors of encroaching war, with his grandmother seemingly nearing death, Fa-An is married: "this death and the wedding, so close, so similar, and both so noisy and so hideous that one might forget where to draw the line to tell them apart."[15] Along with the war that creates havoc and destruction comes also the opportunity to test one's courage, to make sacrifices, to be heroic, necessary, and useful as Lo-Yin, Dragon Eye, Tsa Tse, and others demonstrate. With his thigh blown away, leaving only a mass of torn tissue and bits of flesh hanging by thin tendons, a soldier hears beautiful music all around him:

> The wind blew and the butterflies' wings shone purple and blue from the windows, and the flowers smelled sweet from the air, and the room was spattered with red blood and charred clothing and burned flesh. (216)

Beauty compensates for ugliness, birth and new life for death: the Old Lady dies just after Royal Pearl bears a baby girl; Mr. Tai drowns, but Lo-Yin finds an orphaned baby cooing in a pool of blood. Shen, who becomes Lo-Yin's fiancé, begins as a male chauvinist who dislikes clever women and wants only a pretty wife, while Lo-Yin begins with disdain for men who need weak women to boost their egos. They end up with each other and with a fuller understanding of the Other. Life goes on in the midst of horror and death. Only hope never dies.

Though the plot and the characters are engrossing, the most remarkable and original element in *War Tide* is Lin Tai-yi's stylistic experimentation. During moments of intense emotion, the language suddenly grows heightened, unreal, surreal. Here, for example, is Lo-Yin's reaction to her brother's wedding feast:

> . . . she saw the food on the table, the half-eaten chicken with its pierced wings and its meat sunk in black gravy, and she saw the slices of fat pig meat, and the thick soup and the chicken feet and the overturned winecups, and it seemed this feast was rotting before her eyes, and the red scrolls fell from the wall, and the people fell and rotted and there came a strong sickening odor of decay . . . (28)

From a detailed, realistic description of the banquet dishes—chicken in black gravy, slices of fat pork, thick soup, chicken feet—the text suddenly moves to surreal elements—"the red scrolls fell from the wall, and the people fell and rotted." The only indication of the shift in modes, from the naturalistic to the surrealistic, is the verb "seem." The falling of the red scrolls, emblems of honor and celebration; the falling of the wedding party and guests and the sickening odor that ensues graphically convey Lo-Yin's sensual and spiritual nausea. The wedding was taking place only because the family had capitulated to the Old Lady's insistence on her need for a great-grandson. But a marriage during a time of national crisis simply to cater to the whims of an old lady, a marriage that leaves Lo-Yin with two additional mouths to feed when her brother goes back to war and Royal Pearl bears a child, is ridiculous and oppressive. When the Old Lady begins to make arrangements for Lo-Yin's own marriage, Lo-Yin, unlike her older brother, becomes outspokenly defiant and says she will not "be sold like a piece of meat to some man" simply to please her old grandmother.

In Lin Tai-yi's description of the Japanese soldiers invading Hangzhou, the colors again are exaggerated, the features distorted, contorted. The text itself seems to rise to a shriek:

> They hobbled their way like monkeys hopping among trees, and their long, hairy hands were claws, and they let out monstrous sizzlings or shrieks; they opened their mouths wide and let out shrieks into the open purple winter air, shrieks into the white sky, and their bloody claws scratched over everything they saw, and their eyes were lit by some evil green fire, evil, bitter fire. They scratched the winter sky and broke it like a crust, and from behind the sky rain had poured—black rain, blacker than blood, and the sky was bleeding—When the devils were tired of scratching . . . they sought something warm, something warm and human because they were so afraid, and they sought and found the sight and touch of warm, pale, soft female flesh, and their dirty claws tore the flesh apart, screeching as they did—and the warmth in the flesh had gone with the tearing—and that was how they went. . . . And the city lay rotting, red, wasted, smelling and burning, and on the streets hungry devils and stray dogs hunted; the devils sought among both living and dead to shame them, but the dogs sought for a bone to gnaw from the dead only. (96–7)

The author's disgust and hatred are conveyed not through direct editorial comment but word choice and selective detail. The verb "hobbled" to imply crippled legs; the focus on hairy hands (body hair is considered animalistic in Asia rather than virile); the overlapping repetition of "shrieks," "fire," "blood," "devils"; the use of strong colors: the "evil green fire" fueling the demon's scratching through "open purple air" to the "white sky" which bleeds black rain; the startling imagery of the sky as a crust broken by this blasphemous scratching, and then coming down to earth to another desecration; the extreme contrast between the soft pale flesh of women and the dirty claws tearing at this flesh till warmth and life disappear; and the final comparison making starving dogs in the street more honorable than these men—all this is powerful writing in anyone at any time, but particularly extraordinary for a young woman of 17. War itself, of course, is an unspeakable, surreal experience calling forth the most intense of emotions. With originality and boldness, Lin Tai-yi created the expressionistic language and grotesque imagery appropriate both to her subject and to her emotions.

Her startling imagery, her expressionistic style, her broad vision and large concerns (the feminist and racist protests in this book we will reserve for a later chapter); her skill in individualizing characters through the very language they use as well as through their actions; the variety and inventiveness of character and incident—all emerging at the uncommon age of 17 in a young woman for whom English was second language combine to make Lin Tai-yi an extraordinary writer and *War Tide* an extraordinary achievement. Contemporary critics recognized her accomplishment, for they clearly saw that *War Tide* was "not the autobiographical or lyrical work which so often is the first offering of a young writer."[16] Instead, it has strong claims to being the work of genius that Pearl Buck saw as early as the publication of *Our Family*, when Anor was only 13: "I should not be surprised one day to see an actual genius declare itself in those clear eyes of hers. I sometimes think I see it now."[17]

1.2.4. Helena Kuo's *Westward to Chungking* and *I've Come a Long Way*

Helena Kuo's war novel, *Westward to Chungking* (1944), resembles *War Tide* in that it too is the story of the effect of war on a multigenerational Chinese family, but is less iconoclastic and more conventional. Here too is a tyrannical grandmother whom Kuo describes as having "the heart of a lion and the determination of a mule." However, the mainstay of this family is not a teenage daughter but the 60-year-old father, Lee Tien-min (whose given name translates into Citizen of Heaven). At the beginning of the novel, Lee Tien-min is a prosperous owner of a department store in Soochow, with a fine house, servants, and three children at the university. At the end of the book, having lost store and home, having trekked thousands of miles inland, he is suffering daily bombing raids in Chungking and eking out a living selling soy bean milk and cruellers, but he and his family have survived.

Westward to Chungking is less original than *War Tide* but nonetheless interesting. Its theme is straightforward; its tone optimistic. Kuo's hatred of the Japanese is more moderated than Lin's, and the emphasis in this book falls on the quiet courage of the ordinary Chinese. The characters are well drawn, and there is a large cast, including a series of minor foil characters whose presence serves to highlight certain of the major characters. For example, to offset the integrity and patriotism of Lee Tien-min, who gives away his merchandise so that the Japanese will not benefit from it, Kuo gives us Pan I-Fei, Lee's unscrupulous cousin, who makes a fortune collaborating with the Japanese. In contrast to the two Lee daughters, one of whom stays with the students from her university to work in hospitals, while the younger is raped by three Japanese soldiers but continues to work with her soldier husband at the front, is the beautiful, pampered, and totally useless wife of Pan I-Fei. After the death of her husband, this woman comes to realize that, prepared as she was for nothing in life but to be a plaything for rich men, she was victim of the traditional Chinese oppression of women. Diametrically opposed to this widow, whose major concern is her appearance, is the Lee family's eldest daughter, Fu-yi, who replies to her mother when the latter scolds her for wearing men's clothing, worrying about what people will say, "It is not what they say that matters. It is that I am comfortable" (261). For her, vanity is not a consideration. Furthermore, Fu-yi is the daughter of her father, who "had decided very early in life that one had to do things other people disapproved of if one wanted to progress" (6).

For American readers, *Westward to Chungking* is set apart from the other war novels by its inclusion of a number of American characters and the occasions for comments on the United States interwoven into the plot. The most prominent American character is Sam Hupper, a soldier of fortune, a personable man and a loyal friend, who buys a car and helps the Lee family flee west. Later, he converts a Ford truck into an ambulance and works indefatiguably at the front. American missionaries, Dr. and Mrs. Winter, devote themselves to the medical and evangelistic care of the Chinese, perform the wedding ceremony for the second Lee son, and graciously hold the reception at their home. To Dr. Winter, Lee Tien-min remarks on the similarity between the teachings of Jesus and Confucius, particularly in the Sermon on the Mount. Dr. Winter replies on the most general level, "I agree with you that our beliefs are almost the same. Life is but man's struggle to perfect himself and to rid himself of sin."

The family's oldest son, Tai-Ho, is sent to the United States for pilot training, which gives Kuo an opportunity to comment on the United States through the letters Tai-Ho writes home about his impressions and experiences. Most of them are positive, for he praises the greatness of Americans, delights in the warm-hearted reception which he as a soldier of Chiang Kai-shek enjoys, and bluntly spells out the difference between his native land and the United States: "Here you can eat anything you want. In China, you eat anything you can get. Such is the difference" (268).

However, Tai-Ho cannot help but notice American racial discrimination and Kuo seems to follow in Edith Eaton's footsteps by using the same device as in "Mrs. Spring Fragrance"—a letter home—to express criticism of a serious American shortcoming:

Some Americans do not like the Negroes . . . There is here, what is difficult to understand, a color line between the white and the black. Into this black division, some Americans put our own people . . . but because we are in uniform we are accepted anywhere. . . . I have made friends with a Chinese-American now serving in the American army. Although he is one hundred per cent Chinese except for his American upbringing, he could not mix with the Chinese, and because he was Chinese he could not get work with Americans, except as a waiter, even though he went to college . . . I hope that some day the Americans will realize that the Chinese can also do something besides laundry work and waiting at tables. (269–70)

This is a simple, direct statement of the between-world condition of the Chinese American—Chinese by race but American by culture and education and totally accepted by neither. As though Kuo felt uncomfortable with such an outspoken complaint when she had been so hospitably received in America, Tai-Ho ends his letter cheerfully, observing that the Chinese were presently benefitting from the distinctions Americans were drawing between the Chinese and the Japanese:

> Americans hold the Chinese character in high esteem. Our people are known for their honesty. They say you can never trust a Japanese, but you can always rely on a Chinese to keep his word and pay his debts, so we have something in our favor. (270)

Though Tai-Ho expresses pleasure in this state of affairs presently favorable to the Chinese, Helena Kuo's tone is ironic and shows her awareness of the racism inherent in this pitting of one group against another, and her realization of the ephemeral and tenuous quality of the distinctions being drawn. Finally, the stress demanded by the word "something" in the last line emphasizes the insignificance of this small comfort compared to the overwhelmingly negative condition of being a racial minority in the United States.

Compared to Lin Tai-yi's *War Tide*, Kuo's *Westward to Chungking* is more traditional in that the protagonist is the patriarch, a good man whose perspective is never forgotten. For example, when he worries about his eldest daughter, who is trekking inland with her entire university as it moves west to avoid the Japanese, he consoles himself with these thoughts: "It was true that she belonged to the family, but she belonged also to China. She was one of his contributions to the war" (139). The daughter is not her own person but her father's gift to the nation. The mother is a devout Buddhist whose dreams about her endangered pilot son are so disquieting that she can only be comforted by a perilous pilgrimage 30 miles into the mountains to consult a holy man in his cave. She follows her own path with little effect on the rest of her family. Though the daughters are strong, they are not the mainstay of the family, as is the heroine of *War Tide*. The father is the focal point.

Westward to Chungking ends with a dinner in honor of the first visit of the younger daughter and her husband to the Lee family home. Though reduced to poverty, the family prepares a large feast. Sam Hupper, the family's American friend, marvels at how well Tien-min, the father, manages. Tien-min answers:

> Man is no different from a plant, except that he has better intelligence. My tomato plants grew in Soochow, they grew in the village, and they are growing here. Tomorrow I shall make you a present, Sam . . . Some big ripe fruit. (297)

Lee Tien-min epitomizes "China at war," suffering defeats and deprivations, but spiritually strong and, like his beloved tomatoes, physically hardy. He shall endure, and if not he then his children and theirs after them.

The title of Helena Kuo's autobiography, *I've Come a Long Way* (1942), which has unfortunately been appropriated with slight modifications by a cigarette company, alludes literally to the geographical distances she traveled from her home in Macao to the United States, as well as the cultural, linguistic, and psychological distances she has traversed between an ancient Confucian China and the modern West. The book tells of her childhood home, her liberal father who provided his daughters as well as his sons with both a Chinese and a Western education, her experience of the war, an unhappy love affair, and how she managed to become, as she calls it, "a fragment of old China come West" (3).

Though she voluntarily exiled herself from her country, her patriotism remained strong, as evidenced in this vivid description of the nightmarish trip she took on a ship crammed with refugees panicked by Japanese bombs:

> I looked down on an inferno of misery. No slave ship of the dark ages ever carried such a sad burden. From below rose the most indescribable smell . . . the smell of closely packed humanity, of sweat, urine, decay and death . . . And these were my people, some of the four hundred and fifty millions of Chinese beginning a new Calvary because the politicians in Europe had decided to sell China down the river . . . and here was the prelude to the most forceful tactics of modern war, assault on the morale of the civilian population. Immediately below me a woman had died in the crush. Her face was upturned, terribly contorted . . . She had died trying to force her baby up to enable it to breathe. (233)

For a Chinese writing in English to a Western audience, Kuo is audacious in placing the blame for China's suffering on "the politicians in Europe" who had (continuing her slave image) "decided to sell China down the river." And as a woman with more expensive accommodations on this ship (since she is looking down on the others), she is horrified to see the high cost of mother love for a woman less fortunate than she.

The immediate impetus for her leaving China was her decision to break an engagement that had become oppressive, her need to remain an independent woman rather than the self-abnegating future wife of an abusive husband. As an undergraduate at Shanghai University, she had fallen in love with a young patriot, Lien, who shortly thereafter travelled to Europe to pursue graduate studies. On his return, he postponed their marriage while he sought a suitable position in government but nonetheless put her to work in an old house in Beijing caring for his aged mother, his nonworking brother, his sister-in-law, and his grown-up nephew. When Lien was arrested and nearly executed, he blamed Helena for his troubles, and became alcoholic and abusive. Learning that he had lived with a European woman while abroad, and that he demanded that Helena give up her career in journalism, she boldly broke the engagement and left China.

In style, her autobiography as well as her novel, are written in a straightforward and unpretentious manner. Her English is fluent and at times even colloquial, at other times highly metaphoric. When inspired she produces startling images, as in these examples from *I've Come a Long Way*:

> Zeal for getting knowledge burned inside me like an overdeveloped thyroid. (58)

> We waited listlessly. We hung the harps of our good spirits on the trees of bitterness, and waited. (144)

> Peiping still remains in my memory as one of the most civilized towns I have ever visited. Beside it, London is like a clerk and New York like an impudent street urchin. (196)

She is particularly effective when describing moods:

> But I was not back in the hotel long before there descended on me an awful feeling of damp and dismal loneliness . . . loneliness that smells like a dark cellar, and is as crumpled and forlorn as a discarded shoe . . . The furniture seemed to be on strike against any suggestion of comfort . . . (250)

She can be humorous and visually acute, as in this description of Lee Tienmin's clerk who ran around the store:

> like a fat duck straightening the goods, smoothing a fabric with his plump hands that were like yellow hot-water bottles. (*Westward to Chungking*, 41–2)

or sensuous, as in this description of an oppressive summer day:

> a hot day, with thick damp heat like cotton wool against your face, and the sweat everywhere inside your clothing." (*Westward to Chungking*, 57)

Both Helena Kuo's novel, *Westward to Chungking*, and her autobiography, *I've Come a Long Way*, are clearly the writing of a courageous, independent, yet deeply patriotic young woman who sees herself in a literary ambassadorial role, for her stated purpose is "to print something worth reading—something that would make China better known to the world" (343).

1.2.5. Lin Tai-yi's *The Golden Coin*

Lin Tai-yi was apparently so moved by the war experience that one novel was not sufficient to contain all she had to say on the subject; she wrote three. Her second novel, *The Golden Coin* (1946), pushes her symbolic, expressionistic tendency further and becomes almost allegory in unusual combination with naturalism. Written in the United States but set in China, the book spans the years from 1919 until roughly 1940 with the war as a backdrop for the central theme—the conflict between faith and reason. It is the story of the unequal marriage between Sha, an illiterate, life-affirming woman, who represents faith, and Wen Lang, a cautious, cowardly, life-negating scientist/professor, representing reason.

Lin Tai-yi, circa 1979

The naturalistic strain is found in closely observed details of such unexpected subjects as mosquitoes and flies, as in this example:

> Summers there were flies. They were as large as one's thumbnail, green-headed, with red caps. Clusters of them topped piles of garbage until one's hair rose on end and one's flesh became porous. These flies multiplied as heat multiplied in summertime, until the hot baked streets hummed with them. They swarmed around food, and they rested on people's hot arms and feet and faces, and sometimes they got into people's ears and noses and mouths. One could sometimes pick off these big ones with a piece of paper. Sha delighted to hear flies crack as she squeezed them between two fingers with a piece of paper. When she opened the paper, there the fly lay, crushed to a pulp, eggs crowded out of the body. (13)

Mingling naturalism and expressionism, humor with horror, Lin Tai-yi describes the effect of repeated childbearing and poverty on Sha's mother:

> Her face looked as though it had been hanging out on the washline for a long time, after having been put in a basin and scrubbed and wrung out many times. It was beaten, faded, crinkled, pale, tired, shapeless. It was almost flat, the button nose rising from it only out of necessity. There were no unnecessary features on the face: no bridge, no arch, no brows, little hair; but there were two necessary large eyes and a necessary large mouth. (22)

With a drunkard father and a coarse, worn-out mother, with barely enough food to feed her numerous brothers and sisters, Sha views her family and her surroundings with pessimism:

> She pictured her people as living in a decaying well, at the forgotten dark, maggot-ridden bottom, amid slime and mud and mildew. She pictured these people as the growths of unhealthy poison plants, deserted by those richer on top. These poor saw only the one-foot diameter of sky from the bottom of the

well and knew not enough to climb out, nor did they think there was anything outside. She, for one, longed to come up to the top. (16)

Sha is surprisingly unlike either of her parents and though she does "climb out" with the help of marriage to Wen Lang, professor of biology, she finds that the "top" has its ugliness as well. The dean is found embezzling university funds, and to divert attention from himself he scoffs at Sha for pulling the emergency cord on her first train ride. Wen Lang, afraid of losing his job, neither defends his wife nor attacks the dean. When the crisis blows over, the dean offers Wen a $30 raise, which Sha rightly sees as a bribe to keep silence, but which Wen happily accepts.

The book's dedication to the author's sister Adet invites a comparison with Adet's novel *Flame from the Rock*. Both novels involve a relationship that crosses class lines; however, *The Golden Coin* counters the romanticization of poverty embodied in Adet's soldier Wang Tsai, for the passages quoted above demonstrate that Lin Tai-yi sees no poetry in poverty. While *Flame from the Rock* celebrates a romantic love that comes to fruition despite class differences, *The Golden Coin* portrays a marriage that results because of class differences and the attraction of opposites: Sha marries Professor Wen Lang to escape from the slums while effete Wen Lang lusts after Sha because she is physical and sensual. In both novels, the lower-class person possesses more strength and common-sense intelligence than the upper-class better-educated spouse, but *The Golden Coin* has the additional theme of faith. Sha's belief in the efficacy of the golden coin and of her lucky baby to protect the town seems blessed and rewarded by heaven and is finally undermined only by the disbelief and rationalism of her "superior" professor husband.

As though in answer to Adet's implied criticism of their father's physical withdrawal from China in her time of need, Lin Tai-yi avows that intellectual/spiritual needs can only be satisfied when physical/material needs have been met, writing of her heroine:

> First she had to be satisfied within her body—material satisfaction of the five senses. And only then could the body carry out the wishes of the spirit sanely, healthily, and capably. The other need was to know of a truth and goodness—the spiritual comfort and time-sustaining goodness which must be the reason of all life. This feeling was something which had to satisfy not just one person, but generation after generation. (5)

In grinding poverty where life is a constant struggle to meet basic physical needs, one has no opportunity to consider spiritual needs. The spiritual self, which is nourished by art, philosophy, faith, requires for its development an economic base as well as peace and tranquility. Lin Tai-yi thus removes the question of their family's leaving China from Adet's nationalistic perspective (in which it seems like perfidy) and places it in a larger human context (in which it is reasonable).

Like *Flame From the Rock*, *The Golden Coin* is in many ways a repudiation of the intellectual who wants only to be safe. The author's sympathies are clearly with her heroine and against the thin, pale, bespectacled, coldly analytical Wen Lan. Educated both in China and at Oberlin, the 32-year-old professor finds himself attracted, against all reason, to Sha, a beautiful, robust 17-year-old selling semi-rotten fruits on the streets of Shanghai. Wen proposes to her, is surprised to find his offer accepted, and then worries about having married beneath his station. Later, when his wife has the entire village believing that their son brings luck, he secretly works to undermine this faith. He does not stand up to the dean he knows to be dishonest; in short, he is cowardly, cold, and calculating. Sha, by contrast, is a mythic earth goddess whose belief in goodness and truth defeats, for a time, the forces of cowardice and accommodation. Sha believes that her baby, Lucky Loo, is responsible for the rain that comes to the drought-stricken village just after his birth, that his presence heals disease and brings luck, that the air raid shelter named for him will be bomb-proof, and that the bridge built with his blessing will withstand floods. For a time, she is right. Despite the plot of her husband and his colleague to build a weak bridge and thus sabotage the village's faith in Lucky Loo, the completed bridge defies all laws of physics and miraculously stands. But as the years pass, the beautiful baby is discovered to be slightly retarded; the bomb shelter is destroyed by a direct hit; Lucky Loo is wounded in the knee and crippled; Sha finds herself falling in love with her husband's student, a man whose spirit is closer to her own; and, finally, the bridge, with a blinded Sha and her limping son on it, collapses, drowning them in a rushing torrent.

In light of the ending, the author seems to be saying that idealism and blind faith are doomed, and only with realism and accommodation, ugly as they may be, can one survive in the world. Yet realism is not enough, for in time of great stress and hardship the golden coin, which Sha's baby wears around his neck like a saint's medal, is a means of "prolonging a faith in mankind which otherwise would have been hard to keep. The golden coin was an excuse for living" (192). Myth though it may be, idealism and faith are nonetheless beautiful and necessary, because life-sustaining. *The Golden Coin* is thus the story of the uses of idealism and illusion. The reader is invited to identify with Sha's optimism, her radiant energy, goodness, and moral strength and to denounce hypocrisy and cold rationalism. Even though the power of faith and passion are ultimately physically defeated, they can indeed work miracles for a time and are nonetheless vastly preferable to cynicism and "safety."

1.2.6. Mai-mai Sze's *Silent Children*

The last of this series of wartime novels is Mai-mai Sze's *Silent Children* (1948), a text unlike any of the others. It is centered on a band of homeless children, ranging in age from 5 to 15, whose names (Cruzz, Jolo, Solen, Rull, Mulla, Vara, and Pin) reveal no nationality. The children live in a makeshift camp on a muddy bank across the river from an unnamed city "not indicated on most of the available maps." All of the action takes place at dusk or in the dark, giving *Silent Children* a strangely unmoored, haunting quality. With no identifiable bearings, the novel is obviously unrealistic and thus hardly an outburst of national pride like the other books in this chapter. Instead, Mai-mai Sze seems to be using homeless, hungry orphans to underline the dehumanization of war and perhaps to symbolize an inner psychological condition. She deliberately evokes pity and horror, but she is not maudlin. In showing the children as well organized, calm, and rational, surviving nightmarish conditions, she affirms the strength of the life instinct, but she is not sentimental. Reviewing this book, Richard McLaughlin of the *Saturday Review of Literature* wrote: "There can be few books today which have such emotional impact on the reader and yet are written with such a cool detachment."[18] In fact, the entire book seems to have a surreal, dream-like quality.

Recently occupied by enemy troops, the city across the river from the homeless children's camp is now reluctant host to the army of a foreign ally, and seems to have been forgotten by the outside world, for food supplies are dwindling and the army has not received any orders for many months. Thus, the nameless city is cut off from whatever center there is, and the band of children who survive by stealing forays into this city are more peripheral still.

Yet this band of children is shown to be a closely knit, well-organized community. Sze draws a striking contrast between the children, who share what little they can steal, even if it is only a loaf of bread, and the prominent citizens of the city, who hoard provisions, which they guard with guns. The children place those too weak to walk inside their only shelter, a shack, and give them a share of food. The children turn no one away from their fire, even the adults who intrude and eventually break up their community. The adult hoarders, however, are intent on "exterminating the little rats," their name for the children, and think nothing of killing a child for stealing a loaf of bread.

The book develops along a chronologically organized narrative line through a series of strikingly graphic scenes, which attest to the painterly talents of the author. The most memorable of these scenes occurs when Rull and Jollo, two of the older boys, return from the city with a large trunk and two loaves of bread. The children are disappointed by the meagerness of their supper but are delighted to discover treasures in the trunk: metallic cloth, long velvet gowns, lace parasols, silk robes, petticoats, boots. Though half-starved, they don the items that please them and, silhouetted by the campfire, parade in the mud in a mockery of worldly splendor. When Rull discovers a sack of gold coins at the bottom of the trunk, the children toss the coins into the air, showering themselves with gold until they drop exhausted to sleep wherever they happen to be. Though glittery and attractive, the gold coins are useless because nothing can be bought. The scene is replete with symbolism.

Of the six adult intruders to the children's camp, two are particularly noteworthy for our study: Manus, an American soldier, "a curious combination of puerility and worldliness" (125), and Lo, a Chinese doctor trained in the West. Prisoners of war, both were inexplicably freed and set adrift to search for their ways home. Lo is developed most fully, both from the omniscient author's perspective and from the impressions of Manus. Lo's description, however, verges on stereotype: he is neat, spare, compact, straight almost to stiffness, in appearance younger than his years, a little supercilious because he comes from an ancient culture. He has a precise manner of speech and is the only one in the group who has learned the language of this city. But he is ineffectual, for the children ignore him when he asks in their language where the nearest city is. Manus finds Lo "inscrutable" and notes "mainly that peculiar placidity in the man which offered itself either as a reserve derived from genuine humility or as an air of practised aloofness" (116). Manus is annoyed by Lo's stoicism and "impassive calm"; yet, since their paths have been thrown together, he thinks they ought to be more friendly. Lo, however, is busy with his own thoughts, wondering about the strength of the survival instinct in these children, reminiscing about his own childhood and the difference between himself and his brother. His brother had chosen to immerse himself in traditional Chinese arts, specifically calligraphy, while he

> rejected those ways as antiquated, negative and bankrupt. Can we both be right? We may both be wrong; for perhaps it is not really possible to completely accept or completely reject our heritage; we cannot today live imitating our ancestors, but neither can we discard them. Fortunately for us there is no choice; it is not either the one way or the denial of it. One becomes and that process of becoming includes both acceptance and denial of that heritage; at the same time, however, one is independent of it. The results at various stages in the process may appear defective, even ridiculous at times, but they have the vitality of growth and change, and therefore also the potentialities for fuller development. (129)

In these philosophical, existential musings, the author seems to enter into her narrative, and the reader can see her engaged in an inner debate, perhaps lamenting the time she had spent immersed in traditional Chinese painting (for Mai-mai Sze's second book, as noted above, was *The Tao of Painting: A Study of the Ritual Disposition of Chinese Painting*) but finally reconciling herself to the process of growth and change. Expressing the between-world condition, Mai-mai Sze here states that both acceptance and rejection of the past are the inescapable condition to her independence, her own life and her identity.

Manus and Lo attempt to strike up a conversation but Manus confesses he is hampered by "oriental" stereotypes in his head:

> "I suppose I attach to you all the romantic notions I've ever had about your part of the world and I expect you to be completely different from myself and different from anyone I've known. But you aren't! . . . I think I expected you to be mysterious, contemplative, removed." (132)

Lo, however, is homesick, tired of war, eager for a warm bath and a hearty meal—all down-to-earth desires, just like Manus' own. Manus initially glorifies their meeting as the proverbial "East meets West" and remembers having anticipated such a meeting "as though it were something new and extraordinary," but he suddenly realizes that "East and West met ages ago! But people go on proclaiming the meeting, don't they? I suppose the point is that we've never really succeeded in getting together" (133). What Manus remembers, however, is inaccurate, colored by his American optimism, for the famous Kipling line is not about the meeting of East and West but about their never meeting. In this passage, Sze seems to be agreeing with Kipling; though East and West have physically met, they still remain so ignorant of one another that each meeting seems to be the first one all over again.

As though she didn't know what to do with Lo after interesting her reader in him, Sze suddenly has him killed by Rull. Frustrated and wounded, Rull had discovered a large horde of food in the city across the river and was nearly killed trying to steal from it. Bringing it back, Rull encounters Lo, who, traumatized by the gun Rull points at him, forgets to speak Rull's language, cannot make himself understood, and is shot.

Silent Children ends with the disbanding of the children's camp. When Rull returns wounded, Toor realizes it is no longer safe for them to remain at that spot and leads the majority of the children away with him. Jolo, Vara, and the little deaf-mute Vara cares for remain to bury the body of Solen, their philosophical, wise leader. After the men with a machine gun track Rull down and kill him, the deaf-mute suddenly screams. The book ends with Jollo and Vara leading the no-longer deaf-mute child away. Their destination is unknown, but Jollo has faith that "There would never be an end so long as they had life and breath and strength to move . . . he did not ask how long their strength would last and how far they could proceed without nourishment. The answers were beyond him and in the hands of others, who were unknown to him and to whom he was unknown" (189). The departure is an act of trust, for they launch themselves into the unknown, wanting only to survive.

Silent Children seems to be an existential parable of the condition of life.

There is no benign force in the universe; in fact, to the contrary, if a force exists it is malign. Violence and death startle the deaf-mute into finding her voice. Struggle, hunger, and hardship characterize the human condition. What good there is seems frail and almost futile in the face of the overwhelmingly negative surrounding conditions. The dark pessimism of this book— almost unrelieved by examples of hope, humor, or courage and even physical light—sets it apart from the other novels of this period and also seems out of place, since this novel was published several years after the conclusion of the war. Perhaps the trauma of the war lingered long in the imagination of Mai-mai Sze or, what is more likely, perhaps she used this particular aftermath of war, the silent children, to express an internal trauma, her own sense of a symbolic orphaned condition between worlds.

2. LIFE IN THE PEOPLE'S REPUBLIC OF CHINA: THE CRITICAL STANCE

In sharp contrast to the ebullient patriotism of the majority of books that came out of World War II, those that focused on China after the Communist Party gained control tended, on the whole, to be critical and negative. The authors in the earlier group, with the exception of Helena Kuo and Han Suyin, were brought out of China as children accompanying their families to the West at a time when China was under attack by a foreign power. Thus, their patriotism was unalloyed. The majority of authors in the later group, however, were adults who themselves chose to leave China out of dissatisfaction and disagreement with the government. Making their new homes in an anti-Communist West, they found publishers and a ready audience for expressions of discontent. Thus, our subject as we have defined it—women of Chinese ancestry who have written books in English and published them in the United States—has preselected the political dispositions of the people involved.

Furthermore, the political climate was ripe for anti-Chinese books, for the United States in the early 1950s had done another about-face and now regarded China as an enemy nation. Politicians searched for a scapegoat to blame for "losing China" to the Communists. Senator Joseph McCarthy's House UnAmerican Activities Committee was fine-tooth-combing all of America to root out Communist infection. It is not surprising, then, that the books published about China by Chinese living in the United States from the early 1950s until the early 1970s would be critical in stance. Yet, taking the political atmosphere and preselection into consideration, much may be learned from the authors in this group, for their books provide a window into a country holding one-fifth of the world's people that for nearly three decades was closed to the West.

The earliest of these books in English about life in Communist China was Maria Yen's *The Umbrella Garden: A Picture of Student Life in Red China* (1954). Originally written in Chinese and published in Hong Kong under the title *University Life Under the Red Flag*, the book was later translated into English by the author, with the assistance of Richard M. McCarthy. Since few firsthand accounts about life behind the Bamboo Curtain were available in the 1950s, *The Umbrella Garden* initially received a good deal of favorable attention. A student at National Beijing University during the most momentous period in modern Chinese history, Maria Yen documented in great detail all the changes in student life from January 1949, when she anticipated with great hope the arrival of the Liberation Army into Beijing, until the autumn of 1950, when, fearing "a tyranny more thorough and efficient than any we had ever known,"[19] she fled to Hong Kong. Because Yen is meticulous and detailed, the reader is given the full experience of what it was to be a student during that critical period.

Yen's most serious objection to the Communist government was its methods of coercion and total control. Every aspect of a student's life—academic, political, and even personal—came under close and constant scrutiny and was subject to criticism not only by Communist cadres but also by friends and roommates, who were encouraged, even required, to report any deviations from the official line. Soon nonconformity and independence of thought were virtually impossible. The regulating hierarchy became so elaborate that a person could be required to participate in more than a dozen different circles of graduated sizes, each holding regular meetings: living circles of 5 or 10 students, floor groups within a dormitory, interdormitory groups, "mutual-aid circles" in each class, groups classified by major subjects, squads, and sections. Though the Party's benevolence was given as the reason for the imposition of each new regulating circle, in practice, as Yen saw it, individual freedom was being gradually eliminated. Labelled "democratic centralism," this elaborate hierarchy was touted as a system that enabled the people at the bottom to voice their will through the chain to the top. Instead, Yen noted, it was a highly efficient machine for transmitting commands from the top downward and for rooting out dissension at all levels.

Mincing no words, Yen dubbed the new government "the People's Democratic Dictatorship," and described further harsh and unjust measures it instituted. Upheavals in the university, which anticipated the Cultural Revolution two decades later, brought about the elimination of courses traditionally taught at the university, foreign studies and especially English (Yen's major) fell into disrepute, respected professors and deans were publicly humiliated. After graduation, graduates were assigned to jobs without regard to personal preference, unless they were part of the new elite: Party or Youth League members. Everyone else had to serve willingly wherever he or she was needed and no appeals were possible. Such conditions eventually became intolerable to Maria Yen, who, after careful planning and under disguise, successfully crossed the border and joined other self-exiles in Hong Kong.

Eighth Moon by Sansan (1964), as told to Bette Bao Lord (wife of Winston Lord, the US ambassador to China 1985–1989), has a somewhat different slant since it is the unusual story of a child, Bette Bao Lord's youngest sister, who grew up in the Peoples' Republic of China separated for 17 years from the rest of her immediate family by political events. Sansan was left behind as an infant when her parents and two older sisters took what they thought would be a short trip to the United States. While the family was abroad, however, diplomatic relations between the United States and China were severed. The family could not return, and Sansan could not leave. Adopted by a somewhat begrudging aunt and uncle, Sansan was not told her true identity until she was 16, when her grandmother, fearing that the truth might die with her, told Sansan her full story. Sansan became fired by the dream of reconciliation with her family, a dream that, after much difficulty, was eventually realized, creating the climax of the book.

Eighth Moon, like *The Umbrella Garden*, stresses the hardship of daily life in Communist China, but the narrative voice is straightforward and uncomplaining, able even to see humor in hardship. In one anecdote, for example, Sansan explains that though everything was rationed, one could only purchase what the government allowed to be sold, at which time long lines would form. One woman joined a line not knowing what it was for because everything was in such short supply that she assumed she could use whatever was being sold. To her dismay, hours later, she learned they were selling coffins. Another time, suffering a cloth shortage, the government decreed it was patriotic to wear patches for China and inventively created the "campaign of the glorious patches."

Sansan survived years of famine when the staple of her diet was corn husk meal and years of want when each person was allotted two feet of cloth a year, not enough even to make patches for the old clothes. She participated in the youth labor teams when China tried to industrialize with little equipment and a great reliance on people power. She tended homemade steel furnaces 7 days a week on 8-hour shifts 24 hours a day; she was part of a human conveyor belt passing along buckets of fertilizing manure for one mile to the fields. Like Maria Yen, Sansan was disappointed in the government's disposition of her future. Though she had studied very hard to earn grades high enough for medical school, she was assigned to teach elementary school at age 17 with no prospect for further education. Her friends suffered similar disappointments. One academically strong boy had openly complained about the forced labor, seeing no difference between their work on the farms and the drafted labor gangs of previous emperors; at graduation from middle school, he was assigned to labor instead of college.

Despite all the vicissitudes of her early life, Sansan displayed a remarkable resilience and resourcefulness. She sat through compulsory political theory classes devoted to propaganda but stubbornly maintained her independence of mind: "I did not always believe what I learned in politics class. I could only guess that America was either very rich or very poor—otherwise the party would not dwell upon it so much."[20] Though young, her survival instincts were strong, and she quickly learned to be wary about expressing her real opinions and careful to dissimulate her wariness:

> I realized that while it was not smart to keep quiet and thus arouse suspicion, I was expected to express only opinions that echoed the ones suggested by the group leader. Sometimes it was very hard to find a new way of saying the same thing, and I often spoke up early in the discussion so that no one else could steal my ideas. Later, I discovered an even better method; I would volunteer to take minutes of the meetings; knowing that the recorder was always the last one asked for an opinion. Usually time ran out before the group leader could call on me. (48)

The adaptive strategies demonstrated in this passage are highly developed and testify poignantly to the severity of the constraints imposed on her.

When her adoptive mother learned that Sansan was anxious to be reunited with her biological mother, the distraught woman called a family council, gathering together Sansan's paternal uncles and aunts to pressure the girl into obedience. All advised the girl to remain in China and to view her parents as capitalist enemies. But Sansan held firmly to her dream and after various anxiety-producing subterfuges finally found herself on the train to Hong Kong thinking:

> How foolish they were. What did I care for governments? I would have journeyed anywhere to be with my real family; had mother lived in China, India, Spain or the North Pole, it would have made no difference. (3)

Eighth Moon ends climatically at the railroad station in Hong Kong when Sansan first sees her mother. A motherland without one's mother is an unsatisfactory place.

Yuan-tsung Chen's autobiographical novel, *The Dragon's Village*, published in 1980, discusses the same period as the two books above—the early years of the Peoples' Republic—but from a somewhat more positive stance. Yuan-tsung Chen was born in Shanghai and educated at a Shanghai missionary high school for girls, just graduating in 1949 when the Communists won the war. She worked at the Film Bureau in Peking and in 1951 joined a team working on land redistribution in Gansu Province, the setting for her novel. For the next 20 years, she participated in several land reform campaigns before immigrating to the United States in 1972. She and her husband, historian Jack Chen, now make their home in El Cerrito, California.

The more positive stance of her book may be accounted for by the lapse of 30 years between the events narrated and the recording of them and also by the thawing in relations between the United States and China by the time of publication. After Richard Nixon's visit to China in 1972 and the resumption of diplomacy between the two nations, Americans were once again ready to hear favorable things about their former ally.

The very aspects of coercion and control that Yen and Sansan criticized Chen sets into acceptable contexts, describing the "self-criticism" sessions as "a cross between a family council [an ancient Chinese tradition], a group therapy session, and a Roman Catholic confessional." The *yanko,* or Rice Sprout Song, the powerful symbol of desolation at the end of Eileen Chang's novel of the same name, is compared to the French Carmagnole, "the dance of the revolution," whose steps "come from the movements of working in the fields."[21] Joining in the dance, Chen says, the peasants "shed their shyness . . . and discover their real, vital selves in the gay, bold rhythm" (281) as they go to the land redistribution meeting, which is the climax of the novel.

Guan Ling-ling, the novel's protagonist is a Catholic-missionary-educated 17-year-old who refuses to flee to Hong Kong with her industrialist uncle and aunt when the Communists gain control and instead volunteers with a group of theatre people to be part of a land reform mission. The group is sent to a tiny village in northwestern China, and though many of the consequences of this mission are tragic and shocking the book has the aura of an adventure with friends, an escapade into the countryside culminating in the goal these worthy young people firmly believe is right: taking from the rich and giving to the poor in the process called land redistribution. That suicide, rape, and murder occur as side effects of this process seems the unfortunate price that must be paid; they are the means—tainted by human error—to an ultimate goal that is good.

Land redistribution, idealistic as it sounds in theory, was, in practice, however, no easy task. Where does one draw the line between rich land-owner and middling landowner, for example? What methods of coercion does one use to force recalcitrant wealthy landowners into giving up what they own? When do these methods of coercion become unjustifiable torture? What basic human rights do the wealthy landowners have? When does power corrupt? Can educated urban youths, who feel vastly superior to the poor peasants into whose midst they have been suddenly dropped, really do the peasants any good? Can centuries-old value systems and customs be uprooted overnight? Chen's novel poses all these difficult questions and shows this group of Shanghai film and theatre people struggling with the difficult task of realizing the dream of communism in a remote corner of China.

The best portions of the book are those touching the conscience of the young protagonist. When one of the lesser peasant landlords is harassed by mistake and commits suicide, the senior cadre is less concerned by the man's death than by the negative effect that death might have on the peasant's view of the land reform mission. "As Wang Sha, the official, saw it, committing suicide was an unforgivable sin, an indictment against the new society. I was repulsed by his seeming callousness" (219). Yet, in Wang Sha's absence, when Guan Ling-ling is in charge and her protégé makes two seemingly ill-advised arrests on suspicion alone, Ling-ling supports her and even partici-pates in a nasty cross-examination. When the young activists suggest throw-ing cold water on their prisoner—it is winter and the building is unheated—Ling-ling, with callousness, replies:

> "I wouldn't shed a tear if he dropped dead somewhere else but I don't want him to get pneumonia and die in our hands." I surprised myself with these words; it was as if the spirit of brutality which I myself had condemned had entered my soul and was taking me over. (125)

But the prisoner, a big landlord, is finally revealed to have been bribing the peasants and Ling-ling's mistreatment of him is retroactively justified. The dark revelations that one of the newly elected cadres of a neighboring village is the rapist they were searching for, that one of the cadres in their own village is a murderer, and that one of the members of the Shanghai theatre group is murdered are presented as the side effects of the idealistic venture for which this group had been sent forth.

Chen portrays well the peasant disbelief in these brash young strangers from the city, who come mouthing what seem like fairy tales about gifts of land which they claim are government decrees. The peasants have never before gotten anything they haven't paid for dearly; furthermore, they fear that this government will be short-lived and that the next group in power will only give the land back to the landlords, so why should they stick their necks out now? The horrific mistreatment of women, brutalized and bereft of dig-nity, is portrayed vividly in the characters of Sun's wife and the virgin widow. The energetic young Xiu-ying, so nervous about her election as a cadre that she is literally speechless before her neighbors as she mouths a memorized speech without realizing that no sounds are coming out, brings the book a moment of lightness. However, there is more material here than Chen does justice to, ambiguities she touches upon but does not probe deeply, dark and tragic events that she quickly passes over.

The most recent book by an immigrant from Communist China is Nien Cheng's *Life and Death in Shanghai* (1987), a powerful text by an extraordi-nary woman, who was for nearly seven years a political prisoner. Gracefully and straightforwardly, Nien Cheng describes her ordeal during the Cultural Revolution, her arrest in 1966, the six and a half years of her imprisonment, and the seven years of searching for the truth behind her daughter's death. It is the story of a remarkable woman whose inner resources, high intelligence, strong faith, and, most important of all, anger made possible her survival under extremely difficult circumstances:

The misery of hunger and cold, the interminable days of waiting, the persistent yearning for freedom, the nagging worry for my daughter, and this latest abuse by the female guard produced the cumulative effect of making me very angry. When I got out of bed the next morning, I was no longer depressed; I felt as if something inside me were about to explode. I told myself that in my present circumstances such civilized virtues as tolerance, forgiveness, and even a sense of humor were luxuries I could ill afford. The Maoists were deadly serious in their design to destroy me. I must be equally serious in my efforts to frustrate them. (218)

And frustrate them she did. Using the words of their own leader, whom she studied to good purpose, to foil and frustrate their efforts to wrest a confession from her and wear her down. Instead, she wore down her captors. Her release, ironically, was hastened by the misdiagnosis of cancer by an untrained prison "doctor." After her release, she lived seven years under close surveillance, searching discreetly to discover the facts of her daughter's death, and only after emigrating to the United States in 1980 did she learn that her daughter's murderer had been given a commuted sentence.

Nien Cheng was an obvious target during the Cultural Revolution, for her background had been upper class, her life style comfortable and elegant, and her connections Western. While the rest of the country underwent the throes of change, or, as she put it, "was being taken over by proletarian realism" (3), she preserved her old lifestyle, maintaining for 17 years, as an English friend expressed it, "an oasis of comfort and elegance in the midst of the city's drabness." (3) She was one of approximately a dozen in a city of millions able to maintain their original homes and a staff of servants. Her book gives the reader a glimpse of the aesthetic and cultured life of the privileged upper class before it pitches us into the whirlwind of fanatic revolutionaries intent on destroying all that smacked of privilege and bent on reducing everyone to the lowest common denominator. How she survived this whirlwind is the riveting story of *Life and Death in Shanghai.*

Nien Cheng was born January 28, 1915, in Beijing, the eldest of five children (three girls and two boys) born to a Rear Admiral in the Chinese Navy. Her father had studied at a naval academy in Japan and was the commander of a destroyer. Her mother was 20 when she married and 21 when she bore her first child. Nien Cheng began to study English in middle school and went on to Yenjing University, where her classmate Han Suyin noted in her autobiography that Nien was a "brilliant student."[22] In 1935, Nien, an idealistic 20-year-old, entered the London School of Economics and met her future husband, Kangshi Cheng, who was then working on a PhD in International Relations. Kanghsi Cheng was an ambassador under Chiang Kaishek but in 1949 decided, because of his aging mother, to remain in Shanghai and accept a post as foreign affairs adviser to the new mayor of the city. A year later, he became general manager of the Shanghai office of the Shell International Petroleum Company, one of the few foreign firms that

Communist China allowed to remain, and he and his family were treated with courtesy for many years. When he died of cancer in 1957, his wife took over his work at Shell until 1966. After the events described in her book, she immigrated to the United States and is now living in Washington, DC. The bare facts of her life do not reveal the character that her ordeal brought forth, but the excesses of the Cultural Revolution brought out the woman warrior in her, a fighter for sanity, justice, and truth as she saw it with the weapons at her disposal: her courage, resistance, physical endurance, keen intelligence, and her justified anger.

The four books about life in Communist China discussed so far have all, by and large, been autobiographical. In contrast, the works of Eileen Chang— *The Rice Sprout Song* (1955), *The Naked Earth* (1956), and *Rouge of the North* (1967)—are novels. Eileen Chang has been called "the only novelist of real competence who has deserted Red China and written of life in that country from this side of the Bamboo Curtain,"[23] and "the best and most important writer in Chinese today" whose work, according to C. T. Hsia, a leading Chinese literary scholar, is not only comparable to but in some respects superior to such writers as "Katherine Mansfield, Katherine Anne Porter, Eudora Welty, and Carson McCullers. *The Rice Sprout Song* is already to be placed among the classics of Chinese fiction."[24] This praise, particularly in the case of *The Rice Sprout Song*, is not overstated.

Eileen Chang's background, like Nien Cheng's, was upper-class, educated, and urban but much less fortunate and less stable than Nien Cheng's. Eileen Chang's father, addicted to opium and morphine, was abusive toward his wife and daughter. When her father took a concubine, her mother left her husband, Eileen, and her younger brother for several years to study in France. Returning when Eileen was eight years old and attempting abortively to resume family life, her mother finally divorced her father and returned to France. For a while Eileen lived with her father and stepmother, but after being locked up for nearly half a year she left her father's home permanently. Admitted to the University of London, but unable to travel because of the war, Eileen Chang attended the University of Hong Kong. When the Japanese took Hong Kong, her studies were interrupted in her junior year, and she returned to Shanghai, where she began to write. Professor C. T. Hsia reports that "For the remainder of the war period she was the outstanding writer in Shanghai, her essays and stories being eagerly awaited by readers . . . " (392). After the war, she wrote film scenarios but, finding the literary climate hostile under the new government, she fled to Hong Kong in 1952. In the mid-1950s, she emigrated to the United States and she is now living reclusively in California.

Asked about her tastes in reading during an interview in Berkeley in 1973, Eileen Chang replied that she likes many classic Chinese novels including *The Dream of the Red Chamber*, for which she wrote a textual study. Among Western writers, her tastes are eclectic; she favors Kafka, Brecht (who was a good friend of her husband, Fred Rehyer), Harold Pinter, Stephen Crane, Sinclair Lewis, Emile Zola, Aldous Huxley, H. G. Wells, G. B. Shaw, Mary Renault, and James Jones (a family friend). When queried about how she could write English so well, she replied that she had studied English in a middle school that was run by foreign missionaries and had gone to the University of Hong Kong expressly to study the language.[25]

Her works in English include the novella "The Golden Cangue," originally written in 1943 and based on the opium smoking she was exposed to in her father's house. The story is a brilliant character study of a crafty woman, an addict, corrupted by selfishness and greed, and of the havoc she creates around her. Eileen Chang later produced a novel-length version of this story, which she entitled *The Rouge of the North* (London, 1967). In 1955, she published her masterpiece, *The Rice Sprout Song*, and in the following year another novel, *The Naked Earth*. Both books were originally written in Chinese and later translated by the author herself into English. Both deal with the failure of the Communist government in China, and both were commissioned by the United States Information Agency. *The Naked Earth* is a flawed novel with a particularly weak ending. The author herself expressed displeasure in this book, confessing that she was constrained by a plot contractually agreed upon beforehand. *The Rice Sprout Song*, however, appears to have had a powerful impetus of its own, and seems unaffected by any external constraints. It is a beautifully crafted piece of fiction, undoubtedly her best novel, the one most tightly organized, most artistically and economically rendered, and, after more than 30 years, it still remains the finest novel written in English about life in the People's Republic of China.

The genesis of *The Rice Sprout Song* was a newspaper article written by a Communist Party cadre who had participated in the quelling of a peasant assault on a granary during a severe famine. He had written an article about his doubts at the time, questioning how things could have gone so far awry that the government's guns were turned against the very people for whom the revolution had been fought. Later he wrote a retraction. Which attitude was the right one, Eileen Chang asks, before she launches us into her brilliant imaginative recreation of the story.

The book opens with a description of a string of seven or eight thatched privies, the first buildings of this particular village, followed by a single row of small shops, and across the road a ravine, where a woman dumps a basin of dirty water. "The action was somehow shocking, like pouring slops off the end of the world." With these few well-chosen details, Eileen Chang immediately establishes an atmosphere of dirt and desolation. The book then proceeds to an account of the peasant Gold Root's sister's wedding, a ceremony totally devoid of color, joy, romance. The groom and bride are asked whom they want to marry and why. They give each other's names and respond "Because she/he can work." Each puts a thumb print at the bottom of the forms, and the marriage is complete. Asked to sing a song at the wedding banquet, the bride gives a rendition of the marching song of the Eighth Route Army, model Communist soldiers. The implication is that in Communist China, patriotism has become the only permissible passion, and every individual is totally subordinated to the state. Even as personal and intimate a ritual as a wedding is no longer the individual's to plan or to enjoy. One marries not for one's self or one's family, but for the good of the state, or at least this is what one must claim.

Chang's distaste for the life and conditions she describes is implicit but never obtrusive, for her writing is spare and lucid. Her tone is deftly suggested through striking images and carefully selected details. An image particularly effective and unusual is her use of sunshine, generally a symbol of life and indestructible energy but in Eileen Chang's world: "Sunlight lay across the street like an old yellow dog, barring the way. The sun had grown old here" (3). The implications here run counter to the popular notion that China's venerable age is awesome and praiseworthy and suggest, instead, that with age comes exhaustion, for everything possible has been said and done. There is no longer anything new under the sun so that even the sun itself has grown old and tired in this land. The effect of this environment on its inhabitants can only be debilitating: "His heart was a trodden and squashed thing that stuck to the bottom of his soles" (25).

The theme of *The Rice Sprout Song* is that the government has gone nightmarishly awry. Beginning with Robin Hood idealism, it has now created a new tyranny with its own armies and cadres oppressing the people as blatantly as any past emperor. The book shows the high cost in human suffering exacted from all the people, privileged and nonprivileged, cadre and peasant; it takes no in-between stance as does *The Dragon's Village*. It dramatizes the terrorism by which the government enforces its will. For the cadres at the top of the new hierarchy, survival depends on hypocrisy, paranoia, and self-deception. For those on the bottom, survival itself is not even always possible. Modifying Marx's famous dictum about religion, Eileen Chang notes that Communism in China "had become like opium for the intellectuals . . . a faith which would enable them to suffer privations cheerfully, deaden all disquieting thoughts, still the conscience, and generally make life bearable" (166–7). Chang is clearly on the side of an active conscience.

The most blatant case of the self-deceiving Communist intellectual in this novel is Ku, a director-writer, member of the Literary and Artistic Workers' Association, a "new recruit to The Cause after the Liberation" (64), thus one who jumped on the bandwagon late. Ku's ostensible purpose in this village was to live as the peasants live and to collect materials for his next film, but he finds he cannot subsist on his hosts' thin rice gruel, and he secretly hoards food; he even walks 30 miles to town under a false pretext to have a meal at a restaurant. The more he learns about the life of the peasants around him, the more he sees the Party's failures and excesses. But his advancement depends on his good standing in the Party; thus, he twists reality to suit his politics. Irrationally, he attributes his own gluttony and lust to Kuomintang agents and discounts the peasants' storming of the government granary as a "mere accident, an isolated instance which had no place in the general picture" (167). Witness to a story of the utmost poignancy and significance, Ku rejects it as unusable and invents a formulaic story about the happy cooperation of the villagers in the construction of a dam. Ku's motto, which he repeats to himself "for the thousandth time since the Communists came," is to "Believe—for your own good" (166). The Party must be right, even if in this particular instance it appears to be wrong. The fault lies in the instance, not in the Party.

Slightly higher up on the moral ladder is Comrade Wong, a veteran Communist and the cadre in charge of the village. Though initially an idealist in his youth, he has consistently placed the good of the Party above the good of any individual, including his own wife, whom he abandoned. Now he is in charge of repeatedly pressing already hard-pressed peasants to contribute to one government cause after another; shoes for the soldiers fighting "American imperialists" in Korea, the "Support-Frontlines-Contribution," the "Contribute-Airplanes-and-Big-Guns-Movement," and a half a pig and 40 catties of rice cakes for army veterans at New Year. This final taxation is the cause of the rebellion, for the peasants themselves have been half-starved for months, subsisting on thin rice gruel and a few strands of vegetables boiled with the rice to extract all their nutritional value. Pork and white rice cakes are luxuries the peasants themselves have not tasted in many long months. Thus, pressed beyond endurance, the peasants riot in protest led by Gold Root, and Wong finds himself shooting at the very people for whom he had fought the revolution. He has a brief moment of lucidity and tragic stature when he tells Ku, immediately afterward, "We have failed. We have had to shoot at our people" (146).

Ku's response at this moment is an excellent example of the twisted logic required for self-preservation in the Communist Party:

> Ku avoided looking at him. In his present overwrought state Wong probably did not realize that this admission of failure in a moment of weakness and lack of faith amounted to a virtual betrayal of The Party and could be brought up against him in any purge. But sooner or later it would occur to him. And it would be only natural if he should want to dispose of the sole witness of his crime. Humble as his rank might be, within this village his power was absolute. And what was one more casualty amid all this shooting? (146)

Shocked by Wong's avowal of wrongdoing, for one's faith in the Party must be absolute, Ku contemplates turning in Wong for his traitorous remark and then, realizing that Wong has control over life and death in this village, pretends not to hear this remark. Ku's mind goes through tortuous paths, but he cannot see beyond fears for his own skin and he seems to possess neither heart nor conscience.

Wong, at least, still has a conscience. But as Ku expected, his loyalty to the Party has priority over everything else. To reconcile his conscience with his political beliefs, Wong decides the revolt could only have been instigated by a Kuomintang agent, and he proceeds to torture the peasants into revealing a scapegoat. He refuses to believe that the government can be wrong and that all his years of dedicated service have been wasted.

The tragic protagonists of *The Rice Sprout Song* are the scapegoats: a peasant couple, Gold Root and his wife Moon Scent. Gold Root, ironically, at the beginning of the novel, was awarded special recognition as a model worker and given the title Labor Model and seven acres of land. By the novel's end, Gold Root is labeled counterrevolutionary, a state akin to excommunication in the Catholic Church. Though the peasants are literally scraping the bottom of the barrel, still more is asked of them while the government guards with guns the granary filled with the fruits of the peasants' labor. When Gold Root shows the leadership qualities that were recognized by the Labor Model award by demanding the return of some of his own grain, he is branded a counterrevoluntionary and forced into hiding. Even his own family members cannot assist him without risking their own lives. He is hunted down and finally shot. Moon Scent, his wife, dies heroically continuing the storming of the government granary and setting fire to the stores. The aged aunt and uncle of this couple are forced to denounce them and to join in the Rice Sprout dance at the end. Following immediately upon the tragic deaths of the protagonists, the Rice Sprout song is no dance of joy, as in *The Dragon's Village*, no dance of new life taken from movements of peasants in the fields; it is a whitening of the sepulchre, for the old people are filling in the gaps left by the young peasants killed by government soldiers. The pathetic movements they are forced to make are a bitter mockery of the very nature of song and dance.

The novel's final line backs away like a movie camera zoom lens, distancing the viewer/reader from the scene: "But under the immense open sky the sound was muffled and strangely faint" (182). This line, with its tone of sadness, is tinged with hope, for it implies that the world is larger than this nightmarish corner where right and wrong, justice and injustice, love and honor have been turned upside down. Thankfully, there are still places under "the immense open sky" where one can breathe freely and stand straight, and where such chaos is unknown.

The Rice Sprout Song is a short novel, but its impact is great. Its images reverberate far beyond the text. These images have the condensation of poetry and carry the burden not only of the emotional impact but also of the intellectual and philosophical import. One final example from the end of the novel will drive the point home. The day after the government grain store-house was burned, Moon Scent's body is discovered "in a cave made be-tween two walls propped up by each other when they had caved in. It was in sitting position and was a smooth, bright pinkish red all over. The color had stood out glaringly against the charred ruins. It had occurred to Big Aunt—to all of them, in fact, who had been there—that the seated figure suggested one of the bald, slim images of Arhans lined up on both sides of a temple. She had been deeply shocked and awed" (176). With this allusion to a Buddhist saint, Eileen Chang not only makes clear her sympathy for her protagonist but also vividly concretizes the climax of her novel, the resolution of the conflict. The victory not in earthly but in spiritual terms goes to the peasants. Thus, para-doxically, Chang sides with the peasants against a government that is nomi-nally for the peasants. Undoubtedly, Eileen Chang is a complex and highly skilled artist.

3. LANDSCAPES OF MEMORY: THE NOSTALGIC STANCE

For some people whom time has distanced from their ancestral homeland, memory has become amber-tinted by nostalgia and the landscapes that they paint in this condition reflect more the imagination of the artists than the reality of the land being depicted. Such is the case with the authors in this section who focus on China in their books, but theirs is a China recollected from memory or never known personally but pieced together from the remi-niscences of elders or from romanticized images prevalent in the West. Such nostalgic and romanticized tones may be found in the writings of people with differing lengths of stay in the United States: those who immigrated to the United States from China as children—such as Bette Bao Lord; those who have lived many years in the United States—Dr. Hazel Lin; or those whose families have been many generations in America—Virginia Lee, fourth-generation Chinese American. The longing of these three women for their ancestral homeland finds concrete expression in the important role that a literal ancestral home plays in their novels: *The Physicians* (1951) by Hazel Lin, *The House That Tai Ming Built* (1963) by Virginia Lee, and *Spring Moon* (1981) by Bette Bao Lord.

Hazel Lin was herself a physician, a gynecologist, and endocrinologist in Jersey City, New Jersey. She was born in 1913 in Foochow, Fukien, received a BS from Yenjing University in 1932, an MS from the University of Michigan in 1938, and lived in the United States until her death of a stroke on August 6, 1986. The ancestral home in her novel, *The Physicians*, belongs to Wang Kung, one of pre-Revolutionary Peking's most renowned practitioners of Chi-nese medicine and grandfather of the protagonist. In this home, all is harmo-

Dr. Hazel Lin by Edward Martin Studios, Jersey City, N.J., 1976

nious. The servants love their master and are not only happy and proud to serve him but honored, incredibly, by increased responsibilities. Here Wang Kung's son brings home his bride, whose graceful manners and charm (she brings the doctor hot water and tea upon rising) readily win the great doctor's heart. The atmosphere of peace and harmony are shattered, however, at the birth of the doctor's granddaughter, for the mother dies at childbirth, and her husband, the doctor's son, retreats from the world into a monastery.

Five years pass during which Wang Kung is inconsolable and will not see his granddaughter, allowing the servants to care for her in their quarters. When he is finally persuaded to allow her to live with him, her brightness and liveliness bring him great joy. Despite his opposition, she pursues the study of Western medicine. When she graduates, he is not only reconciled but proud of her accomplishment and even visits her in her new adopted country where the two doctors pool their knowledge—Eastern and Western medicine—to cure a difficult case of nephritis.

The house that Tai Ming built, in the novel of that name by Virginia Lee, was constructed in southern China with the money earned by great-great-grandfather Tai Ming in the gold mines of California. Though most of the book takes place in San Francisco, the emotional center of the Kwong family remains in this house in China where the grandmother and aunts live. From this house, despite the distance, the women wield a great deal of control over events on the other side of the world. Virginia Lee describes the house in loving detail, incorporating every element of Chinese architecture that would most charm the Western reader:

> The edges of the roofs on the magnificent home curved upward, as the spirit of man should always look upward. The glazed, deep blue tiles of the roofs glistened like amethyst on a bright sunny day. The adjacent garden was spacious, and within, on a hill, was an octagonal pavilion . . . This was a home consisting of many one-storied buildings surrounded by a high brick wall. Each building opened on a courtyard where flowers grew in earthen pots lined against the walls . . . The windows were in designs of fans and leaves, the doors in the shapes of half-moon, full moon and flower vase . . . The original builder studied and read much in his late years in the octagonal pavilion on a low hill in the garden, pausing often to look at the peach and plum trees below. Beyond was a camelback bridge, its reflection in the water making a silvery circle on the surface of the lotus pool. In a far corner, against delicate blades of heavenly bamboo, was a huge green jardiniere filled with beautiful goldfish, their trembling fins like a lovely thin haze of pure white silk. (14–15)

Certainly, the architectural features described above do exist in China but the accumulation of so many exotic and pretty details calls to mind the landscape on lacquered furniture or painted china, the Blue Willow pattern, for example. And the profusion of extravagant adjectives near the end of the passage: "*heavenly* bamboo", "*beautiful* goldfish," "*lovely thin* haze," "*pure white* silk" result in a text that almost resembles a fairy tale.

Not only are the house and grounds picture-book flawless, but the inhabitants seem to be as well. For generation after generation, the wives left behind in this house contentedly remain separated from their husbands for decades, and dutifully send their sons to America when the boys reach age 14 or 15. Thereafter, the women remain involved in the lives of their loved ones only through letters, though they often continue to exert considerable pressure on those in the New World to maintain the language and cultural patterns of the Old. Their husbands return to them only to await death and their sons only to marry the women their mothers have selected; then these young wives are in turn left behind in China. No one complains of this fractured family life, but all accept it as the norm.

An actual drawing of the ancestral House of Chang serves as the end papers for *Spring Moon* and a great deal of space is given to its description. The house itself reflects the history of China and the fortunes of the family that built it. Spacious and grand, the Chang compound was a small palace, encompassing 30 courts and separate residences surrounded by a park complete with a pond, willow trees, decorative rocks, and arching bridges. In its full splendor at the opening of the book, the year 1892, it housed the Old Venerable, the patriarch, his wives, concubines, sons and their wives, concubines and children; and a large assortment of slaves and servants. Life did not always run smoothly, however, for the book opens with the suicide of nine-year-old Spring Moon's personal slave girl, Plum Blossom. Over the years, as the Chang family's wealth declines, the ancestral home is also diminished. At the end of the book, in 1973, when Enduring Promise, Spring Moon's son, returns from America after an absence of 25 years, the once-splendid home has undergone so many changes that it is barely recognizable:

> At last he reached the entrance. But when he peered inside he was suddenly unsure, wondering if his memory had played a trick and these walls were not the right ones after all. For huddled in the receiving court was a jumble of tiny dwellings jammed one beside the next, filling the space so that there was barely enough room for a thin man to pass between them.
>
> If any man was there. The place was unnaturally silent, like an empty stage, the cakes of charcoal in doorways and the laundry overhead part of the set. He took a step and turned to look back at the entrance. It was the right height and width. And there, in the third stone from the bottom on the left, the first character of his school name. He had time to carve only the first before his uncle, Bold Talent, had caught him . . . Slowly he made his way down the narrow alley, which twisted this way and that as if it were a pathway through a maze.
>
> . . . At one place he thought he saw a fragment of the inner wall of the receiving court, the back wall now a score of hovels. And one building, larger than the rest, could have been the Hall of Ancestors, though nothing of the red columns remained, the shutter doors had been replaced by masonry and rows of tiny windows. (414)

The house of Chang had suffered a dramatic decline. No longer could one privileged family enjoy the luxury of such vast space; nor could a single family proclaim its self-importance through a Hall of Ancestors. China had undergone a levelling process: the high had been brought down; the low had been raised up. No longer was a girl forced, by the accident of her birth into poverty, to be the slave of another born into wealth. Spring Moon at the end of the novel is no longer the pampered daughter of a great house mourning the suicide of her slave girl who would not accept the marriage arrangements made for her. Spring Moon, now the family matriarch, lives simply in one tiny room in a narrow alley on the grounds of what was once her family's magnificent residence. But her spirit has remained unchanged, lively, indomitable, "her eyes, too, were the same, clear and bright, though wrinkles surrounded them . . . " (416).

In all three books, the traditional arts and materials of China are alluded to with reverence and provide the authors with metaphors; in *The Physicians*, the great doctor's son cherishes his wife "like a rare piece of jade or a precious Ming vase" (25). In *Spring Moon*, when Bold Talent returns from his studies at Harvard and takes the three-day journey up the Soochow Creek to his home, he notices that "life along the meandering stream seemed to unfurl like an endless scroll, as it always had" (34). The matriarch's skin "seemed like antique silk, without sheen but still fine" (84). And later, in this passage, luxurious materials abound:

> On the eve of the Year of the Boar, 1911, the courtyards had been transformed overnight by snow, barren earth sheathed in white velvet. In the morning the sun, which for days had glimmered faintly in an iron bowl, shone in heavens of blue porcelain. Icicles sparkled on rain pipes. The green tile roofs, varnished with frost, gleamed like finest jade. (182)

The occasional Chinese art metaphor in *The Physicians* and *Spring Moon* becomes a literal element in *The House That Tai Ming Built*, for the Kwong family makes its living importing and selling the art and artifacts of imperial China. Since the family owns two Chinese antiques shops in San Francisco's Chinatown, "Tai Ming Co., since 1855," and "The House of Tong," Uncle Fook's antique store next door, Virginia Lee is able to indulge in lengthy historic backgrounds and sensuous descriptions of China's porcelains, ivory carvings, enamels, silks, and jade. Lee uses the material arts of China as metaphors as well, at times overusing them, as may be seen in the following descriptions of the heroine's mother: "For Fay, with her sleek hair like rich brocade and her small bones like shafts of fine ivory, was a mixture of the old and the new" (89); "But it was always a voice with the tone of a *jade* bell, not brass. And she never ruled so much with an iron hand as she did with a *porcelain* hand" (92); "Fay's hands would appear in the sketch for they were lovely hands, lovely *porcelain* hands" (112); "she talked in *jade* tones" (123), "the hours went by quickly, day passing into night as smoothly as *jade* passed through her fingers" (146); "the thick snow of winter sounded like the falling of broken *jade*" (155) (emphases added). These images have been scattered throughout the text, but the readiness with which the author falls into their use is nonetheless apparent.

However, Lee's use of cultural artifacts must be set into the context of the entire novel, something earlier commentators have failed to do. Frank Chin and the group of angry young men who compiled the introduction to one of the earliest anthologies of Asian American literature vehemently rejected Virginia Lee's emphasis on beautiful artifacts as falsely exoticizing Chinatown life and catering to white stereotypes; Chin called Virginia Lee a victim who is "completely brainwashed."[26] Elaine Kim objected to what she calls Lee's assumption of the "tour guide" role (291). However, one must remember that

The House That Tai Ming Built is essentially a tale of interracial love thwarted by racist American laws, discussion of which we shall reserve until Chapter 5. In this context, at a time when a Chinese was not considered good enough to marry a white person, Virginia Lee's nostalgia for a homeland is altogether natural, and her insistence on the long and glorious tradition of Chinese arts and culture is but the means to counter the prejudice that creates such agony for her heroine. This was the same means of self-defense and self-affirmation employed by Edith Eaton when faced with racial taunts:

> Whenever I have the opportunity, I steal away to the library and read every book I can find on China and the Chinese. I learn that China is the oldest civilized nation on the face of the earth and a few other things. At eighteen years of age what troubles me is not that I am what I am, but that others are ignorant of my superiority. ("Leaves," 128)

In her life, as well, Virginia Lee asserted her Chineseness. Though born in San Francisco in 1923, the fourth generation of her family in that city, she attended both Chinese and American schools, studied Asian history in college, and married a man from South China. Thus, despite her American birth, her emotional attachment to China was not only strong but self-defining. This lack of assimilation speaks either to the success of her parents in maintaining Old World customs and loyalties or to the coldness of the hospitality extended to minorities in the New World, or both.

The feature that I find more disturbing and distorting than the allusions to China's artistic past is the custom, in *Spring Moon* and many other preceding novels, of calling characters not by their Chinese names but by the English translations of these names. The purpose of this practice, obviously, is to render the names more recognizable to the Western reader for whom Chinese words are totally meaningless and thus difficult to remember. However, the effect of these translations—taking some examples from *Spring Moon*: Bold Talent, Noble Talent, Fragrant Snow, Resolute Spirit, Golden Virtue, Grand Vista, Enduring Promise, Lustrous Jade—is to make the Chinese appear to be quaint, naive people whose tastes are exotic, charming, and fanciful.[27] An analogy will make my objection clearer. Suppose an English novel were translated into Chinese and its characters, Theodore and Amy, were called by the Chinese translations of the meanings of their names: Gift of God and Beloved. The effect would be a distortion of the original text. The meaning of a name may have affected the parents' choice at a child's birth, or the parents may have been totally ignorant of any original meanings and simply decided on the basis of pleasant connotations. Whatever the case, etymological meanings have little significance, for the names become simply signifiers for the person. To translate the name is to place undue insistence on the lexical significance. When the original cultural context for a particular name is not explained, but the name is nonetheless translated, the translated name takes on connotations from the new culture that may be totally inappropriate.

The single exception to my objection to this practice occurs in *The House That Tai Ming Built*, when grandfather wants to call Bo Lin (which means precious lotus) Fragrance from Books, a ridiculous name in English but a distinctive one in Chinese since it stands apart from the usual flower names given to most girls. Grandmother's preference, however, prevails. In this case, discussion of the English meanings of the names has significance and relevance. The preferred names reveal character—grandfather's intellectual aspirations for his granddaughter and grandmother's conventionality—and the chosen name reveals the family power structure—grandmother has the final word. Apart from this single episode, Virginia Lee wisely uses the Chinese names for her characters throughout *The House that Tai Ming Built* and does not translate any others.

As we cannot forget our parents, though we may all have varying opinions and reactions to them at different times, so China, the motherland, exerts a tremendous influence on her daughters scattered far afield on the other side of the planet. They may remember her with fierce pride, cynical bitterness, or amber-tinted nostalgia, but they remember her.

Chapter 4

Focus on America:
Seeking a Self and a Place

The question of one's identity is at the same time a simple and a very complex issue. Is one to be identified by one's race, nationality, sex, place of birth, place of death, place of longest residence, occupation, class, relationships to others, personality traits, size, age, interests, religion, astrological sign, salary, by how one perceives oneself, by how one is perceived by others? The possibilities seem endless. The most fundamental means of identification are the first three listed, and for the writers of this study the first three are also the most problematic. When born to parents of different races or nationalities, or when born in one country, reared in another, and finally settled in a third, one cannot give a simple answer to the question of racial or national identity. When one is born female in a world dominated by males of two different races, further complications ensue. The gender issue is the same for all the authors in this study, regardless of their racial or national origins, and we have discussed this at some length in earlier chapters. The racial and nationality issue, however, has multiple and complex variations, almost as numerous as there are individuals.

How does one define a Chinese American? At what point does an immigrant become an American? How does one identify one's nationality if one's life has been characterized by a great deal of moving about? Mai-mai Sze, for example, was born in China to Chinese parents, taken to England as a young child, cared for by an Irish nanny, sent to a private high school and college in the United States, to a painting school in France, and now lives in New York City. Another example is Diana Chang, whose mother was Eurasian (one half Irish) and father Chinese; she was born in New York City, taken to China as an infant, reared in the International Sector in Shanghai where she attended American schools, then brought back to the United States for high school and college (Barnard). In the early 1970s, she was included in anthologies of Asian American literature, but also castigated for the lack of ethnic pride and themes in her novels.

To further complicate the question of identity, not only are biological and geographical factors significant, but external or social factors impinge as well. That recent immigrants feel a sense of alienation and strangeness in a new country is to be expected, but when American-born Chinese Americans, from families many generations in the United States, are asked where they learned such good English, they too are made to feel foreign and alien. The "double consciousness" with which W. E. B. Du Bois characterized the black American: "this sense of always looking at one's self through the eyes of others, of measuring one's soul by the tape of a world that looks on in amused contempt and pity"[1] equally characterizes Chinese Americans. However, if they should go to China, they would soon realize, by their unfamiliarity with conditions and customs and by the reactions of the Chinese to them, how American they are. As Lindo Jong tells her daughter in Amy Tan's *The Joy Luck Club*, "When you go to China . . . you don't even need to open your mouth. They already know you are an outsider . . . Even if you put on their clothes, even if you take off your makeup and hide your fancy jewelry, they know. They know just watching the way you walk, the way you carry your face. They know you do not belong" (253).

Thus, the feeling of being between worlds, totally at home nowhere, is at the core of all the writers in this study and, consequently, of the books they write.

Helena Kuo, whose wartime novel and autobiography were discussed in the previous chapter, described the between-world condition at the beginning of her 1942 autobiography:

> I have seen America as a powerful young nation that foreshadows for me the future of China. I live now in a happy if sometimes puzzling state of divided mind; the old Chinese mind and the new mind of the West. I am educated and progressive to the point of being aggressive, but always with me is my happy heritage of Chinese civilization which gives me a heaven-sent balance, and I believe I shall never be wholly westernized, even if sometimes I seem to be walking on the edge of a dangerous chasm. (*I've Come A Long Way*, 4)

Recently arrived from China, as a college-educated adult with her sense of identity and her sensibilities already shaped, Kuo considered her Chinese heritage to be a familiar, stabilizing force to counterbalance the dizzying Western progressivism she encountered in the United States. Yet she too acknowledged her awareness of the precariousness of the balancing act that was her life as a Chinese in the United States.

1. THE COSMOPOLITAN ÉMIGRÉ

For those who immigrate as children, the sense of "walking on the edge of a dangerous chasm" is perhaps even more acute. Mai-mai Sze's autobiography, *Echo of a Cry* (1945), and Chuang Hua's autobiographical novel, *Crossings* (1968), make an interesting pairing in this regard, for the authors have similar backgrounds, their books similar themes, and Sze's book seems, in psychological and thematic ways, to be a mother-text for Chuang Hua's. *Echo of a Cry* focuses on the author's early years, from early childhood until college; Chuang Hua's *Crossings* is devoted primarily to the adult years.

Both authors come from privileged and complex backgrounds: Mai-mai Sze's father, as noted previously, was ambassador to England from 1914 to 1927 and thereafter ambassador to the United States; Chuang Hua's father was a surgeon and later a stockbroker. Both authors were taken from China as small children, introduced to Western culture in England, and both have settled in the United States, in or near New York City, with forays into France. Both are true citizens of the world with all the outward polish and adaptability attendant on such cosmopolitanism, but both also reveal, in their books, an inner sense of loss and fragmentation that is the cost of these multiple transplantations, or "reshufflings," as Mai-mai Sze calls them. Although their books are different in form, they carry the same theme: the struggle for a stable sense of self amid changing surroundings and conflicting contexts.

The opening episode of *Echo of a Cry* is emblematic of the between-world condition expressed in both books. For the celebration of her deceased grandmother's one hundredth birthday, Mai-mai Sze and her mother pay a visit to Shanghai. Before seeing the family matriarch, an elderly aunt, Mai-mai is nervous. Having lived abroad most of her life, she is unfamiliar with Chinese customs, like how low to bow or the proper honorifics for addressing the matriarch whom she had heard described as "imperious" and "formidable." To her surprise and relief, the aunt is a loving, grandmotherly type, who does not require any bows at all and urges sweets upon her. The aunt's wall is covered with old photographs of the family, including Mai-mai at different periods, and her conversation is no more intimidating than the complaint that her dentures hadn't been properly fitted.

Despite the unexpected warmth and informality of this reception, Mai-mai

Sze confesses to a sense of alienation as she looks at her baby photograph on her great-aunt's wall:

> What a lot of places had been home since the time of that first photography in a Peking courtyard. I was then a Chinese baby, sitting in my mother's arms with pink pompoms on my head. Now home was half a dozen other places across the seas. I could feel no connection with that comfortable bundle in a padded coat.

In spite of the visible sign of belonging here, Sze's own sense of self had been shaped by experiences worlds away from her origins and totally disconnected from the Chinese custom that occasioned this return visit: a birthday celebration for a dead relative. How far her travels—geographic and psychological—have taken her from the baby in the photograph on her great aunt's wall is the subject of her book.

Echo of a Cry combines humor and wit with existential angst and social awareness as the author briefly recounts early childhood memories of China and then extensively details the process of Westernization in England, France, and the United States. Despite a breezy, cheerful tone, however, Sze's sense of alienation in Western countries also comes through forcefully. During one childhood summer in England, spent with a fervently religious Quaker family, she was punished for any infraction, even a spill at table, by having to deposit coins into the China Inland Mission box decorated with a picture of a little Chinese girl who resembled her. Her only comment on this episode is "It irked me no end to throw my pennies away in this manner" (Sze 1945, 111). Nonetheless, she reveals that her attitude toward "visiting missionaries was therefore a bit colored by this vexatious penalty." Being forced to contribute to the China mission allied her with her white hosts, with white missionaries, and thus with their patronizing condescension toward her own people, an alliance that was discomforting. Her further remarks about missionaries express this discomfort and are quite outspoken for an ambassador's daughter, "They were of all nationalities and all engaged in 'saving the poor heathen.' It may have been my prejudiced imagination, but they seemed much too satisfied with themselves . . . " (111). Her use of quotations around the expression "saving the poor heathen" clearly shows her disaffection from the missionaries' perspective and her recognition that their attitude of superiority is objectionable.

Later, as a resident in the United States and a student at Wellesley College, she encounters racial prejudice when a black student is snubbed at a lunch counter by two white girls who refuse to sit "by any damn nigger!" Mai-mai sits beside the black woman and asks if she objects to the term "colored people," and when the woman replies that it's better than "nigger," Mai-mai continues, "It still implies inferiority of a kind, doesn't it, as if 'colored people' were not up to others? When you think of it, we're all colored except the pure white man. And is there such a thing?" (163). Her realization of the absurdity of distinctions based on skin color and her empathy for the young black woman leads to her recognition of their identical position in a society that so discriminates, and she concludes, "We're cause people, whether we like it or not" (1965). For an ambassador's daughter from a privileged background to make such a statement is a revolutionary act.

On a painting trip to a village in southern France, Mai-mai Sze is regarded as a curiosity and everyone calls her "Chine." In France, someone had told her, "'Ah, but you are déracinée—up-rooted!' It seemed an apt way of putting it, and irrefutable, if one insisted on pigeonholing by nationality" (173). And because this kind of pigeonholing is still the way of a world not yet prepared to accept world citizens instead of nationals of a single country, Mai-mai Sze ends her autobiography with this poignant passage, which supplies the book's title:

> Fervently we have wanted to belong somewhere at the same time that we have often wanted to run away. We reached out for something, and when by chance grasped it, we often found that it wasn't what we wanted at all. There is one part of us that is always lost and searching. It is an echo of a cry that was a longing for warmth and safety. And through our adolescent fantasies, and however our adult reasoning may disguise it, the search continues. (202)

The cry she refers to is the equivalent of the primal scream, the newborn's reaction to the lost security and warmth of the womb. This cry becomes symbolic of the existential human condition, representing as it does the loss of an absolute good. Sze's autobiography, like her novel, *Silent Children*, emphasizes the pain of this loss. For the person between worlds, the loss is intensified: it is both physical and psychological, for it is loss of the mother as well as loss of the motherland.

Though not intended as a sequel to *Echo of a Cry*, *Crossings* lends itself to such a reading, for it continues the story of a déracinée cosmopolitan Chinese woman, now grown up and struggling to find herself in the Western world. In theme and authorial persona, it follows from Sze's *Echo of a Cry*; in form and style it anticipates Kingston's *The Woman Warrior*. *Crossings* is an experimental novel that requires and rewards the reader's closest attention. Fragmented in narration, poetic yet spare in style, understated yet conveying deep emotion, the text omits quotation marks and proper names, and yet the plot is conveyed. The book is structured around the growth and decline of a love affair between a Chinese American woman, Fourth Jane, and a Parisian journalist; however, this affair is constantly interrupted by memories of childhood and family, by dreams, nightmares, and images arresting and resonant so that the interruptions, the memories, become the central concern, and the affair with which the book begins and ends merely the most recent episode in the narrator's life.

Fourth Jane is the middle child of seven in a well-to-do family that took her as a child from China to England and then to the United States. Jane, as an adult, spends time in Paris but makes return visits to New York. In all, she crosses the ocean seven times and makes four cultural adjustments. As in the case of Mai-mai Sze, these travels are culturally enriching but their cost is a sense of fragmentation, a loss of centeredness and clear direction. Jane's actions show confusion, an inability to commit herself to any one thing or person for an extended time, a tendency to change direction abruptly, to break off relationships suddenly, in short, to a fragmentation of personality. She seems extremely depressed and spends a great deal of time in France sleeping: "On certain days moving from one room to another in her apartment was the only displacement she felt capable of undertaking" (116). The cumulative effect of so many crossings and displacements for her, at times, is a kind of paralysis.

Because the many crossings required her adjusting and readjusting to different cultures and languages, and perhaps because she is a middle child and female, Jane seeks a stable unchanging center outside herself. The closeness of her parents, their stability and unity, had been one of the main pillars of her life; thus, she feels her own strength and identity threatened when they disagree about her brother Fifth James' marriage to a Caucasian. Jane is shaken when her father relents from his initial objection and goes to the hospital to visit his daughter-in-law and his newborn grandson. Jane stubbornly sides with her mother in remaining adamant against the foreign intruder, but she expresses her anguish over this split to her father: "I feel a terrible danger crossing. The oneness of you and Ngmah [mother] you have built so tightly you can't undo overnight just to accommodate them" (196–7). She feels impelled to have her own separateness for a time, for, as she explains, "I don't know who I am outside of the old context and I'm afraid I might not survive the new" (196). Ironically, while away, she herself becomes romantically involved with a Caucasian.

But this lover also fails to provide a sense of centeredness. For him, Jane is peripheral. He makes time for her only in the interstices of his life between his busy schedule as journalist and husband to another woman, and though he often writes cryptically about or to Jane in his column he just as often does not answer her phone calls and notes. His disinterestedness throws her back upon her family memories for emotional support.

Parallel to the tension created in Jane by her parent's opposing views toward James' wife is the effect of the conflict between her two countries: China and America. When her French lover unlovingly tells her that she is in exile in America as she is in France and that she should go back to China where she really belongs, she explains that she has loved both China and America, "as two separate but equal realities of my existence," and when it was still possible to return to China she had looked forward to being able to "live America there as I had lived China in America." But with the civil war in China and the Korean conflict in progress, she feels herself torn:

> I saw with dread my two lives ebbing. Each additional day of estrangement increased the difficulty of eventual reconciliation, knowing the inflexibility of Chinese pride. In that paralysis I lived in no man's land, having also lost America since the loss of one entailed the loss of the other, I had such longings to make a rumble in the silence. But both parts equally strong canceled out choice. (122)

Even if it were possible to return to China, she decides she could not live there: "I would have to conceal one half of myself. In America I need not hide what I am" (125).

Thus, the forces for fragmentation—both external and internal—have been inexorable. The external forces have included total uprooting and transplanting, war between the two nations she considers her own, and conflict between the two parents she still relies on. The internal force for fragmentation is the conflict between her need for independence and her need for love and security, the desire to please her father by being obedient to his will and the desire to assert her own will. That her father has consistently been loving and concerned makes the break all the more difficult. That he declines, suffers, grows old and helpless, at the mercy of surgeons himself, increases the guilt of her pulling away from him.

At the same time that her father's tyrannical power and smothering love must be rejected, his strength, talent, adaptability, ingenuity, and pride are what has given the family its very substance and shape. One of the major cohesive forces in Jane's life is the memory of her father's strength and tender care: his planting beans in neat rows, his organizing endless rounds of birthday celebrations and family outings, his driving three hours up to her college just to deliver a typewriter. In short, the small but crucial proofs of love, exemplified in the simple tasks of daily life, are the forces that keep us whole and keep us going. The domestic chore of cooking is one of these. In *Crossings*, Chuang Hua devotes pages to the details of the increasingly complex dinners that Jane prepares for her lover—whom she is not always sure will appear—from steak to stuffed chicken to Peking duck; these meals are not only an expression of love but an affirmation of life in spite of depression, confusion, and loss. After Dyadya's protracted death, we follow Ngmah's thorough cleaning of her room. What comes through, forcibly, between the lines, is the woman's determination to conquer her extreme grief by these mundane means. In concentrating all her energies on the most efficient cleaning method, she refuses to give in to despair; she affirms her own life and her usefulness; she snatches a reason, small as it is, for being.

The personality fragmentation of Fourth Jane in *Crossings* is reiterated in the text's style and method of narration. Reminiscent of Faulkner's *The Sound and the Fury*, chronological time is fractured—with a childhood memory following a scene from the present—and the fragmentation occurs on the large level, between chapters, as well as in the smaller units, between paragraphs and sentences. In one instance, two actions proceed simultaneously while the narration cuts back and forth between them, a technique often used by filmmakers but less frequently by novelists. Apparently an interruption, the second action actually illuminates and comments on the first. This is Flaubert's method in the famous scene in *Madame Bovary* in which the suave, seductive speeches by Rodolphe Boulanger are interwoven with and implicitly commented upon by the Agricultural Fair awards for the fattest pig and best pile of manure. In *Crossings*, when Jane and her lover are discussing her return to America and the possible end of their relationship, their conversation is repeatedly interrupted with the sounds and actions of a Chinese opera: "Percussion rushed into the frantic fray of clacking sticks, the savage turbulence of cymbals and gongs quickening to madness" (130). The agitation of the lovers—their wary sparring and emotional pain—is not delineated explicitly but implicitly and metaphorically in the description of the flamboyant operatic battle with its "prolonged shriek of rage" and its "wild weaving wails of tearing anguish."

Not only does the author juxtapose linear narrative elements that reverberate against each other, but, in like fashion, she juxtaposes visual imagery with significant impact on the narration. Some images are integral to the narration and contribute to its progression; others arrest the flow of the narrative and call attention to themselves. An example of the latter, arresting kind may be found in the middle of the conversation between the journalist and Jane on his first visit to her apartment. He speaks first:

> Writers belong in the kitchen. Cooking is an essential part of their imaginative environment.
> Oh. You can put in the steak now.
> A bird plunged like dead weight ten stories from the roof. Two stories from the pavement, with a single flap of wings, it skimmed above the quivering treetops and took off in a sweeping spiral till it disappeared behind the rooftops.
> We can eat now. (24)

In the midst of preparing for a meal, the falling bird has a jarring effect and disturbing implications. But it does not appear to have been noticed by the lovers, who make no reference to it and is therefore the narrator's interjection and an intrusive element in the narration. Its presence may be accounted for only by its effect on the reader and its symbolic resonance. Fourth Jane is falling in love, falling into a hopeless dead-end affair with a married man, but it is a willful fall, for the bird has wings it chooses not to use until the last minute. Then it swoops up easily and takes off in a display of its flying powers. In like manner, Jane enters this relationship with open eyes, trusting that her strength will enable her, when she so decides, to escape relatively unscathed.

The next episode begins with grandmother sitting "still and heavy as a stone," echoing the "dead weight" of the falling bird. The family has gathered for grandmother's birthday celebration, paralleling mother's birthday party two episodes back. And so the book unfolds, with images weaving like shuttles between fragments of past and present, connecting and clarifying the action and characters.

Chuang Hua's synthetic vision and her acute sense of oppositions are sharply realized in her most graphic images, which bring together the beautiful and the horrifying, the dignified and the absurd in the yin yang fashion we noted as characteristic of Lin Tai-yi's *War Tide*. Thus, "bloated corpses" that "flowed in the current of the yellow river" are juxtaposed with the "slenderest, reddest" stalks of sugar cane, "most tender and full of juice inside sweet to chew and suck on" (49). And on the occasion of grandmother's birthday, all the family members line up in order of rank and pay her tribute with great ceremoniousness while she sits enthroned, muttering the only English words she can recall, "machine gun" (26). These disparate images, mixing dignity and absurdity, decay and life, ugliness and beauty, reveal an unflinching, unrestrained vision, one that recognizes the harsh reality of coexisting and unresolvable opposites. As Chuang Hua achieves artistic coherence through images, so Fourth Jane reaches toward personal coherence, through her memories and her acceptance of everyday responsibilities.

2. THE EURASIAN

Coexisting and unresolvable opposites are daily experiences for bicultural people and particularly for Eurasians. Which language, which nationality, which culture will dominate? By which race shall one be known? Though the geographical location of the family and the father's strength of character have some bearing upon the answers, generally the mother sets the tone in a home and establishes its traditions. As a rule, hers is the initial care for the children; she determines their language orientation; she prepares the family food and the holiday celebrations. For the Eaton sisters, living in the United States and Canada, Western ways predominated, for their mother, though biologically

Chinese, was reared in the English culture. For Han Suyin and Diana Chang, though growing up in China, Western ways also predominated, for Han Suyin's mother was Belgian and Diana Chang's mother an American Eurasian.

Though Americans and Europeans were the minority in China, their social status, paradoxically, was higher than that of the Chinese themselves; thus, to follow a Western lifestyle in China was, in certain ways, to be one of the elite. The nineteenth-century Western dominance within China that Han Suyin detailed at length in the first volume of her autobiography *The Crippled Tree* (1968) still held sway into the period of Diana Chang's autobiographical novel, *Frontiers of Love* (1956), set in Shanghai at the end of World War II. Chang describes the atmosphere with great wit and some sarcasm:

> All the hybrids and the cosmopolitans, all that were left in China, all that were not in internment camps, still moved, she knew, with the subtle authority of foreigners. Colonialism was still a perfume behind their ears, still the wicks of their unconscious spirits. They moved among the Chinese and left blondness in their wakes, even when they were brunettes. (86)

In both books, the question of identity is central. Han Suyin answers the question in *The Crippled Tree* in a very Chinese fashion by delving into family history, her father's, and the history of her father's country, China. The text is a blend of genres and voices. Novelistic re-creation fills in where the author does not have firsthand information; poems are interspersed into the text, as well as the oral and written memories and remembered voices of many others. Central, of course, is the voice of Han Suyin herself, but large portions of the story are told by others: the only surviving letter from a trunkful of letters written by her mother to her parents in Belgium; large portions of her father's gracefully written autobiography; her Third Uncle's account of what transpired in China while his brother was in Belgium; Li Chieh-jen, the De Maupassant of China, commenting on the Revolution of 1911; Dr. Cantlie's biography of Dr. Sun Yat-sen; letters from Joseph Hers, her father's employer in the Belgian firm constructing railways in China. Out of these many pieces, Han Suyin creates a collage of the story of her parents' time, their fairy tale courtship in Belgium and their failing marriage in China, set in the history of the late nineteenth century, the turbulent period of China's industrialization and colonization by Western powers. Though the book emphasizes her father's history, it begins on her mother's side with this shocking letter:

> Dear Papa, dear Mama,
>   Today I shall not have time to write you a very long letter, because the bandits were here last night, and the cook has been decapitated. His head is in

the garden, so I have shut the window. The little one is crying with prickly heat, but I cannot get any talcum powder so please send me two dozen tins, it is easy to get in England. I have had to give up my corsets too, and you would not recognize me, I drag myself in slippers all day long. (11)

The traumatic—bandit's raid, decapitation—has become everyday and the everyday—talcum powder and corsets—rare. The world has turned upside down and children are unrelenting in their demands. Little wonder this European woman is distraught, imprisoned as she is through bonds of her own making (husband and children, against her parents' wishes) in barbaric, terrifying China.

In dramatizing and re-creating this scene, which she could not have personally witnessed, Han Suyin demonstrates a novelist's inventiveness and a daughter's empathy. Furthermore, she introduces the major tension and theme of her text: the enormity of the task of bridging East and West. The misunderstandings and conflicts within her own family were but a microcosm of the same struggles on the national level, within China, and on the international level as well. And Han Suyin's critical place is in the middle, as apologist and explainer for both sides. Though she begins with great empathy for her European mother, in the next chapter she delves into the history of her Chinese father's people, the Hakkas, who began migrating from northern China southward as long ago as A.D. 311, and in the detailed faithfulness and length of this account family pride is clearly evident. She is the daughter of both her parents.

The innovative method of *The Crippled Tree* is to provide multiple perspectives for a single subject. For example, the treatment of Chinese engineers on the Belgian railroad is presented from different perspectives: from the Chinese point of view and from the Belgian employer's. All accounts stand side by side, their conflicts of perspective clearly in evidence. Thus, the fact—that truth depends on one's perspective—is irrefutably and brilliantly demonstrated.

Another example is the boat trip through the whirlpools and gorges of the Yangtze River from Chungking to Shanghai, which is described four times, each time from a different perspective: the first, lyrically and hopefully by Han Suyin recreating her 17-year-old father's departure from his home in Chengtu for Belgium; the second, when her father describes his apprehensive return home with his foreign wife; third, her mother's account as a starry-eyed bride entering an exotic and romantic land where she saw green monkeys frolicking on the hillsides; and, finally, years later, when Han Suyin takes the trip looking unsuccessfully for the green monkeys her mother reported seeing. The journeys up and down the Yangtze take on resonance as symbolic searches for one's dream, taken boldly and hopefully by each of the family members in turn; each journey results ultimately in disillusionment.

Writing of herself in the third person, using one of her European names, Rosalie, Han Suyin describes the condition of the Eurasian who does not deny one part of herself but struggles to live with contradiction and fragmentation:

> In Rosalie a fragmentation of the total self occurred, each piece recreating from its own sum of facts a person, each person functioning separately withholding itself from the other, yet throughout maintaining a secret vigilance, boneless coherence, fragile as the thread that guided Theseus in his labyrinth. Others born like her of two worlds, who chose not to accept this splitting, fragmentation of monolithic identity into several selves, found themselves later unable to face the contradictions latent in their own beings. Consistency left them crippled for the world's incoherence.
>
> In Rosalie the necessity of knowing mutually contradictory truths without assuming any one of them to be the whole truth, became in childhood the only way to live on, to live and to remain substantial. And she was astonished that others were unwilling to accept the discomfort of always being partly wrong, of never knowing a total answer; they became so sure, believing one thing only, preferring a cosy semi-blindness to the pricking clarity of doubt.
>
> Of course, thought Rosalie, it is more comfortable. It is like never moving the furniture about. (369)

Fragmentation, contradictory truths, "the discomfort of always being partly wrong, of never knowing a total answer" when called by their positive names are tolerance, openness, and flexibility, the ability to see and understand many perspectives. Han Suyin turns handicaps into advantages; the legacy of her bicultural, biracial heritage, she proudly asserts, has prepared her for the world's incoherence and inconsistencies. Out of external fragmentation, disparateness, and difference, like pieces of a quilt, she has created for herself a "boneless coherence," an interior sense of comfort, unity, and design. She prefers the "pricking clarity of doubt" to the "semi-cosiness" of surety, and Maxine Hong Kingston, a generation later, would assert the same preference: "I learned to make my mind large, as the universe is large, so that there is room for paradoxes" (*Woman Warrior*, 29).

In contrast to Han Suyin's *The Crippled Tree*, Diana Chang in *The Frontiers of Love* explores the question of Amerasian identity within a narrower frame of reference, a shorter span of time, and with much less weight of history bearing down on the individual. Identity, for Chang, who is decidedly American in her thinking, is a purely individual choice, and for the Amerasian, the choice is broader than for most. In *Frontiers of Love*, Chang makes

Photo of Diana Chang by Gordon Robotham, 1986

a tripartite division of the question of an Amerasian's choice of identity and offers her reader three possible answers: two (Feng Huang's and Mimi Lambert's) are extremes; the third (Sylvia Chen's), the most reasonable way.

Twenty-six-year-old Feng Huang, intense and purposeful, rejects the name Farrington and the English culture provided by his divorced English mother, as well as the arrogant wealth of his distant Chinese father, and becomes an ardent Chinese communist, subordinating everything and everyone to what he believes to be the good of the Party and of China. Nineteen-year-old Mimi Lambert, "carelessly beautiful, lazily feminine, casually flirtatious" (32), daughter of an "Australian adventurer" and a "reckless Chinese socialite" (11), vehemently rejects China and things Chinese. When her Swiss lover does not have enough backbone to withstand his father's objections to their marriage, she throws herself at any American male in the desperate hope of obtaining the lifeline she seeks: passage out of China.

The novel focuses, however, on 20-year-old Sylvia Chen, the daughter of an American woman, Helen, and a Chinese man, Liyi, manager of a Shanghai plant. Though Liyi would prefer the quiet life of the traditional Chinese scholar brushing beautiful calligraphic ink strokes on rice paper, his actual life is presently embroiled in a labor struggle brought to a head by Communist agitators at his plant. An admirer of Western ways, he married an American and then found that the two children he had fathered were "foreign" to him. Life seems to have galloped past, leaving him out of step, confused and ineffectual:

"Do you know anything about labor unions?" his daughter had once asked him and, involuntarily, he had replied, "No, I'm above those things," and moved his arm in an ancient gesture. It seemed he had wanted to fling back a non-existent silk sleeve. But his shirt cuff had merely rested stiffly on his wrist . . . (159)

He seems to embody the old China, ignorant of and therefore dismissive of the modern world, elegant but anachronistic, willfully blind and dangerously unrealistic.

His wife, Helen, on the other hand, torn between homesickness for America, disgust for China, and love for her husband and children, is unhappy and volatile (much like Han Suyin's mother) and freely expresses her frustration. China is "out here in the jungle, out here in the desert, out here among savages, out here in the leper colony. And the Chinese to her were part savage, part leprous and totally mysterious" (48). When Liyi's nephew, Peiyuan, a "country bumpkin" comes to live with them, Helen's aesthetic sense is offended:

He had the features that Helen found so antagonizing on some Chinese. Such small eyes (What's the matter with you Chinese, having such small black eyes?), the kind of Chinese nose that looked stuffed and adenoidal, and such large, uneven white teeth. The cowlick made him look unkempt, indolent, unmannered as only the Chinese could be, what with their spitting out of tramcars, picking their ears at movies, belching at meals. His whole appearance was slack, except for the activity of his eyes, bright and eager (but they were small, tight-lidded, like Korean eyes), and the mobility of his mouth (hardly ever closing upon teeth.) (54–55)

Such a description written by a Caucasian would be considered tactless if not racist. Written by a Chinese, however, it reveals W. E. B. Du Bois' double consciousness—an acute awareness of Western standards of beauty against which such Chinese features fail miserably. At the same time, as borne out by the rest of the novel, the author has an affection for this "ugly" character; Peiyuan, is, after all Sylvia's first cousin and a person that she grows fond of. His untimely death, at the hands of fanatic Communists, is a tragic waste that proves to be a catalyst in Sylvia's life.

When her parents quarrel, Sylvia's position, between her American mother and Chinese father, is tense and difficult. Sympathizing with her father, Sylvia is hurt when her mother rails against Peiyuan and the Chinese in general; yet seeing her father's evasive and ineffectual ways, she understands her mother's impatience. Walking down the street, she is aware of the curious eyes of onlookers who notice that her brown hair looks reddish in the sunlight and who see that "she walk[s] with all the freedom and impatience of a foreigner, yet in her there [is] something inescapably Oriental" (5). Young and unformed, she is attracted to Feng Huang, who has chosen with fierce determination to be Chinese. "But she was both as American as her own mother, and as Chinese as her father. She could not deny her ambivalence"

(19). When she later discovers that Feng is interested in her mainly as a source of information about her father's factory, and that Feng was involved in the imprisonment and eventual death of her cousin, the romance dissipates. Released from her dependency on others for her own identity, she realizes, with the abruptness of an awakening, that the energy she had loved in Feng, and in Peiyuan, is hers as well:

> By residing fully and carefully in her own (body), she would be able to engage her emotions, her mind and her days with pride. Abruptly, she had no longer felt accidental, but responsible. She was Sylvia Chen, and she would speak out for herself—an entity composed of both her parents, but ready to act and not merely react, for one individual—herself. She had seemed to take her first breath of life. (237)

In *Frontiers of Love*, Chang makes clear that one's identity is the sum of all of one's past, not the choice of one half of one's ancestry at the expense of the other, the mistake made by Feng Huang and Mimi Lambert. For Sylvia Chen and for Diana Chang, this past includes nostalgic memories of early childhood in Peiping (Beijing):

> Peiping, the old walled city, was her first home. Sylvia remembered a medieval incandescence flaring in all its seasons. Life there, between walls that divided and secluded and marked off in patterns of regular and irregular squares, was as fully *now* as the warm grasp of a hand, as quilts tucked thickly under the chin, as minutes spent coin by coin by an old man in the sun. She remembered childhood and hot cereal and soft-boiled eggs. She thought, tasting these again, that one's first memories should be of loving and that these should be under the Peiping sky; that one's early eyes should grow deep with looking upon that northern largeness; that one's proportions might embrace both the utter intricacy of the new moon . . . and the boldness, the lustiness, the full-blown wonder of solid sunlight and blackest artesian depths—that these should be and remain and live at the young core of every adult, be the solid unwavering pivot of the unchanging child in every grown person, the point of eternal return, the memory which is the person, beyond which no history can recede! (57)

How different is Diana Chang's sun—"the boldness, the lustiness, the full-blown wonder of solid sunlight"—from Eileen Chang's (no relation) exhausted sun—lying "across the street like an old yellow dog, barring the way"—in *The Rice Sprout Song*. In this passage, Diana Chang strongly affirms the centrality of her own past. The depth of feeling for these childhood memories of her natal city goes beyond fondness or affection; it is an attachment like an umbilical cord: the central and essential sustenance necessary to the life of every adult. Chang makes no apologies but simply and boldly states that *everyone's* "first memories . . . should be under the Peiping sky." This proud assertion counteracts the painfully alienated description of Peiyuan's Chinese ugliness. Taken together, the two passages express the double consciousness of what it means to be Chinese in a white world. *Frontiers of*

Love ends with Liyi's realization that he cannot reject what he has wrought, for

> that had been the bravest thing he had done—to marry Helen and bring two Eurasians into the world. But that had been done with the courage of innocence. Now the courage of understanding was required . . . To be Chinese was not enough; it did not define one's beliefs any more. The times were demanding new loyalties, more discriminating, more humanitarian. His children, free from any narrow chauvinism, were the new citizens for an expanding century. (245)

The golden memory of Peiping is but the foundation for building a cosmopolitanism and expatriation "free from any narrow chauvinism." Indeed, for Diana Chang "to be Chinese was not enough," for her five later novels, with a single minor exception, do not have Chinese or Amerasian characters in them at all. Asked why her later protagonists were all Caucasian, she replied that "exoticism" can stand in the way of the "universal" she strives for in her themes and, therefore, she has "often subsumed aspects of her background in the interest of other truths." Asked why a Chinese or Chinese American can't also be "universal," she responded that we are living in the United States and "Everyman" here is white.[2] Though an ethnic minority writer is not bound to write of her own ethnicity, as women writers are not bound to create only heroines nor to adopt a feminist perspective, nonetheless, prolonged avoidance of that which is closest to one's self when self-hood is one's major theme is a difficult stand to defend. The explanation may be that Diana Chang's formative years were spent in the United States, in New York City, during the McCarthy era, when all Americans, including Chinese Americans, had to disavow everything having to do with a Communist country, and China, of course, was Communist. Thus, the central characters of five of her six novels are white Anglo-Saxon Protestants with the occasional "exotic," a Jew. In her poetry and recent short fiction, however, Chang has treated Chinese American subjects.

3. THE AMERICAN-BORN CHINESE AMERICAN

3.1. Jade Snow Wong and Maxine Hong Kingston

Even if one's life is not complicated by parents of different races or by geographic relocations, one cannot escape the between-world condition as a nonwhite in the United States. Both Jade Snow Wong and Maxine Hong Kingston, a generation later, were born to two Chinese parents in the United States and reared in California Chinatowns, San Francisco and Stockton. And the between-world consciousness is central to their autobiographical texts,

Fifth Chinese Daughter (1945) and *The Woman Warrior* (1976). Though Jade Snow Wong's autobiography has been disparaged by a number of Asian American commentators,[3] Kingston herself considers Jade Snow Wong a literary mentor, describing her as "the Mother of Chinese American literature" and the only Chinese American author she read before writing her own book. "I found Jade Snow Wong's book myself in the library, and was flabbergasted, helped, inspired, affirmed, made possible as a writer—for the first time I saw a person who looked like me as a heroine of a book, as a maker of a book."[4]

The two books are greatly divergent in style and temperament, each text largely affected by the personalities of the two women and by the period in which each was produced. *Fifth Chinese Daughter*, as noted earlier, was written for a white audience during World War II, and its popularity, to a large extent, was due to white readers' need to distinguish between friend and foe; thus, of necessity, it contains many explanations of Chinese culture and customs. Another reason for its popularity may be that it was, as critic Patricia Lin Blinde put it, "a Horatio Alger account in Chinese guise,"[5] demonstrating the greatness of America in that even a minority woman much repressed by her family could attain the American Dream. *The Woman Warrior*, an outgrowth of the Civil Rights and Women's Liberation movements of the 1960s and 1970s, is a much more personal text, written not as an exemplum for others but as a means of exorcising the personal ghosts that haunt the author. It is written for the author herself, as well as for other women, and for Chinese Americans, whom at one point she directly addresses (5–6).

Fifth Chinese Daughter is subdued in tone, polite, restrained, well-brought up. *The Woman Warrior* is angry, bitter, rebellious, and outspoken. *Fifth Chinese Daughter* is a sober, straightforward narrative delivered in chronological order, as though to tell this much were effort enough. *The Woman Warrior* is poetic, experimental, fragmented in narrative line, a virtuoso performance of imaginative power and verbal dexterity.

Fifth Chinese Daughter is written in the third person, for Jade Snow Wong was rigorously trained in traditional Chinese ways and followed them, even though her resentment often shows through between the lines and in the details of some of the episodes. Writing of herself in the third person, however, though stilted and stylized,[6] shows that she is a properly modest Chinese daughter and demonstrates her filial respect for her father. Only after his death, could she refer to herself in the first person in her second book, *No Chinese Stranger* (1976). Jade Snow Wong is apologetic for writing an autobiography so early in life (she was only 24), but, true to her upbringing, gives credit for her book's existence to authority figures who helped her shape it: her editor and teacher. She claims not to judge the right or wrong of the experiences she relates but to include them because they are "significant episodes which . . . shaped my life" (vii).

In *The Woman Warrior*, not only does Maxine Hong Kingston use the first person freely, but she ranges widely through the polyglossia and images of her multicultural upbringing, from male locker room talk—"I hope the man my aunt loved wasn't just a tits and ass man" (9) to allusions to Virginia Woolf—"by giving women what they wanted: a job and a room of their own" (62)—to Chinese myth—"As the water shook, then settled, the colors and lights shimmered into a picture, not reflecting anything I could see around me. There at the bottom of the gourd were my mother and father scanning the sky, which was where I was" (22)—to open tirades against her mother: "You lie with your stories. You won't tell me a story and then say, 'This is a true story,' or, 'This is just a story.' I can't tell the difference. I don't even know what your real names are. I can't tell what's real and what you make up. Ha! You can't stop me from talking. You tried to cut off my tongue, but it didn't work" (202). This polyglossia is a verbal portrait of the Chinese American girl Maxine, who "being young is still creating herself."[7] Maxine is American-bold in protesting the misogyny of traditional Chinese culture and the tyrannical methods her mother used to impose her will on her family. Kingston is poetic and imaginative in creating dramas that she did not witness: the No Name aunt's adultery and punishment, Fa Mulan's mystical training, Brave Orchid's exorcising of the sitting ghost. In fact, the line between fantasy and reality, in Kingston's book as in her mother's stories, is never strictly maintained and the narrative frequently crosses the border.[8]

Both books, however, seek to resolve psychological conflicts and come to terms with an unresolved past in order to move into the future. As daughters of Southern Chinese parents born and reared in the United States, both authors share the same cultural conflicts. By the third grade, Jade Snow "decided that the American School was going to be continuously different in more and more ways from Chinese studies and that there would be little point in wondering why" (18). In the fourth grade, Jade Snow was conscious that not only were American ways different from Chinese ways but that she was caught between the two:

> the specific differences would involve a choice of action. Jade Snow had begun to compare American ways with those of her mother and father, and the comparison made her uncomfortable. (21)

Maxine Hong Kingston, in her first chapter, spells out the purpose of her book as an attempt to bridge the gulf between the two separate halves of her ancestry and upbringing: "Those of us in the first American generations have had to figure out how the invisible world the emigrants built around our childhoods fit in solid America" (5). How does she reconcile her mother's ghost stories with American neon and plastic? Is she more American than Chinese? What is American? What is Chinese? She asks her compatriots:

> Chinese-Americans, when you try to understand what things in you are Chinese, how do you separate what is peculiar to childhood, to poverty, insanities, one family, your mother who marked your growing with stories, from what is Chinese? What is Chinese tradition and what is the movies? (5–6)

Can a Chinese American growing up in America ever know what is Chinese? Isn't her experience limited to her own family, which may be atypical, and to the images of Chinese acted by white actors that she has seen in movies made by whites? In other words, Maxine is posing the questions, Who am I? How do I sift out all this contradictory and confusing stuff to the kernel that is my center? Is there such a neat, hard kernel or am I all this amorphous and contradictory stuff? At the end of her book, she is still working at her self-definition: "I continue to sort out what's just my childhood, just my imagination, just my family, just the village, just movies, just living" (205).

What is peculiar to me and my family? What is typical of many? These are questions both women ask as they write their books. That which is peculiar to their own families distinguishes them from others; that which they share with others brings them the comfort of membership in a larger community. They can only answer the first question with assurance, but in giving their answers they hope that others in the larger community will recognize a similarity and nod in concurrence and solidarity.

One aspect common to both the Wong and Hong families, despite the more than three decades separating them, is the sense of being merely sojourners in an alien land. The older generation of both families tried with mixed success to impress this notion upon the younger generation. Jade Snow Wong learned this lesson so well that she repeated it at the end of the speech she made at her graduation from college: "It seems to me that the most effective application that American-Chinese can make of their education would be in China, which needs all the Chinese talent she can muster" (135). However, her words spoke one thing, and her actions another, for she did not "return" to China except briefly as a tourist (on a tour of Asia sponsored by the US State Department); her home and her life have been and are in California. Nonetheless, in calling herself American-Chinese, she implies that she's essentially Chinese with only a veneer of American. This would have been the socially approved stance in the 1940s.

Maxine Hong Kingston, on the other hand, calls herself Chinese American without a hyphen, so that Chinese is only the adjective for American. Kingston is unequivocally rebellious and American: "Whenever my parents said 'home,' they suspended America. They suspended enjoyment, but I did not want to go to China. In China my parents would sell my sisters and me" (99). Her mother's use of the word "ghosts" to designate the non-Chinese "barbarians" is indicative of the older generation's need to set apart their family from the world around them, a world that is ignorant of the customs brought from China, which from the mother's perspective, was the only right way to do anything. But Maxine's desire is to get away from all these ghosts from China with which her mother has haunted her childhood to the places that are "ghost-free."

Therefore, a minority individual's sense of alienation results not only from rejection by the dominant culture but also rejection of parental strictures. Minority parents' own fear of losing their cultural heritage is intensified by the fear of losing their children to the "foreign" culture, and therefore they insist with greater vehemence on their children's acceptance of family traditions and Old World ties. Thus, though born in the United States, both Wong and Kingston are prevented in childhood from identifying themselves as American by parents who tell them that they should eventually "go back" to China. In *The Woman Warrior*, Kingston writes: "Not when we were afraid, but when we were wide awake and lucid, my mother funneled China into our ears: Kwangtung Province, New Society Village, the river Kwoo, which runs past the village. 'Go the way we came so that you will be able to find our house. Don't forget. Just give your father's name, and any villager can point out our house.' I am to return to China where I have never been" (76). Kingston shows the gulf between a mother's insistence that her daughter's real home is her father's boyhood home and the daughter who sees only the impossibility of "returning" to a place where she has never been. Nor can she understand her parents' persistence in holding tightly for 40 years to the idea of returning to China. When the last uncle in China dies and the villagers take over the Hong family land, her mother laments, "We're not going back to China for sure now" (106).

As children attending schools with Americans and accepting American ways as the norm, both Jade Snow Wong and Maxine Hong Kingston found the Old World teachings of their parents inappropriate and often embarrassing. Though Maxine was forthright in her expressions of rejection, Jade Snow's reaction was typically Chinese. Jade Snow, brought up with the old Chinese virtues of absolute obedience to authority, honesty, hard work, repression of anger, and sensitivity to the opinions of others, describes how these virtues were reinforced throughout childhood by physical punishment and public humiliation. Early in the book, she recalls one episode in which she ran to her mother to complain that a neighbor's child had spit on her. Instead of sympathizing with her child as an American mother would, her mother immediately concluded that Jade Snow must have provoked such a reaction and that she should be punished. In front of all the women working in their factory, her mother spanked her with a wooden hanger: "Again the shame was almost worse than the pain, and the pain was bad enough, for Mother usually spanked until the wooden hanger broke" (3). For a wooden hanger to break, the mother's anger and strength had to have been great. But what is difficult for contemporary American readers to comprehend is that Jade Snow's reaction at the time was not openly expressed resentment and protest but a redoubling of efforts to be approved by her elders. After such incidents, she would pray: "To make up for this neglect and prejudice, please help me to do my best in striving to [be] a person respected and honored by my family, when I grow up." What after the 1960s would be denounced as Uncle Tomism is the approved Chinese way to behave: "Anger and resentment towards superiors are supposed to make the individual work harder to achieve the objectively defined standards of behavior that can bring universal praise. One has to work out crises of anger by being a model of social propriety."9 However, the fact that wooden hanger incident appears at the very beginning of the book and that Jade Snow describes many similar instances of parental harshness indicates the very real and deep, lingering presence of anger and resentment, though this anger is never forthrightly expressed.

Maxine Hong Kingston, on the other hand, is openly and vociferously critical of things Chinese—"I don't see how they kept up a continuous culture for five thousand years. Maybe they didn't; maybe everyone makes it up as they go along" (185). She retreats into "American-normal": "To make my waking life American-normal, I turn on the lights before anything untoward makes an appearance. I push the deformed into my dreams, which are in Chinese, the language of impossible stories. Before we can leave our parents, they stuff our heads like the suitcases which they jam-pack with homemade underwear" (87). "Chinese people are very weird" (158), Kingston's brothers and sisters tell each other, unable to comprehend the actions of either their mother or their aunt recently arrived from China. After describing some of the unusual meals her mother cooked and forced her children to eat—squid eye, blood pudding, skunk, raccoon, city pigeons, snakes, and snails—Kingston concludes, "I would live on plastic" (92). Surfeited with her mother's stories of ghosts and spirits, Kingston wants to escape: "I've found some places in this country that are ghost-free. And I think I belong there" (108).

One tragicomic incident in *The Woman Warrior* epitomizes the between-world condition. When the neighborhood drugstore mistakenly delivers another family's prescription to the Hong home, Brave Orchid forces Maxine to go to the druggist to ask for candy as retribution. For the mother, this is a necessary measure to ward off the illness that would surely follow the medicine to their home; for the daughter, this is a humiliating act of begging, confirmed by the druggist's giving her out-of-season candy: "Halloween candy in December, Christmas candy around Valentine's day, candy hearts at Easter, and Easter eggs at Halloween" (171). Uncomprehending the insult, their mother is pleased, thinking she has taught "the Druggist Ghosts a lesson in good manners." For his part, the druggist feels that these little Chinese children, living behind their parents' laundry, are to be pitied, for they cannot afford to buy treats. Neither party understood the other; only Maxine understood both, but, as a child, she was powerless to explain one to the other. Furthermore, to add to her own psychic pain and confusion, Maxine found the druggist (an outsider) more comprehensible than her mother (to whom she owes her life), and as a small child she had to carry out the wishes of this incomprehensible mother.

The Woman Warrior is a brilliantly developed exposition of the between-world condition from the very first line, in which Kingston breaks her mother's injunction to silence by telling the story of the adulterous aunt that she is told never to tell, to the last story of Ts'ai Yen. The American daughter needs to gain independence from family traditions, seen in the No Name aunt's story as constraint to the point of annihilation, while the Chinese mother's purpose in passing on family stories and custom is to mold the next generation into conformity with time-honored tradition. The dutiful mother tells the story to her daughter as a cautionary tale, but the rebellious daughter calls this aunt "my forerunner" and admires her for defying conventions, breaking taboos, and being her own person, regardless of the cost. The mother wants the daughter to participate in the family's punishment by never speaking of this aunt, but the daughter begins her book by making public the aunt's story and even embroidering on it with her own poetic speculations as to why and how the woman committed adultery and suicide. Out of a victim, one whom the villagers punished by raiding her family's house and destroying or taking all their stores, and whom her family punishes by never speaking her name, Kingston creates a victor, of sorts, and a threat: the No Name aunt killed herself and her child as she was expected to do, but she did it by jumping into the family's drinking well, thus polluting the water and getting her revenge. Furthermore, as a spite suicide, she does not even mean Maxine well, but a "weeping ghost, wet hair hanging and skin bloated, [she] waits silently by the water to pull down a substitute" (16).

Though seemingly disconnected, the episodes in The Woman Warrior are carefully structured and organized to illuminate the themes of woman as victim and woman as victor. Each theme is manifested primarily in one story at a time, and these stories alternate and balance one another throughout the text: the No Name aunt is followed by the warrior Fa Mulan; the indomitable Brave Orchid's feats by the tragedy of her pale, weak sister Moon Orchid; the crazy women who have only one story that they repeat over and over; by Maxine herself, who has a list of more than 200 items that she finally gives voice to.

Often, however, the victim and victor are in the same person at different times, as we saw above with the No Name aunt. Brave Orchid, normally a victor, is vanquished in her interference with her sister's life. Had Brave

Orchid not provided her sister's passage to America, not insisted on pushing her sister to reclaim her rights as the first wife to a man who was much younger and had remarried, Moon Orchid would be still living peaceably in Hong Kong. Brave Orchid's inappropriate insistence on importing to the United States the traditional Chinese custom, in which one man could have several wives under one roof and the first wife would have preeminence, brought about her sister's madness and death. Another example, comparable to the Brave Orchid/Moon Orchid episode is the story of Maxine's tormenting the silent Chinese girl: the strong one, the aggressor, is not necessarily the victor, for though Maxine pulled the silent girl's hair and pinched her cheeks, cajoled, threatened, and tormented her to speak, not a word came from the girl's lips. As an aftermath of this self-contemptuous act, Maxine was ill and bedridden for 18 months. Kingston demonstrates that victim and victor are intermingled and often inseparable.

Both *Fifth Chinese Daughter* and *The Woman Warrior* record the confusion of young girls' attempting to reconcile conflicting self-images; at times, American teachers and friends seem more accepting and encouraging than parents. Maxine earns A's in school, but the mother, unimpressed, tells her she must defend her village, like Fa Mulan, the woman warrior. "I could not figure out what was my village" (45), Maxine complains. Jade Snow comes home elated at having been skipped a grade in school—"The teacher and her friends all seemed very much excited, and Jade Snow caught their excitement" (18)—only to have her excitement squelched by her fathers' bland reaction—"'That is as it should be.' That was all he said, with finality" (19).

Both Jade Snow Wong and Maxine Hong Kingston felt the weight of a Chinese tradition which demanded the repression and subordination of the individual will: "In every way, every day, Jade Snow was molded to be trouble-free, unobtrusive, quiescent, cooperative."[10] For both women, the attempted repression of their individualities took the form of silencing their voices; as Kingston put it, "If you don't talk, you can't have a personality" (180). From the parents' perspective, the less strong the child's own personality, the easier the job of molding it as it should be molded.[11] Silence was literally imposed by Jade Snow's father's injunctions: "one was not supposed to talk when one was either eating or thinking, and when one was not eating, one should be thinking. Only when in bed did one neither eat nor think" (4). But in bed, one was supposed to sleep. The only talking her father did permit was the rote repetition of Chinese history lessons. For Kingston, silence was the result of being a Chinese in America and being a daughter in the Hong family. Being silent before whites was common among Chinese Americans, particularly those who entered the country under false or "paper" names and thus feared that too close contact with whites would eventually lead to deportation. As they built zigzagging bridges to confuse the gods, so Chinese took steps to confuse the gods in this country, the whites. Kingston writes,

"The Chinese I know hide their names; sojourners take new names when their lives change and guard their real names with silence" (5). Perhaps, a mature Maxine muses, the older generation felt threatened by its own young—"always trying to get things straight, always trying to name the unspeakable" (5). Being a Chinese girl in an American school, having to cope in a foreign language with people of another race and culture, was another reason for reticence. Ignorant of English when she entered American school, Maxine was totally silent, flunked kindergarten, and was given an IQ of zero, an indication not of her intelligence, obviously, but of the inadequacy of the tools of measurement.

> It was when I found out I had to talk that school became a misery, that the silence became a misery. I did not speak and felt bad each time that I did not speak. I read aloud in first grade, though, and heard the barest whisper with little squeaks come out of my throat . . . The other Chinese girls did not talk either, so I knew the silence had to do with being a Chinese girl (166).

And at home the situation was also not conducive to speaking. She had been told that her mother had cut her frenum at birth, an act both terrifying and powerful, which her mother had justified by explaining that: "Your tongue would be able to move in any language. You'll be able to speak languages that are completely different from one another. You'll be able to pronounce anything" (164). The result, however, was just the opposite, Maxine became tongue-tied and silent. The cut tongue becomes the symbol of the mother's overwhelming power over the daughter, in a sense, a castrating power. Brave Orchid did so much talking, was so much commanding a presence, and "never explained anything that was really important" (121) that her children lapsed into silence around her. The daughters grew up hearing sexist maxims from their parents' mouths: "When fishing for treasures in the flood, be careful not to pull in girls" (52). "Feeding girls is feeding cowbirds." "There's no profit in raising girls. Better to raise geese than girls" (46). Such sayings elicited anger that the child Maxine expressed by being sullen, disobedient, and unobliging. When Moon Orchid fresh from China found her nieces and nephews rude and asked her sister, "Why didn't you teach your girls to be demure?" . . . Brave Orchid yelled, "They *are* demure. They're so demure, they barely talk" (133). Told she is ugly, unmarriageable, that she "quacks like a pressed duck" (192) and looks like a "furry wild animal" (134), little wonder Maxine was silent around her elders. Even now as an adult, Maxine says "A dumbness—a shame—still cracks my voice in two" (165).

For Jade Snow Wong, silence was an externally imposed condition. When she broke free of her father's control, she broke into words, reporting the conditions she had overcome to arrive where she had. For Maxine Hong Kingston, silence was a refuge from her mother, a place for her own creativity to blossom. As she covered her school paintings with black paint as curtains hiding her "mighty operas" from probing eyes, so she remained silent in school and around her mother until her outburst at the end of high school freed her voice and until her book, *The Woman Warrior*, drew apart the curtains.

Despite the complaints, implied or fully expressed, against the constraints of domineering parents and a restrictive cultural legacy, both Wong and Kingston are, to a certain extent, also proud of their cultural legacy. Jade Snow writes lovingly of her father's patience in teaching her Chinese, and she is touched and proud when she discovers among his personal things after his death her own Chinese exercise books, which he had valued so long. Brave Orchid tells Maxine, "It is better to feed geese than girls," but the mother's own example speaks to the contrary: earning a medical degree while her husband was halfway around the world, exorcising a ghost that terrified everyone in the dormitory, bearing six children after the age of 45 (106), carrying a hundred pounds of Texas rice up- and downstairs, working at the laundry from 6:30 a.m. until midnight—this mother's indefatigable energy sustains the entire family and her example, like that of the woman warrior, is an inspiration to her daughter. She may cook strange foods, but "all heroes are bold toward food." Little wonder Maxine had to learn to enlarge her mind to make "room for paradoxes" (29).

Both Wong and Kingston, gaining maturity, push aside the leaden weight of familial oppression; both find and develop their own talents. From the position of personal strength and self-assertion, they can look back with greater tolerance on their parents' attempts to shape their identities. Though her brothers are supported through college, Jade Snow is not and must earn her own way as a housekeeper and cook; this she succeeds in doing, and at the book's end she sets up her own pottery business in Chinatown. The discipline, the capacity for patient, hard work that her parents instilled in her from girlhood stands her in good stead at the potter's wheel, and the individuality that was so long repressed finds expression in the malleable clay. Though her shop is an oddity in the eyes of Chinatown, her work is admired enough by Caucasians to be purchased by prestigious New York museums, both the Metropolitan and the Modern Art. *Fifth Chinese Daughter* ends with a reconciliation between the father and daughter; he admires her accomplishments despite his initial disapproval of her even attempting them, and he is not too proud to tell her so. She is proud and happy that she has succeeded in winning his approval.

For her part, Maxine eventually finds her voice. Having accumulated a list of over 200 items about herself that she needed to confess to her mother "so that she would know the true things about me and to stop the pain in my throat" (197), Maxine decides to be brave and let them out, a few a day, but her mother rebuffs her, "Senseless gabbings every night. I wish you would stop . . . I don't feel like hearing your craziness" (200). One evening, Maxine's throat "burst open" (201), and she lashed out, voicing the most difficult items on her list, complaints against her parents and assertions of her own worth:

> I want you to tell that hulk, that gorrila-ape, to go away and never bother us again . . . You think you can give us away to freaks. You better not do that, Mother. I may be ugly and clumsy, but one thing I'm not, I'm not retarded . . . I can do ghost things even better than ghosts can. Not everybody thinks I'm nothing. I am not going to be a slave or a wife. I can't stand living here anymore. I am going to get scholarships and I'm going away . . . And I'm not going to Chinese school anymore . . . And I don't want to listen to anymore of your stories; they have no logic . . . You lie with stories . . . (201–2)

To her surprise, as she pours forth this tirade, she finds that the authority she was resisting so furiously is no longer there: "No higher listener. No listener by myself" (204). This existential realization frees her, and only after this, with greater maturity and from a safe distance away, can she look back and see that she "had been in the presence of great power, my mother talking-story" (19, 20). Only then, can she acknowledge that she and her mother were both born in the year of the dragon, and that she, like her mother, also talks-story.

The Woman Warrior consciously seeks to break stereotypes by providing an insider's perspective. In informing us that she and her mother were both born in the year of the dragon, Maxine subverts and converts the white stereotype of "dragon-lady" from an image of sinister threat to one of strength of will and courage; Brave Orchid and Maxine do not endanger the lives of others but are fierce in defending their own against encroachments and repressions. Kingston devotes a great deal of space to an analysis of the "quiet, demure Chinese girl," who may indeed be outwardly silent, but whose silence hides a tormented, squashed speech. Non-Chinese may find Chinese food tasty, but Kingston, unflinching, shows there is another side, nightmarish and seemingly unspeakable.

The Woman Warrior ends with a resolution of the conflict between parent and child, metaphorically, in their collaboration in the final story of Ts'ai Yen, a story begun by the mother and ended by the daughter. Not only is Ts'ai Yen's story narrated by mother and daughter but it symbolizes both their lives. Ts'ai Yen, the victim, abducted by barbarians and forced to live among them many years, ridiculed and misunderstood by even her own children is Brave Orchid, who had a great falling off in coming to America, where hard physical labor and uncomprehending "half-ghost" children are her lot. And Ts'ai Yen is Maxine as a child, unprepared for American school, alienated by the fearful "ghosts" created all around her by her mother. Ts'ai Yen, the victor, inspired by the barbarians' flutes reaching over and over for a high note, which they found and held "an icicle in the desert," who begins to sing in a way that communicates her sadness and anger to the barbarians and touches her children who then sing with her, is Brave Orchid after Maxine has reached a level of maturity when resentment and anger are replaced by understanding and affection. And it is Kingston, whose retelling of her mother's stories "translated well." Embracing her confused childhood, translating her mother's stories, revealing their beauty and power, Kingston transforms her victim's state of cut frenum into a victor's state of full-throated song.

The national recognition and the numerous awards both *The Woman Warrior* and *China Men* have received attest to Kingston's victory and demonstrate how successful she has been in making central and complexly beautiful what had seemed a peripheral and confusing between-world condition. Testifying to her accomplishment are the many rave reviews and articles about her in national papers and magazines, of which the following is merely a small sampling: "the most exciting new writer in years," "a brilliant polished gemstone" writes Susan Brownmiller in *Mademoiselle*[12]; "a brilliant memoir . . . it is as fierce as a warrior's voice and as eloquent as any artist's," says Jane Kramer in *The New York Times*[13]; "this searing, beautiful memoir . . . this dazzling mixture of prerevolutionary Chinese village life and myth, set against its almost unbearable contradictions in contemporary American life, could unfold as almost a psychic transcript of every woman I know— class, age, race, or ethnicity be damned. Here is the real meaning of America as melting pot," writes Sara Blackburn for *Ms*.[14]; "Four years ago in this space I said '*The Woman Warrior*' was the best book I'd read in years. '*China Men*' is, at the very least, the best book I've read in the four years since," declared John Leonard in *The New York Times*.[15] In the People's Republic of China, too, her work is known. During a visit to the First Foreign Language Institute in Beijing, I learned that one of the faculty members there, a young man, had translated part of Kingston's book and published an article about her. Kingston's first visit to her parents' country was noted in the Beijing English publication *China Daily* on May 21, 1982, and she has paid subsequent visits to China since. In her way, then, she has accomplished the goal she thought impossible "conquered and united both North America and Asia."

3.2. Maxine Hong Kingston and Amy Tan

Creating as great a furor on the literary scene as did Maxine Hong Kingston's *The Woman Warrior* 13 years earlier, Amy Tan's first novel, *The Joy Luck Club* (1989), is in parts an echo and a response and in parts a continuation and expansion of Kingston's book. Focused on Mandarin-speaking Chinese rather than Cantonese, less angry in tone, but equally poetic, painful, and often funny, Amy Tan continues to probe the problematic Chinese mother–American daughter relationship in four separate stories of two gener-

Maxine Hong Kingston at the Viet Nam Veterans Memorial, Washington,
D.C., April 1989 Photograph by Amy Ling

ations of women. The stories are rich in imagery and sharp detail while the individual personalities (within each generation) are less defined. In fact, in existential fashion, actions and events define and identify the characters, who become who they are because of what they have chosen to do. Thus, though the eight characters are divided into four families and given different names, the book itself is concerned more with a simple bifurcation along generational lines: mothers, whose stories all took place in China, and daughters, whose stories are being lived in America; mothers who are possessively trying to hold fast and daughters who are battling for autonomy. The one story, the Woo's, in which the mother/daughter bond is broken by the mother's death, ceases to be a battle and becomes a devastating loss, a loss compensated for by the daughter's taking the place of the mother and finding mother substitutes. The lost mother is entangled with the story of two lost daughters, who when found and returned to the family become a means of recovering the mother. Further, the lost mother in Jing-mei's story develops into a trope for the lost motherland for all the daughters.

The four sides of the mahjong table, called "winds" in the game, serve both as a structural and a symbolic device. The novel is divided into four main sections with the focus shifting from one family to the next in each section, allowing mothers and daughters to tell their stories in the first person and making two complete rounds of the table. The exception is Suyuan Woo, who, having recently died, does not speak for herself but whose daughter, Jing-mei, speaks four times, telling her mother's story as she takes her mother's place at the mahjong table and on the fateful trip to China. The symbolic purpose of the cardinal point winds is apparent in Tan's giving a preeminent place to Jing-mei Woo's position at "the East, where things begin" and where the novel begins and ends, making the Woo story central and alluding, of course, to China, where the mothers' lives began.

Further, the winds play a metaphoric role. In mother Lindo Jong's early life, though forced into an arranged marriage, she discovers her own inner strength, and says "I was strong. I was pure . . . I was like the wind" (58). She uses her wind, her breath, to blow out her husband's end of the wedding candle, a courageous act of sabotage that she later makes use of to free herself from this unhappy marriage. Much later in life, she instructs her daughter Waverly on "the art of invisible strength," applicable equally to the game of chess and to life: "Wise guy, he not go against wind. In Chinese we say, Come from South, blow with wind—poom!—North will follow. Strongest wind cannot be seen" (89). In other words, victory over hostile forces (the cold North wind) may be achieved not through direct confrontation but by apparent accommodation and giving in (warm South wind). A simple maneuver in Chinese martial arts illustrates this principle well. If someone of greater weight pushes against you, attempting to knock you over, instead of pushing back you simply step backward, and your opponent, expecting resistance, will be knocked off balance by the force of his own thrust.

Extending the wind imagery in *The Joy Luck Club*, daughter Rose Hsu Jordan says, "I still listened to my mother, but I also learned how to let her words blow through me" (191). And, finally, the balance and imbalance of winds reflects the balance or imbalance in the emotional lives and the power struggles of the characters, most vividly exemplified in the stories of Ying-ying and Lena St. Clair.

Each of the four sections of *The Joy Luck Club* begins with a prologue, a brief narrative, emblematic of that section's theme. The first paragraph of the first prologue contains a rich image that resonates throughout the entire novel:

> The old woman remembered a swan she had bought many years ago in Shanghai for a foolish sum. This bird, boasted the market vendor, was once a duck that stretched its neck in hopes of becoming a goose, and now look!—it is too beautiful to eat.

The parable of the once useful duck whose overweaning pride and vanity transformed it into an aesthetic but useless swan has multiple ramifications; it is an emblem of the mother herself in her emigration to the United States in search of a materially more prosperous life, as well as a metaphor of every mother's unrealistic ambitions for her daughter (who is merely a duck but whom the mother wants to see as a swan). Suyuan Woo, for example, possessing enormous faith that everything is possible in America and expecting her child to be a prodigy, first wanted Jing-mei to be another Shirley Temple, and when that seemed unlikely, then at least a concert pianist. Simultaneously touching and ludicrous, such dreams characterize the bittersweet tone of the mother–daughter relationships in this book, as they did in *The Woman Warrior*. The daughters are proud of their mothers' strength and ingenuity; moved by their tragic, beautiful stories from the Old Country, and touched by their fierce love; but at the same time the daughters are exasperated by their mothers' impossible demands; resentful of their mothers' intrusions on their lives, and sometimes humiliated and ashamed of their stubborn, superstitious, out-of-place Old World ways.

In the rest of the first prologue, when the woman from China arrived in the United States, American officials confiscated the swan, leaving her with only one feather and the memory of the beautiful bird. She wants to tell her daughter about the bird, but, though an old woman now, she is still waiting for the day when she can tell her story in "perfect American English." The swan thus becomes transmuted into a symbol of the mother's past life in China, an experience she wants to communicate to her daughter, but because the daughter has achieved the mother's dream—"Over there, nobody will look down on her, because I will make her speak only perfect American English"—the mother herself, who has not mastered English, cannot speak with her own daughter. Ironically and tragically, the achievement of the mother's dreams for her daughter, which entailed physical removal from the motherland, results in the alienation of mother and daughter, for the daughter readily and entirely adapted to the customs and language of the new land while the mother still held onto those of the old. As mother Lindo Jong succinctly put it, "I wanted my children to have the best combination: American circumstances and Chinese character. How could I know these two things do not mix?" (254).

The gulf between the Old World and the New, between Chinese mother and American daughter, and the painful difficulties resulting from attempts to bridge this gulf show *The Joy Luck Club* to be a continuation of Kingston's *Woman Warrior*. However, Tan's independence is evident in her occasional light, even hilarious, touches. For example, though Suyuan Woo expects her daughter to be a concert pianist, she inadvertently arranges for music lessons from a piano teacher who turns out to be deaf. The mother remains ignorant of this significant fact, but the daughter quickly learns to her delight that all she has to do to please this piano teacher is to maintain the rhythm and not worry about the notes. In another example, when Lindo Jong meets the man who will eventually be her second husband, they are unable to communicate since he speaks Cantonese and she Mandarin. They attend English class together, where their courtship begins, "But we could talk only in the manner of our English teacher. I see cat. I see rat. I see hat" (263). Hardly the language of a romantic courtship. In a third example, Jing-mei Woo speaks of her mother's crab dinners, "I was not too fond of crab . . . but I knew I could not refuse. That's the way Chinese mothers show they love their children, not through hugs and kisses but with stern offerings of steamed dumplings, duck's gizzards, and crab" (202). Incorporated within this passage are both a lighthearted joke and a serious complaint; the paradoxical usage of the adjective "stern" for an offering of love seems antithetical and yet sadly appropriate for a gift that cannot be refused because it carries the weight of authority.

In the final example of Tan's lightness of touch straining with ambivalence, Lindo Jong is speaking to her daughter with great pride about Taiyuan, her hometown; but Waverly thinks her mother is saying Taiwan,

> "Ai!" she cried loudly. "I'm not from Taiwan."
> And just like that, the fragile connection we were starting to build snapped.
> "I was born in China, in *Taiyuan*," she said, "Taiwan is not China."
> "Well, I only thought you said 'Taiwan' because it sounds the same," I argued, irritated that she was upset by such an unintentional mistake.
> "Sound is completely different! Country is completely different!" she said in a huff. "People there only dream that is China, because if you are Chinese you can never let go of China in your mind." (183)

This tragi-comic incident perfectly exemplifies the mother–daughter gulf, for the mother cannot understand how a daughter of hers could be so ignorant as to confuse Taiwan and Taiyuan while the daughter cannot understand why the mother is in a passion over such an inadvertent, minor slip. Clearly, they share neither the same realm of experience and knowledge nor the same priorities. Their differences, however, are not marked by a slip of the tongue or even the generational gap, but by a deep cultural and geographical chasm.

Like Maxine's, the childhoods of the daughters of the Joy Luck Club are marked by their mother's stories, their mother's mystical and mysterious powers, and by ghosts, whose perimeters Tan expands even further. An-mei

Hsu tells us, "When I was a young girl in China, my grandmother told me my mother was a ghost. This did not mean my mother was dead. In those days, a ghost was anything we were forbidden to talk about" (42). Intensifying the poignancy, An-mei is conjoined to silence about her own mother, as Maxine was told not to speak about a more distant relation, her no name aunt. Like Brave Orchid, An-mei Hsu fills her daughter's imagination with ghosts, telling her she knows it will rain because

> lost ghosts were circling near our windows, calling "Woo-woo" to be let in. She said doors would unlock themselves in the middle of the night unless we checked twice. She said a mirror could see only my face, but she could see me inside out even when I was not in the room.
>
> And all these things seemed true to me. *The power of her words was that strong*. (185) (emphasis added)

Ying-ying St. Clair, emotionally drained by the cruelty of a philandering husband, allows herself to be turned into "a tiger ghost" and much later she marries a Caucasian man, "but it was the love of a ghost" (251). Later still, Ying-ying complains to her son-in-law that her daughter has become "so thin now you cannot see her. She like a ghost, disappear" (263). For Tan, ghosts are not only restless spirits who haunt particular sites, or non-Chinese in general, as for Kingston, but what remains of a living person after her spirit has suffered the worst that it can endure.

Tan seems, at times, to be answering Kingston's character Maxine. Maxine, for example, complains: "sometimes I hated the secrecy of the Chinese. 'Don't tell,' said my parents, though we couldn't tell if we wanted to because we didn't know" (183). Tan explains, in her chapter "Rules of the Game," that secrecy is equivalent to hidden power: "A little knowledge withheld is a great advantage one should store for future use. That is the power of chess. It is a game of secrets in which one must show and never tell" (95). Furthermore, when the child An-mei Hsu is told of the rape that led to her mother's shameful position as the third concubine of a wealthy man, she concludes:

> In truth, this was a bad thing that Yan Chang [her mother's maid] had done, telling me my mother's story. Secrets are kept from children, a lid on top of the soup kettle, so they do not boil over with too much truth. (237)

Tan finds reasonable explanations for silence where Maxine found perverseness and confusion.

Maxine is uncomprehending and resentful when she reports that even her mother voiced the misogynist sayings that so infuriated her as a child:

> They only say, "When fishing for treasures in the flood, be careful not to pull in girls," because that is what one says about daughters. But I watched such words come out of my own mother's and father's mouths . . . And I had to get out of hating range. (52)

Amy Tan, however, gives a sympathetic explanation for the mother that seems to be misogynist and rejecting in Lindo Jong's story, "The Red Candle." At age two, Lindo was affianced to the Huang family's son, after which she says,

> my own family began treating me as if I belonged to somebody else. My mother would say to me when the rice bowl went up to my face too many times, "Look how much Huang Taitai's daughter can eat."
> My mother did not treat me this way because she didn't love me. She would say this biting back her tongue, so she wouldn't wish for something that was no longer hers. (51)

Seeking the motivation behind a hurtful remark—"Look how much Huang Taitai's daughter can eat"—leads Tan to an understanding of and sympathy for the mother whose seeming rejection is but a self-defensive mask for her own vulnerability and love. The conventional words are not spoken with glibness and hostility but with difficulty, as bitter pills the mother herself must swallow and learn to like the taste of.

Amy Tan's *The Joy Luck Club*, as if told by a more mature narrator, more often takes a sympathetic stand toward the mother. Though all the stories of *The Joy Luck Club* mothers are poignant, the most affecting one is Suyuan Woo's. She had been forced to leave behind twin baby girls when she was running away on foot, in panic and exhaustion, from Japanese soldiers during World War II. In the clothes of these babies, she hid jewels to pay for their care, her photograph, name, and the address of her family in Shanghai so that the babies could later be returned. But her house was bombed, her family totally annihilated, and all her efforts to recover her children were in vain. For 40 years, from America, she tried to find these lost daughters in China; at last, they were found and wrote to her, but not before her sudden death. Her daughter Jing-mei is asked to go to China to tell these sisters whom she has never met all about their mother. These sisters live in the motherland that Jing-mei has never known, and Jing-mei has lived with the mother that the sisters have never known. But when Jing-mei is first asked by her mother's friends from the Joy Luck Club to go to China on this mission, her immediate response is bewilderment: "What will I say? What can I tell them about my mother? I don't know anything. She was my mother" (40).

Tan's implication is clear: we all take our mothers (and motherlands) for granted. They are just there, like air or water, impossible really to know or understand because we are so intimate, and more often than not they have seemed a force to struggle against. Not until they are gone do we give them any thought. Ying-ying St. Clair realizes this truth in regard to her Amah or Nanny, the mother-figure in her childhood: "Amah loved me better than her own . . . But I was very spoiled because of her; she had never taught me to think about her feelings. So I thought of Amah only as someone for my comfort, the way you might think of a fan in the summer or a heater in the winter, a blessing you appreciate and love only when it is no longer there"

(73). Only then, because of their absence, do we expend emotion and energy on them. Perhaps the more conciliatory tone of Jing-mei Woo as compared to Maxine's anger may be attributed to the fact that Jing-mei's is an absent, silenced mother, irrevocably separated from her daughter by death, while Maxine's mother is still very much alive and very vocal.

By extension of this analogy, the absent motherland looms large on the horizon of the emigrant mothers whose "unspeakable tragedies left behind in China" (20), recorded and recounted in vivid detail in *The Joy Luck Club*, resonate in their daughters, Amy Tan herself being one of the daughters. Some of the elements of Tan's life have been incorporated into her novel. A comparison of her life and her novel will enable us to see the extent that Tan has reshaped her materials into fiction.

Amy Tan was born in Oakland, California, in 1952; her parents had emigrated from China in 1949, leaving behind three young daughters. They had planned to find a place to live first and then send for the daughters, but the Communist Revolution prevented their carrying out this plan. Despite years of effort on her mother's part, contact was lost. Not until Amy was 12 did she learn of the existence of these sisters. The lost, absent daughters haunted the mother, in whose mind they became the perfect, good daughters, and their example was raised aloft to haunt Amy Tan, the bad, present daughter. "A few years ago, we found them," says Amy Tan in an interview with Susan Kepner. "It was an incredible experience. We met them in China, and now one of them is here. They write to me in Chinese, and my mother reads the letters to me."[16]

Amy Tan's life has been marked by death and change. When Amy was 15, her 16-year-old brother died of a brain tumor, the following year, her engineer-Baptist-minister father also died of a brain tumor. Her grief-stricken mother, believing that their house in Santa Clara was imbalanced in *feng shui* (wind and water), fled with her two remaining children to Switzerland, where Amy attended the College Monte Rosa Internationale in Montreux and from which she nearly eloped with an escaped mental patient who claimed to be a German army deserter. Back in the United States, she completed her bachelor's and master's degrees in English and linguistics at San Jose State University, where she met her husband, Lou DeMattei, now a tax attorney. She studied one year toward a PhD in linguistics at the University of California at Berkeley, but the sudden murder of a close friend brought to the fore all the grief and anger over the deaths of her father and brother that she had suppressed for five years. She dropped her studies and took a position as a language development specialist working with handicapped children, where she was rewarded by what she considered a miracle: a two-year-old blind boy who had never spoken spoke to her. She then took up freelance writing and joined a writing group out of which *The Joy Luck Club* grew.

When visiting a Buddhist retreat in Marin County once with her husband,

Amy Tan was amazed to see so many people "trying to learn how to act Chinese. . . . I couldn't help thinking, 'If you really want to learn how to act Chinese, go live with a Chinese mother for twenty years. Then you'll act Chinese'" (Kepner, 58). What she heard from her Chinese mother for 20 years boiled down to three precepts: "First, if it's too easy, it's not worth pursuing. Second, you have to try harder, no matter what other people might have to do in the same situation—that's your lot in life. And if you're a woman, you're supposed to suffer in silence." Tan adds that she was never good at the last precept. She further explains that Chinese mothers map out your life and won't take no for an answer. If you tell them to "'shut up'" "you could be held as an accessory to your own murder. Or worse . . . " to their suicide. "So the ground rule is, *there is no way the daughter wins*" (Kepner, 59).

The *Joy Luck Club* has clearly been inspired by two forces in Amy Tan's life: her relationship with her mother and the loss of loved ones through death. Tan fictionalizes the circumstances, but gives expression to the emotional trauma of the death of a loved one in Rose Hsu Jordan's story, "Half and Half." Rose, then 14 and the middle child of seven, had been asked to watch her younger brothers during a family outing at the beach. Though she sees her smallest brother, four-year-old Bing, slip off the reef into the water, she is paralyzed into shocked silence. His body never emerges. But, curiously, the story is not focused on her guilt, though she certainly is filled with it; the focus is on her mother's pain, on her fierce but futile efforts to change fate and to recover her son through her faith in God and her will power. Though her mother performs uncanny acts, like driving the family car (when she had never driven before) back along the dangerous road to the beach the next day, she is unable to bring back her son, and thereafter loses her faith in God.

By transferring her own father's death to the mother in her novel, Tan decidedly centers her book on women, and further heightens the emotional intensity of the mother/daughter bond/bondage. In life, the mother/daughter relationship disintegrates into a battle for power/autonomy, and Tan's imagination is fertile in portraying the variety of battle tactics whether it is Waverly Jong's anger at her mother's pride in her success at chess—"Why do you have to use me to show off? If you want to show off, then why don't you learn to play chess" (99)—or Jing-mei Woo's desire during her piano recital to expose the ridiculousness of her mother's desire for a concert pianist daughter—"I was determined to put a stop to her foolish pride" (138).

Though the mothers all have different names and individual stories, they seem interchangeable in that the role of mother supersedes all other roles and is performed with the utmost seriousness and determination. Like Brave Orchid in *The Woman Warrior*, all the mothers in *The Joy Luck Club* are strong, powerful women. Maxine's mother is a dragon, and Ying-ying St.

Clair a tiger, whose first husband told her, "Ying-ying, you have tiger eyes. They gather fire in the day. At night they shine golden" (246). Ying-ying, with the cunning of a tiger, uses the camouflage of her stripes to lie in wait between the trees, hiding her power and ferocity until the time is ripe:

> So this is what I will do. I will gather together my past and look. I will see a thing that has already happened. The pain that cut my spirit loose. I will hold that pain in my hand until it becomes hard and shiny, more clear. And then my fierceness can come back, my golden side, my black side. I will use this sharp pain to penetrate my daughter's tough skin and cut her tiger spirit loose. She will fight me, because this is the nature of two tigers. But I will win and give her my spirit, because this is the way a mother loves her daughter. (252)

The mother/daughter relationship is clearly a painful one; an overt battle between two equally strong forces in which the mother uses the pain of her past experience both to "cut loose" the spirit of her daughter and to instill in the daughter the mother's own spirit. The daughter will struggle because she is also a tiger and fiercely independent, fighting against invasion, even from her own mother.

In the deeply affecting story "Magpies," An-mei Hsu tells how her mother sacrificed herself, embracing the pain of her existence by commiting suicide, but carefully planning her death so that her daughter would be the beneficiary. The mothers are so strong that they endure all manner of pain to enforce their will, to show their love. The daughters, equally strong, find ways to rebel, if not openly then in secret. Even in dreams, the battle of wills does not cease, for example, in Rose Hsu's dream:

> I came to a giant playgound filled with row after row of square sandboxes. In each sandbox was a new doll. And my mother, who was not there but could see me inside out, told Old Mr. Chou [guardian of the door to dreams] she knew which doll I would pick. So I decided to pick one that was entirely different.
> "Stop her! Stop her!" cried my mother. As I tried to run away, Old Mr. Chou chased me, shouting, "See what happens when you don't listen to your mother!" And I became paralyzed, too scared to move in any direction. (186)

Jing-mei's self-protective strategy against the mother who expected her to be a child prodigy is to disappoint her mother whenever possible: "I failed her so many times, each time asserting my own will, my right to fall short of expectations. I didn't get straight A's. I didn't become class president. I didn't get into Stanford. I dropped out of college" (142). Ironically, Maxine did get straight A's, but her mother was disinterested. Though their actions were opposite, both daughters' strategies were the same: counter to their mother's wishes. When Maxine's mother made it clear she was concerned about her daughter's marriage, Maxine did her best to appear unmarriageable.

The daughters' battles for independence from powerful commanding mothers is fierce, but eventually, as in Kingston's book, a reconciliation is reached. The daughters realize that the mothers have always had the daughter's own best interests at heart. Because their own lives in China had been circumscribed by parental and societal constraints that had led invariably to humiliation, pain, and tragedy, the mothers had all come to America to give their daughters a better life, a life of greater choice. Great is the mothers' exasperation, then, when the daughters do not take advantage of the choices available to them or choose unwisely. The daughters realize, too, that their American marriages, with freely chosen mates, have not worked out any better than the arranged marriages of their mothers. An-mei Hsu is puzzled by this:

> I was raised the Chinese way; I was taught to desire nothing, to swallow other people's misery, to eat my own bitterness.
> And even though I taught my daughter the opposite, still she came out the same way! Maybe it is because she was born to me and she was born a girl. And I was born to my mother and I was born a girl. All of us are like stairs, one step after another, going up and down, but all going the same way. (215)

An-mei is at first puzzled by and then philosophically resigned to what seems an irrefutable fact that, despite geographical, cultural, and chronological changes, the fate of womankind has not fundamentally changed; it is inevitably tragic.

With time, the mothers grow old and weak and give up trying to impose their will on now fully grown daughters. As Waverly Jong puts it, "But in the brief instant that I had peered over the barriers I could finally see what was really there: an old woman, a wok for her armor, a knitting needle for her sword, getting a little crabby as she waited patiently for her daughter to invite her in" (184). Once the daughters are aware of their mothers' vulnerability, their weakness, then all danger is past and the mother may be invited in. The ultimate surrender, of course, is death. But the death of the mother, far from a victory for the daughter, is a tremendous loss.

When An-mei Hsu's grandmother is dying, her mother, long rejected because of a shameful marriage, slices off a piece of her arm for her mother's soup to show the extent that her filial devotion will take her. An-mei Hsu herself bears a scar on her throat emblematic of the years of enforced silence and rejection of her mother, which her uncle and aunt required of her. The dead mother, like the lost motherland, casts a much larger shadow on the living than any of the living mothers and she continues to enforce her will. Jing-mei is initially reluctant to carry out her mother's unfulfilled, long-cherished wish to be reunited with her lost twin daughters, and she complains, "My mother and I never really understood one another. We translated each other's meanings and I seemed to hear less than what was said, while my mother heard more" (37). Her mother, when alive, dismissed with vehemence the suggestion that her daughter resembled her:

> A friend once told me that my mother and I were alike, that we had the same wispy hand gestures, the same girlish laugh and sideways look. When I shyly told my mother this, she seemed insulted and said, "You don't even know little percent of me! How can you be me!" And she's right. (27)

However little the daughter knows about her mother, however ill-prepared and insecure she is, Jing-mei does take her mother's place at the mahjong table and does make the trip to China to see the long-lost twins. And in performing this act of filial obedience, with which the book draws to a close, the daughter realizes that she is not filled with resentment or anger. Instead, in her sisters' faces, to her delight and surprise, she finds her mother.

> And then I see her. Her short hair. Her small body. And that same look on her face. She has the back of her hand pressed hard against her mouth. She is crying as though she had gone through a terrible ordeal and were happy it is over . . . And now I see her again, two of her, waving . . . As soon as I get beyond the gate, we run toward each other, all three of us embracing, all hesitations and expectations forgotten.
> "Mama, Mama," we all murmur, as if she is among us. (287)

Though Jing-mei may not know her mother any better in death than in life, she, like her twin sisters, carries her mother in her face and in her gestures. Like *The Woman Warrior*, Tan's *Joy Luck Club* ends on a note of resolution and reconciliation. The struggles, the battles, are over, and when the dust settles what was formerly considered a hated bondage is revealed to be a cherished bond.

To be truly mature, to achieve a balance in the between-world condition then, according to Wong, Kingston, and Tan (American daughters all), one cannot cling solely to the new American ways and reject the old Chinese ways, for that is the way of the child. One must reconcile the two and make one's peace with the old. If the old ways cannot be incorporated into the new life, if they do not "mix" as Lindo Jong put it, then they must nonetheless be respected and preserved in the pictures on one's walls, in the memories in one's head, in the stories that one writes down.

3.3. The Chinese American Male Experience

Crossing the gender barrier to create a literary text focused on a person of the opposite sex would seem, by its relative rarity, to be a difficult task, for, despite several notable exceptions,[17] most male authors choose male protagonists and female authors female protagonists. And yet, a writer's, particularly a fiction writer's, special talent should be the ability to enter imaginatively into the psyche of any person, and to recreate that person's perspective and experience, regardless of geography, time period, or gender.[18]

Among the writers in this limited study, four, a rather disproportionate number, have assumed a male perspective in their fiction: Edith Eaton in certain stories of *Mrs. Spring Fragrance* (1912), particularly "The Wisdom of the New"; Lin Tai-yi in *The Eavesdropper* (1958); Diana Chang in *Eye to Eye* (1974); and Maxine Hong Kingston in two books, *China Men* (1980) and *Tripmaster Monkey: His Fake Book* (1989). Though written from the first person perspective of a male visual artist, Chang's *Eye to Eye* does not concern itself with the Chinese American experience (all its characters are white), and thus falls outside the concern of this chapter. Also outside the boundaries of this chapter, though an interesting topic to pursue, is why authors choose to cross the gender barrier in the first place. We know only that Kingston, who had originally envisioned one large book, discovered that the women and men had very different and often incompatible stories, which seemed better treated separately; thus, she divided her material into two volumes along gender lines. Of the motivation of the other authors, we have no information. Suffice it to say that they all took up a challenge, and let us examine how well each succeeded in meeting it.

3.1.1. "The Wisdom of the New"

Sui Sin Far's "The Wisdom of the New" (briefly discussed in Chapter 2), is the longest story in her entire collection and is told predominantly from the perspective of the male protagonist, Wou Sankwei. Read from his perspective, the tragedy of the story is intensified, for his is the heaviest burden, the greatest sacrifice. In the United States for seven years, Americanized and unconsciously in love with an American woman, Adah Charlton, the niece of his benefactress, Wou Sankwei is nonetheless a Chinese man who has always done and continues to do his duty, whatever the cost to himself. Three weeks before leaving China, he had married a woman his mother chose and had left her pregnant. Seven years later, he sends for his wife and son to join him though both are strangers to him, provides for his family financially, loses a second infant son, plans his first son's American education, and because of this plan loses his first son by his wife's own hand. Though he prefers life in the United States, the story closes with his laconic and euphemistic note to Adah Charlton, "I am returning to China with my wife whose health requires a change" (84).

Though Wou Sankwei's love for Adah Charlton is unacknowledged and undeclared, it is suggested in the respect Sankwei accords the young woman, in the time he continues to spend with her even after his family's arrival, in the American education he wants his son to have. Adah, however, is astute enough to see that Sankwei's wife is jealous with good cause and warns Sankwei to pay greater attention to his wife's wishes, reminding him of his wife's long years of loyalty while they were separated. However, the advice comes too late. Though Sankwei is finally willing the night before school was to begin, to accede to his wife's wishes, if she had protested, the dutiful

Chinese wife does not express her protest verbally. However, because the Americanization of her son seems a monstrous and irrevocable loss, she seeks to save him from it and takes a symbolic and irreversible act. Edith Eaton skillfully transforms an act of poisoning and horror into an act of beauty and natural consequence by not dwelling on the details of the act but by looking back afterward, using the wife's own explanation: "The child is happy. The butterfly mourns not o'er the shed cocoon" (84). An American husband would have considered his wife deranged and had her institutionalized after she had poisoned their son, but Wou Sankwei protects her by not acknowledging her culpability and removes the threat she feels by sacrificing his personal wishes to hers.

Though both husband and wife pay a huge price in this story, the wife at the end is mentally deranged and therefore insensible to suffering. The husband, however, is left with the total burden of consciousness, enormous loss, and profound guilt. His punishment would seem to exceed his crime, for of what is he guilty except being seduced by American ways and wanting his son to share in his pleasure? True, he is guilty of insensitivity to his wife's fears, but her fears, from the perspective of the narration, seemed extreme and irrational. Her flaw was her inability to change and adapt to new ways; his tragic fate was to be married to her. He is trapped between worlds, forced to relinquish the new, his life in America, because of his entrapment in the old, a marriage arranged years before, and compelled by his own faithfulness and loyalty to this old bond.

Because the narrative assumes Wou Sankwei's perspective, the American way of life is given a slight preference; but because of his consideration for his wife at the tale's close, the Chinese way is also presented sympathetically. What is apparent and unambiguous, however, is that the two cultures are incompatible and mutually exclusive: the choice of one necessarily results in the rejection of the other.

3.1.2. China Men

To complete the picture, of which *The Woman Warrior* is but half, Kingston published her second book, *China Men*, four years later. The first book, inspired by Kingston's relationship with her mother, is an emotional text, an intimate, personal wrestling with the seemingly indomitable dragon-figure of Brave Orchid. It is filled with her mother's voice and Kingston's own, audacious, even rude, imaginative, poetic, brilliant. It is a woman's complaint and a woman's song of victory. *China Men*, however, is inspired by Kingston's relationship with her father, a man who was either silent or venting misogynist curses: "Everyday we listened to you swear, 'Dog vomit. Your mother's cunt. Your mother's smelly cunt'" (12). As it was not easy to be Brave Orchid's daughter, so, Kingston imagines, it must have been equally difficult to be her husband. As words were Brave Orchid's weapon, silence was her husband's defense. "Worse than the swearing and the nightly screams were your silences," Kingston tells her father, "when you punished us by not talking . . . you kept up a silence for weeks and months" (14). Since this parent will not tell his stories, claims no past, wants only to live in the present, Kingston is left to her own creative resources to fill in the gaps. Her imaginings become a stratagem as well for getting him to break his silence: "I'll tell you what I suppose from your silences and few words, and you can tell me that I'm mistaken. You'll just have to speak up with the real stories if I've got you wrong" (15). China Men seems to spring more from an intellectual rather than a gut/heart source, as though Kingston felt obliged to give the men their place in the sun, not so much because she was bubbling up with the material but because their side deserved a hearing. Though China Men is equally brilliant, inventive, powerful, the author seems somewhat less personally engaged with her material than she was in The Woman Warrior.

The purpose of China Men, as Kingston herself has said, is "to claim America" for the Chinese. Through the labor of the great-grandfathers in the sugar plantations of Hawaii, of the grandfathers blasting through the Sierra Nevada mountains to build the railway, of the fathers sweating in the laundries and restaurants, of the brothers risking their lives in Viet Nam, Chinese men have earned their place in America; they have earned the right to full and equal citizenship. That such an obvious point needs to be made at all Kingston demonstrates by the chapter she places at the heart and center of her book, "The Laws," which cite chronologically and without comment the laws of the United States concerning the Chinese, from the Burlingame Treaty of 1868 to the latest immigration law of 1978. Blatant racial discrimination characterized the laws for the 75 years before 1943, when the Chinese Exclusion Act was repealed. Clearly, the United States wanted to be a nation of "nordic fiber" (1953), and the hordes of "Mongolians" were only increasing the threat already presented by the "Negroes" and "Indians." The laws of the 1960s and 1970s reveal a more balanced and equitable treatment, at least on paper, of the world's races.

China Men begins and ends with parables about the treatment of Chinese men in the United States. The opening chapter, "On Discovery," adapts an episode from a nineteenth-century Chinese novel, Flowers in the Mirror, by Li Ju-chen,[19] in which a man sails by chance into a country of women and is forced to endure all the tortures that generations of Chinese women have endured for the sake of beauty: pierced ears, plucked eyebrows and foreheads, and bound feet. He is at last transformed into a "pretty" servant fit for the empress. A dialogism informs this parable. On the one hand, as a woman, Kingston seems to take a feminist delight in inverting the gender roles and in giving men a taste of medicine they have forced their women to drink. On the other hand, as a person of Chinese ancestry, in suggesting that the Women's Land is in North America she sides with the men in implying that Chinese men have been metaphorically castrated in the United States. They have been "allowed" to serve the white master through the demeaning work usually relegated to women: cooking, washing, and ironing.

Apart from this first chapter, however, Kingston does not concentrate on the emasculation of Chinese men in the United States. Instead, she focuses her epic[20] narrative on their rebellious acts, on their heroic feats, their achievements against enormous odds, accomplishments requiring great physical strength, intellectual ingenuity, and spiritual endurance.

In *China Men* as in *The Woman Warrior*, speech, language, and stories are the bearers of history, identity, self-hood. Being silenced, whether self-imposed, as in the father's case, or externally imposed by the whip of an overseer at a sugar plantation, as in the case of the Great Grandfather of the Sandalwood Mountains, is to be stifled as a human being and erased from history. The Great Grandfather resists this erasure by breaking the law against speech among the workers, by first disguising his speech as coughs, Chinese single syllable words being conducive to this disguise:

> When the demons howled to work faster, faster, he coughed in reply. The deep, long, loud coughs, barking and wheezing, were almost as satisfying as shouting. He let out scolds disguised as coughs . . . he said, "Get—that—horse—dust—away—from—me—you—dead—white—demon.   Don't—stare—at—me—with—those—glass—eyes. I—can't—take—this—life." He felt better after having his say. (104)

Then, in the evening, Great Grandfather talked story to the silenced men, giving them an idea for relieving themselves of their bottled-up words. And the next day, instead of plowing straight furrows at work, the men dug holes in a circle and shouted all their pent-up emotions and unspoken wishes into these "ears into the world," their telephone lines to China:

> "Hello down there in China!" they shouted. "Hello, Mother." "Hello, my heart and my liver." "I miss you." "What are you doing right now?" "Happy birthday. Happy birthday for last year too." "I've been working hard for you, and I hate it." (117)

Far from docile and willing slaves, these men were assertive, bold, and threatening. After the shout party, the white demon overseers no longer enforced the rule of silence and "in cutting season, the demons no longer accompanied the knife-wielding China Men into deep cane" (118).

The men had covered up the shouting holes after speaking their fill. And, Kingston writes poetically, "Soon the new green shoots would rise, and when in two years the cane grew gold tassels, what stories the wind would tell" (118). She, a daughter, a woman, has gone into the land of the men and brought back their stories. She has had the ears to listen to the stories told by the wind, and sung by the islands. As Fa Mulan successfully entered the men's world of battle, Kingston the "family historian" enters and successfully recreates the men's world of work.[21]

China Men ends with "On Listening," a brief chapter in which a Filipino scholar tells the narrator that the Chinese search for the Gold Mountain led them to the Philippines, but, according to the scholar, who clarifies or befogs the issue by attempting to be more precise, the search was not for a mountain of gold but for a gold needle in the mountain. They built roads, railroads, and cities on their way; they filled swamps, and, finally, while sifting dirt and rock, looking for the gold needle, they were told that all they were looking at was gold. This conclusion parallels that of *The Woman Warrior* in that the state of victimization with which both books began is inverted at the end. The work the China men put into building America—on the railroads, farm-lands, in the cities—is their gold, their reward. Granted, it is only a needle's worth in this land where gold abounds, but it is, nonetheless, a history in which a Chinese American may take some bitter pride. In the book's last line, Kingston watches the young men who listen to this tale for their reaction. Only if they listen and pass on the story will it remain alive and will they have a history, an identity.

3.1.3 *The Eavesdropper* and *Tripmaster Monkey*

Though Lin Tai-yi's *The Eavesdropper* (1959) is set in the 1940s and 1950s in China and the United States and Maxine Hong Kingston's *Tripmaster Monkey* (1989) is set in America of the 1960s, the two novels, nonetheless, make a fruitful comparison and contrast. Both are structured around the between-world condition and both have disaffected male protagonists who are writers/artists at odds with the worlds in which they find themselves. Even more than being at odds, both protagonists, Liang Shutung from *The Eaves-dropper* and Wittman Ah Sing, the Tripmaster Monkey, in fact, define them-selves by their defiance of the material values of the cultures in which they live. Neither owns any material property; both consider themselves spiritu-ally rich; both are confident in their literary powers and secure in the knowl-edge that writing is their intended life's work. Both, however, also feel and resent the constraint and humiliation of poverty. Both disdain conventional mores to such an extent that they long to "drop out" of society: Shutung by "eavesdropping" on life, his own as well as others', and Wittman by "trip-ping" through the use of drugs or through his own "natural high." Neither protagonist marries the girl of his dreams; Shutung only discovers her when he is introduced to the girl, Feina, whom his brother intends to marry; and Wittman's monkey-like antics frighten away Nanci Lee, "the most unforget-table girl of his acquaintance" (10) and the "most beyond girl in the world" (16). Both men are hurried into marriages with women to whom they are only briefly acquainted, without the prelude of a romantic courtship, and almost without love; Shutung marries Lilien Yee because, in a moment of loneliness, he made her pregnant, and Wittman marries Taña De Weese the morning after meeting her at a party, partly to avoid the draft, partly on a lark, and with the full understanding that since neither really "loves" the other (though they both want to go to bed together), "We can each of us cut out whenever we feel like it" (154).

Both novels are, in a sense, books within books, like mirrors reflecting images in other mirrors[22]; they are self-consciously about writers writing, about the love of reading and writing, about the necessity, pain, and joy of self-expression. Using scintillating language, they reveal and revel in language and imagination, in images seemingly effortlessly thrown out, in metaphors, visions, dreams, nightmares. In *Tripmaster Monkey*, Wittman describes a silent movie that seems a fitting image not only of the play he is writing but of the book Kingston has written:

> Remember how bedazzled you felt at black-and-white movies when it rained all up and down the screen? Light and camera through the windowpanes made the lines of rain dripping from the eaves twinkle and sparkle—setting off bodily thrills. And the star in her mermaid cocktail dress shimmered over to the window and crumpled up a letter . . . Remember the pure firing milli-shocks of light, and that sound? . . . Spangling, she crossed the screen, and the camera dollied in a close-up pan around the Christmas tree dangling with foil icicles— tiers of winking metallic rain . . . And the storyline didn't matter nor who she was in the shimmering dress—when that corruscation sparked and popped on the silver screen, you had corresponding feelings. (134)

The visual and auditory sparkling is recreated through verbal pyrotechnics— "the pure firing milli-shocks of light," "tiers of winking metallic rain," "corruscation sparked and popped on the silver screen"—and the power of this display to effect a physical, bodily response is not only the subject being described but also the result of the passage on the reader. The piling up of short phrases using varying words and images for the same sparkling effect recreates the endless line of images when two mirrors are placed opposite each other with reflections bouncing back and forth into infinity. Not only do style and imagery suggest reflecting mirror images, however, but the content explicitly does so as well, for Kingston employs elements from the Chinese classic novel *Journey to the West* in writing her novel *Tripmaster Monkey*, which is about Wittman Ah Sing's writing a play employing elements from *Journey to the West* (42). In *Tripmaster Monkey*, indeed, as the "sparkling" passage states, the storyline doesn't matter, the energy of the author and all her attention has been devoted to the creation of a character through verbal style, through language, and imagery.

In *The Eavesdropper*, too, character is created through language, but the character so created is not the protagonist but his antithesis. Fulton Yee is a American-born Chinese American, totally devoted to practical and business matters, totally devoid of spiritual depth, whose all-American voice becomes almost a caricature of a lower socioeconomic type. Shutung has the misfortune of being Fulton's brother-in-law and is therefore thrown against his will into close contact with this man with whom Shutung has little in common. In recreating Fulton's voice, giving us his language and his pronunciation, Lin Tai-yi conveys Shutung's (and her) disparaging attitude. In the passage below, Fulton is telling Shutung about the brainstorm he had about a name for his new restaurant:

> "It's gotta be a name that sticks in the mind . . . And it's gotta be original. Now I been fooling around with a lot of names, like Lotus Garden or Bamboo Inn and names like that, but I always have to turn them down in the end, and you know why? Cause words like that are redundant; know what I mean? Redundant means something's stale and got no life. But last night, as I was laying there in bed, listening to it come down, suddenly it hit me. Now I want you to imagine you're a motorist driving along Northern Boulevard at forty miles per hour. You're tired and hungry and looking for a place t'eat. You see the name of this restaurant in bright red neon lights up ahead. You got only ten seconds to make up your mind. I want you to tell me if you'd slam on the brakes and come in to eat."
>
> I said, "What name?"
>
> "I'm coming to dat . . . Are you ready? 'Cause if you are, I'm going to spring it, and I want you to tell me your candid reaction the second it hits you. Okay?"
>
> "Okay." . . .
>
> He sat up higher in his seat and straightened his shoulders, and after a moment's deliberate silence, said dramatically, "Fulton Yee's Melting Pot." (15)

Fulton's character is readily apparent through his language alone; he is ungrammatical and inaccurate despite his MBA from NYU, and he is smug and self-righteous with little cause. At the same time, the language imitates the subject it speaks about: the passage is itself indeed redundant, drawn out and circumlocutious as well as cliché-ridden, and the would-be climax is most anticlimactic, in fact, nearly a joke. Shutung's candid response puts Fulton in his place, abruptly deflating his ego: "I'm afraid I don't get the connotation. What are you going to cook in that pot—immigrants?" Fulton thinks a moment and agrees the name may not be inspired after all, remarking, "You gotta good ear, Shutung, you're okay." And he patronizingly pats Shutung, the most famous novelist in postwar China, on the knee as they drive into Manhattan.

The major difference between the two novels, and it is a significant one, is that of tone in regard to the protagonist. The Eavesdropper, narrated in the first person supposedly by Shutung himself, is serious, even tragic in tone; it is satiric only when the spotlight turns on Fulton Yee. Otherwise, the author and narrator/protagonist are in full accord, and at times, especially when writing about writing, author and first person narrator seem to blend into one. In two instances, even, Lin Tai-yi seems to forget the gender of her narrator:

> Folded away like inadequate summer dresses when the smell of winter was in the air, my plans for writing a great novel soon became palled and unreal, for I was writing short articles to make quick cash against the skyrocketing inflation, and I sold them fast and spent the money even faster. (126)

Describing Shutung's exhaustion after a late night game of bridge with his superiors in the Chungkung government, Lin Tai-yi writes: "Like after doing an evening's fine embroidery, I reeled home . . . " (146). It is possible, of course, for a male narrator to think of the lightness of summer dresses and the exhaustion of doing embroidery but these images are less likely to occur to a man than to a woman. These are, however, but isolated lapses in a text filled, for the most part, with very beautiful and striking images, for example: "far-away, crickets were sharpening their scissors and preparing to cut up the night" (52) and "I was tired of wearing frustration like a faded silk garment which had seen better days" (138).

Tripmaster Monkey, on the other hand, is told in the third person by a narrator who is, by turns, affectionate/sympathetic and satiric/mocking towards the protagonist, Wittman Ah Sing. It is immediately clear to anyone who knows him and his work that Wittman Ah Sing is modeled after the playwright Frank Chin. In a personal conversation with me, Kingston admitted that Frank Chin was "an inspiration" for Wittman, but, as if to dilute this confession, she added that her husband (an actor), her son (a musician), and her brother were also models. Both Wittman and Chin are men of letters, specifically playwrights, whose literary style is hip, energetic, scintillating, sometimes bombastic, often angry, aggressively masculinist, fervently espousing "yellow power" while simultaneously lapsing into self-contempt and bitterness against the Chinese American community.

For those unfamiliar with Frank Chin's work, a brief introduction may be helpful. Chin's play "Chickencoop Chinaman" won the East West Players playwrighting contest in 1971 and in 1972 it was produced by the American Place Theatre in New York City, the first play by an Asian American author to be produced since Winnifred Eaton's "A Japanese Nightingale" nearly two generations before. A *New Yorker* critic described the speeches of Tam Lum, the central character, as "a dazzling eruption of verbal legerdemain" (June 24, 1972). Jack Kroll of *Newsweek* (June 19, 1972) found Chin a "natural writer, his language has the beat and brass, the runs and rim-shots of jazz."[23] As one of the editors of *Aiiieeeee!*, one of the early anthologies of Asian American literature, Chin helped to recover lost and neglected Asian American writers. As a critic, however, his judgment is marred by a narrow and amorphous definition of what constitutes an "authentic" Asian American sensibility and voice. For Chin, most Asian American writers, particularly successful women who have married white men, do not have the authentic Asian American sensibility; instead, they've become accomplices to "white racism." Chin has not minced words in denouncing them. For example, in a 1972 letter to Frank Ching, editor of *Bridge* magazine, Chin wrote: "Now let me recommend someone to you whose work I respect and find fucked up as a thinker, a Eurasian, a Chinese-American, a mind and person, fucked up. Diana Chang." Kingston he attacks in the final six pages, like a parting shot, of his latest publication, *The Chinaman Pacific & Frisco R.R. Co.* (Minneapolis: Coffee House Press, 1989). The "Afterword" is not at all an afterword to his collection of short stories but a fierce, somewhat garbled parody of Kingston's *Woman Warrior* and the first chapter of *China Men*. Chin entitles his parody "Unmanly Warrior" and renames Kingston, Smith Mei-jing. Mei-jing may be translated as American gold, emphasizing, perhaps, Chin's sense that Kingston has "sold out" purely for economic gain. His parody takes Kingston to task for complaining about her own people and for contributing to the emasculation of Chinese American men. Aware of his attitude, Kingston cannot help being somewhat ambivalent towards Chin.

Of her character Wittman, Kingston said at a conference at Georgetown University on April 8, 1989, "I liked his personality, his intensity, his tricks." Kingston herself brought up a question about her politics that she thought her audience was too polite to ask: since her novel is focused on a man, has her politics changed, has she abandoned feminism? Her answer was, "No, the omniscient narrator in *Tripmaster Monkey* is a Chinese American woman; she's Kwan Yin (the Goddess of Mercy) and she's me . . . sometimes she's compassionate [towards Wittman] and sometimes she kicks him around." An entire novel, however, devoted to a character whom the author herself does not always like becomes problematic for the reader; if the character is trying the author's patience, why should we readers, at one remove from the fray, remain patient and involved?

Without doubt, the novel is brilliant, the puns witty, and the wealth of allusions from Shakespeare to Rogers and Hammerstein and Hollywood films, from *The Romance of the Three Kingdoms* to *Orlando*, from Rilke to Whitman to Bulosan, from Chang and Eng to the Eaton sisters, from phrases in Chinese to expressions in French—this massive compendium—is fun, dizzying, and impressive, reminiscent of the style of the mature James Joyce. In fact, the interweaving of the sixteenth-century Chinese classic *Monkey* or *Journey to the West* recalls the intricate interweaving of Homer's *Odyssey* into Joyce's *Ulysses*. The use of an earlier mythic source to give substance and shape to a particularized contemporary experience was the method Kingston used to good effect in *Woman Warrior*, and which she employs again with equal success in *Tripmaster Monkey*. The 1960s, with its counterculture of "flower children" and "hippies" protesting the Viet Nam war, was a period particularly well suited to a resurrection of the iconoclastic Monkey King, whom we shall examine next.

Wu Ch'eng-en's classic novel, *Monkey* or *Journey to the West*, "is unique in its combination of beauty with absurdity, of profundity with nonsense. Folk-lore, allegory, religion, history, anti-bureaucratic satire, and pure poetry—such are the singularly diverse elements out of which the book is compounded," writes Arthur Waley, the novel's original translator.[24] Monkey is an irrepressible, irreverent, fun-loving, proud, mischievous, and sometimes foolish creature who accompanies the monk Hsuan Tsang, an historical person, to India to bring back the Buddhist Scriptures. Though Monkey himself must be reprimanded at times for his pranks, he has a serious, philosophical side as revealed in his religious name, Aware-of-Vacuity (or Emptiness), and in the satiric edge of most of his antics. In addition to defending his monk against would-be attackers, Monkey makes it his business to shatter pomposity and self-righteousness wherever he finds it, whether in the Jade Emperor's heavenly court or among the rulers of earth. Nothing is sacred; and no one who deserves it is spared his scorn.

Monkey was born out of a stone "that since the creation of the world had been worked upon by the pure essences of Heaven and the fine savours of Earth, the vigour of sunshine and the grace of moonlight, till at last it became magically pregnant and one day split open, giving birth to a stone egg" (Waley's translation, 9), which in turn developed into a stone monkey. Thus, he is often referred to as the Stone Monkey, which lends itself to a pun that Kingston could not resist: "when he was a younger and more *stoned* monkey" (103). Not only does Wittman Ah Sing (pun intended) resemble the Monkey King; he *is* the Monkey King, for, as he tells Nanci Lee, "Underneath these glasses . . . I am really: the present-day U.S.A. incarnation of the King of the Monkeys" (33). When fired for displaying Barbie dolls and wind-up monkeys in obscene poses in the toy department of the store in which he worked, Wittman literally becomes aware of emptiness. Like a monkey, he can pick up things with his toes; as a child, he wore a monkey suit and passed the hat while his father played the organ; like the original Monkey King, he's the master of 72 transformations and a fighter against pomposity, hypocrisy, and racism.

While he is witty, indefatigable, and outrageous, Wittman is also psychologically insecure, emotionally unstable, lacking confidence with women, and constantly puffing himself up because he fears his own insignificance. In one devastating passage, Kingston describes him as King Kong:

> Swinging his chains—tool-wielding ape—he lassoos the chandelier, pulls himself up, and rides it. [Chin has been described a Chinatown cowboy.[25]] He screams higher and louder than the ladies. Swooping Fay Wray up in his mighty arm, he and she swing across the ceiling of the San Francisco Opera House. Down rain crystal and loose excrement—cee—on to the audience. Balso Snell.

> O, say can you cee? The ape is loose upon America. Crash their party. Open his
> maw mouth, and eat their canapes and drink their champagne. The party is
> mine. (221–2)

The content here is irreverent, even outrageous, and the perspective a fluc-
tuating one. When Wittman, the Chinese American hero in the white man's
world, like the Monkey King in the Jade Emperor's heaven, vents his anger at
the humiliation and rejection he has been dealt by being insulting in return,
Kingston uses indirect discourse, "Open *his* maw mouth, and eat their
canapes and drink their champagne." Though uninvited to the party, he will
not only snatch away the blond beauty but gobble down all the food and
drinks. In the next sentence, the perspective shifts to a triumphant first
person: "The party is *mine.*"

But where is the narrating author in all this? What is the tone? At times, it
seems the author allies herself with her protagonist—"crash *their* party and
eat *their* canapes." At times, she seems to ridicule him—"open his *maw*
mouth"—or is she enjoying his vengeance, the more animalistic the more
satisfying? "He screams higher and louder than the ladies," says our omniscient female narrator, alluding perhaps to the title of Chin's anthology
Aiiieeeee!, which is a scream. Does his ability to scream higher and louder
than the ladies indicate that he is unmanly and ridiculous? Or is he, perhaps,
more sensitive to racism and thus suffering greater pain than the sex that is
supposed to be "emotional" and "gentle"? At still other times, because of
his megalomania, the narrator feels left out—"The party is *mine,*" says he.
Indeed, Frank Chin's work and his pronouncements have undoubtedly been
phallocentric[26] and generally dismissive of women's accomplishments.

Thus, Wittman in this passage, and throughout the book, is shown to be
simultaneously heroic and inane, daring and ridiculous, vulnerable and ego-
centric, sensitive and insensitive. With such a character, little wonder that the
tone is slippery and boundaries unstable. Kingston, skilled in ambivalence
and paradox, is always crossing boundaries. As Maxine in *The Woman Warrior* was never sure of the truth or fiction of her mother's stories, and the
narration itself often crossed the boundary between truth and fiction, so
Tripmaster Monkey does likewise. The "grandmother" whom Wittman and
Taña search for may be his real grandmother, or a stranger woman someone
palmed off on his parents, or a wife his father left in China, or an old Japanese
lady. Wittman and Taña may indeed be married, but then the marriage ceremony was impromptu and casual and was performed by an illegitimate "minister" of an unrecognized church. When Wittman sees his bus seat mate turn
into a blue boar before his eyes, he may be hallucinating or seeing her true
nature. (She is indeed a bore.) When the "winners of the party," those who
stayed the longest, see the sunrise coloring the world in a breathtaking rosy
glow, is this a sign of a benign presence in the universe or the aftermath of a
nuclear bomb test? As Wittman says about his movie made of a deck of cards:

"The same story can be comedy or tragedy, depending on the music" (93). Wittman himself is heroic and ridiculous, admirable and pitiable. When the Chinese American in her is predominant, the author/narrator weeps with her protagonist; when the woman in her is dominant, she laughs at him. Her ambivalence is overtly stated in the very last sentence of the novel: "Dear American monkey, don't be afraid. Here, let us tweak your ear, and kiss your other ear" (340).

At the same lecture/reading at Georgetown University in April 1989, Maxine Hong Kingston said, "When I first started writing, everything was from the first person point of view. I saw this as artistically weak. I've spent a lifetime trying to escape the I. I want to do a classical third person story." On the first page of *Tripmaster Monkey*, Kingston writes "Whose mind is it that doesn't suffer a loud takeover once in a while?" (3). And on the next page, "There is no helping what you see when you let it all come in." *Tripmaster Monkey* gives the impression that Kingston has been taken over by an alien voice; she has, to a large extent, subsumed her "I" for another, and whether this results in an artistically stronger book than her earlier ones is a debatable point.

"I will make of my scaffold, a stage," says Wittman in one of his eloquent moments (30). And indeed the Chinese American between-world condition is his scaffold and his stage; on this stage Kingston and Wittman are united. In the introduction to *Aiiieeeee!* (1974) Frank Chin observed that self-contempt was an inherent and unconscious aspect of Asian American sensibility: "This self-contempt itself is nothing more than the subject's acceptance of white standards of objectivity, beauty, behavior, and achievement as being morally absolute, and his acknowledgment that, because he is not white, he can never fully measure up to white standards" (xxvii–viii). White standards of beauty and the Asian's acceptance of these standards are painfully brought out in Wittman's encounter with Yoshi Ogasawara, "a Nisei girl of Okinawan ancestry, whom he'd never asked out because his sexual hang-up was that he was afraid of smart pretty women" (106). Though she is intelligent enough to be in medical school, she is obsessed with the ugliness of her single-lidded eyes, which she hides under heavy make-up:

> Pushing her face forward to show her eyes, weighted down with false eyelashes, she was entertaining the party with our eyes. She batted two black brushes that were glued on with strips of electricians' tape, black eyeliner tailing out to here, blue-green mascara lids, and the lower lids rimmed with silver paste. Her eyelids were the puffy type, and the tight tape pressed into them at mid-puff; skin sort of lapped over the top edge of the tape, and made a crease per lid. (106)

She plans an eyelid operation not because she has trouble seeing, but because, in her words, "They don't like eyes like ours. We don't find my kind of eyes attractive. We like eyes that . . . We like eyes like his . . . He's got double lids. I've got single lids." Her identification with the white perception is so complete that she unconsciously shifts pronouns from third person to first. Though she is pointing to Wittman's as examples of good eyes, he is disgusted by her self-contempt and will have no part in her self-denigration. However, earlier, when a white man tells Yoshi that her eyes are beautiful, Wittman berates himself. "It was Wittman ought to have done that. Why wasn't he the one to have leapt up, taken her in his arms, and spoken up, 'You are beautiful'? Because he can't stand her; her eyelids are like a pair of skinks" (106). Not only is Wittman aware of how wrong it is that Yoshi has bought into a system that devalues her, but he is also aware that he himself has done likewise. The awareness of his own schizophrenia is tortuous, but he is unable to change. Thus, he marries Taña De Weese, whose long blond hair, as they drive to Reno to look for his missing grandmother, is "a giant brush of a mane painting the hills its own color" (195). When he and Taña photograph themselves together at a coin-operated machine, "she look[s] like a blond movie star; Wittman look[s] like a wanted bandito. El Immigrante, his wetback passport picture i.d." (168). If they were to go on stage together, he would buy Taña a leopard-skin bathing suit so that she could play "Sheena, Queen of the Jungle. Me Chimp" (179). His self-mockery is painfully blatant. He cannot believe his good fortune that a beauty such as she is willing to sleep with and then marry a bandito such as he. At the same time, a "Fifth-generation native Californian" (which Frank Chin happens to be) whose Great-Great-Grandfather came on the *Nootka*, "as ancestral as the *Mayflower*," he is contemptuous of F.O.B.s (fresh-off-the-boat immigrants) (41). Wittman is a man of many contradictions.

Though he is embarrassed by his mother's mahjong friends when he takes Taña to visit his mother, Ruby Long Legs, in Sacramento, he is fiercely loyal and protective of them as well. Despite his marriage, he falls easily into "us" against "them" along racial lines. "'Myself, I am a blonde at heart,' said Auntie Dolly. 'Don't you look askance at her, Taña, with your sanpaku eyes, or else I'm getting a divorce'" (181). It is all right for Wittman to mock his mother and her friends because they are his people, but it is not allowable for Taña, a white woman, to do so. She passes the test and politely reserves her opinions to herself.

Wittman is a monkey capable of many transformations. He's Wittman Ah Sing, U.C. Berkeley graduate with a major in English literature, familiar with all the Western classics, reading Rilke aloud on the bus, spouting Kerouac, Melville, Whitman, Shakespeare. He's "Joang Fu, pronounced like Joan of Arc," whose name means Inner Truth, professional storyteller on a floating restaurant in the bay between Macao and Hong Kong who woos a dark veiled lady with his songs and stories. He's Lance Kamiyama's best friend who comes to Lance's wedding party to wish the blonde bride and the Japanese American husband well and he's Lance's oldest enemy, holding a score against Lance since elementary school which he wants to settle at this party. He's contemptuous of FOBs "So uncool. You wouldn't mislike them on sight if their pants weren't so highwater, gym socks white and noticeable . . . " (5), but he is the artistic voice for the Asian American community, bringing together everyone he knows into his extravaganza of a stage performance at the novel's end.

Defending Asian American pride, he refers to himself and his race as "we umberish–amberish people" (166), and he objects vehemently to the desecration of an Asian god: the Buddha-shaped bottle whose head unscrews so that Jade East aftershave lotion can pour forth; Wittman wonders how Christians would like to see a Jesus-on-the-cross bottle whose head unscrews for their aftershave cologne. Wittman rails against the casting of whites in Asian film roles, or, if Asians are employed, the belittling of them as houseboys and maids or through their being brutally killed (324). He brings up the hated word "inscrutable," remarking, "People who call us inscrutable get their brains sewn shut. . . . They willfully do not learn us, and blame that on us, that we have an essential unknowableness" (310).

For both *The Eavesdropper* and *Tripmaster Monkey* the between-world condition and Asian pride are common grounds. In fact, one of the characters in *The Eavesdropper* provides the epigram and title for this book. "'My pet,' he said, 'we're caught in between times and in between worlds. That's why you see a spectacle like myself. There are no uncomplicated Chinese left any more'" (50). There are the words of Wu Tsunglin, the editor of *Tides*, the foremost literary magazine in China, a PhD from Harvard, the distinguished son of a wealthy Shanghai family. Wu is the mentor and first employer of Liang Shutung, the narrator/protagonist. After graduating from college, Shutung with fear and trembling ("A new untried author was like a virgin girl. There would never be a second time" (35)) shows Wu his manuscripts and is encouraged by the older man who recognizes his talent, and gives him a column to write for *Tides*, every other week. Wu not only possesses literary acumen but also social ease and sophistication; he carries on clandestine affairs with foreign women and a much publicized correspondence with the famous George Bernard Shaw. Though Shutung's first impression is that Wu is "one of the happier symbols of the blending of East and West" (34), later, when Shutung visits him at home, he is surprised to discover that the "domestic" Wu, father of eight, is a man who "would not exercise birth control" and "who loved the comfort of being served by the obedient, illiterate and— he said—totally utilitarian wife his parents picked for him" (49). Shutung sees in this man certain of the conflicts that would eventually be his own: " . . . in his heart, for all that elaborate decor, there was and always would be, the dull pain of frustration, and split loyalties, to himself as an artist and his wife as a human being, to his old Chinese obligations and to the West he knew as a young man" (49).

Shutung himself goes on to earn a master's degree from Yale University, but he is saddled in marriage to a woman he does not love and in love with a woman he cannot marry. Lilien, his "utilitarian" wife, receives the confession that he wants to be a novelist with shocked silence and incomprehension. Feina, his brother's beautiful tubucular wife and Shutung's spiritual mate, is pure sensibility—"except for these emotions there would not be me" (42); she not only understands his need to write but she provides him with the space and time to do so. And after her death, almost as though she had become his guardian spirit, his writing goes very well, and he is a success both as a newspaper editor and as a novelist. China's runaway inflation and total economic collapse, Lilien's desire to return to America, and the Communist victory all push Shutung back to the United States, where one of his selves is fated to sit behind the worn desk in the shabby Chinatown office of the dying insurance/travel business begun by his father-in-law while the other "like a curl of blue smoke, meandered its way up into the white summer sky" (251). Schizophrenia again.

It is impossible for the artist to survive intact in a world where money is the only ruling power. In such a world, survival is only possible if the artist splits himself in two or achieves "such a degree of objectiveness that I would be eavesdropping upon myself" (19). At a party at the Yee home, Shutung reacts negatively, "I felt that I was only an observer in this world and that there was no place for me, and I did not wish to enter it" (90). Compelled, nonetheless, by circumstances to enter this world, Shutung goes through the motions like an automaton: "I moved about as if in a dream, unfeeling and unlike myself" (251). Shutung shuttles back and forth between a chaotic China in the throes of World War II and a civil war (despite four books about the war or set during it, Lin Tai-yi had evidently not finished with the subject) and a materialistic, inhospitable United States. In China, his American clothes and well-fed look were very much resented, for poverty and self-denial had become the necessary order of the day. "Pride in one's ability to do without was, I remembered, the fuel of the intellectuals and it was acid and corroding" (119). Back in the United States, when he translates his most successful novel into English, it is rejected by publishers who find it too "'remote,' for books on China are moving very slowly now; interest in the Orient isn't great at the moment, at least in the book trade" (240–1). Shutung realizes with despair that even the world of publishing is ruled by the marketplace, which is in turn affected by political forces. And he himself is superfluous—a man caught between worlds, a patriot without a country, an artist unable to make use of his talent.

Tripmaster Monkey is, for the most part, written in the spirit of play and fun. Kingston said, explaining the genesis of this book, "I would like us to have come here for a wonderful reason—we came to have fun. After I had that vision, I set out to do research to back it up." She discovered that playing in the form of putting on plays was one of the reasons the earliest Chinese came to the United States. "We came to play . . . We played for a hundred years plays that went on for five hours a night, continuing the next night, the same long play going on for a week with no repeats, like ancient languages with no breaks between words, theatre for a century, then dark. Nothing left but beauty contests" (250).

Though full of rollicking humor, *Tripmaster Monkey*, however, has tragic undertones, for both Wittman and Shutung are disillusioned idealists and unfulfilled artists. "We all had, everyone of us, some rare and secret, splendid dream. All of us were trying to make it come to life, but it never did" (92), says Shutung, who is constantly having to compromise and is invariably disappointed. In defense of Wittman, the sympathetic narrator explains, "Wittman's not crazy and he's not lazy. The reason he doesn't have right livelihood is that our theatre is dead" (249). Like Shutung, he was born at the wrong time and in the wrong place. Both Wittman's bitterness and anger and Shutung's frustration and withdrawal are the result of the discrepancy between things as they are and things as they should be. For both Wittman and Shutung, there should be brotherly love without racial discrimination and a respectable means of living for the readers and writers of this world.

Chapter 5

Righting Wrongs by Writing Wrongs

1. WRITING RACISM AND OPPRESSION

Giving such prominence to the legendary figure of Fa Mulan in her first book, Maxine Hong Kingston decided wisely, for the woman warrior is a powerful symbol running counter to tradition. In most cultures throughout recorded history, men, physically larger and stronger, have assumed the tasks whose success depends on greater size and strength. And women, the child-bearers and caregivers, have been regarded as needing shelter and protection to perform their special function. Thus, the warrior has been the gender role assigned to men while the woman warrior has been an anomaly. But because they are such an anomoly, legends of amazons and historical cases of women taking actual part in battle are arresting. Almost always, these women have had to disguise themselves as men to perform the male role of warrior. In the West, Jeanne d'Arc is the most famous example, but there are others, including an Italian woman warrior, Onorata Rodiana of Castelleone, who served in the calvary under Oldredo Lampugnano in 1423. She fought under various names and guises until she was mortally wounded when Venice laid siege to Castelleone in 1452.[1] In the American Revolution, an African American woman, Deborah Gannet, enlisted under the name Robert Shurtliffe and served in Captain Well's company from May 1782 until October 23, 1783. She was reported to have "discharged the duties of her office and at the same time, preserved inviolate the virtue of her sex, and was granted therefore a pension of 34 pounds."[2] Fa Mulan, Kingston's woman warrior, was a historical Chinese woman who lived in the Liang Dynasty, about A.D. 500, and served 12 years in the army in her father's stead, successfully hiding her identity.[3] Her filial devotion was so extraordinary that a song about her exploits, translated as "Magnolia Lay," has been passed on from generation to generation ever since; it is this song that Kingston remembers singing with her mother and that provides the core of the story Kingston tells in the "White Tigers" chapter.[4] Twentieth-century China seems to have had more than her share of women warriors. In the early decades of the century, women's armies were established to help overthrow the Manchu rule of the Ching dynasty. In the 1930s, there was the example of Hsieh Ping-ying, whose autobiography was translated by the Lin sisters, briefly discussed in Chapter 2. Today, military training for young women students in China is commonplace; as one American observer noted, "There certainly are more women, young and old, in China than anywhere else in the world who have been trained in the use of weapons."[5] And yet, despite the numbers of militarily trained women, a prejudice against women's serving in combat still lingers. The story of Ku'o Ch'ung-ch'ing, a modern day Fa Mulan, whose story we related in Chapter 1, is a case in point.

Thus, when Kingston adds to the traditional legend of Fa Mulan by having her bear a child while still fighting battles disguised as a man, instead of waiting as in the original story until after the battles are won, she increases the woman's stature and asserts that the impossible *is* possible. Kingston's Fa Mulan, like Kingston's mother who bore six children after the age of 45 and who can carry 100 pounds of rice up and down stairs, can perform successfully both male and female roles. If the negative impossible—that girl babies are killed at birth or sold as slaves—is possible, then the positive impossible— that women can bear arms better than men and bear children at the same time—is also possible.

In *The Woman Warrior*, Maxine toys with the idea of taking literally the woman warrior's example and of doing actual battle like Fa Mulan. But she is hard put to find American equivalents for the feats performed by her Chinese heroine, and she realizes that accomplishing these tasks would be next to impossible:

I could not figure out what was my village. (45)

To avenge my family, I'd have to storm across China to take back our farm from the Communists; I'd have to rage across the United States to take back the laundry in New York and the one in California. Nobody in history has conquered and united both North America and Asia. (49)

In the chapter "White Tigers," Kingston elaborates at length on what the woman warrior's training would have to be and throws not a little magic into the arduous physical, mental, and spiritual preparation necessary for the successful deposition of tyrants and the avenging of wrongs. After a lengthy period of training, when finally mature and fully prepared for battle, the woman warrior returns to her parents, who carve a list of words, grievances, on her back; this is her commission. Though this detail of carving on the back has been transposed from the life of a historical male general, Yueh Fei, it is even more appropriate to the story of Fa Mulan, for it effectively symbolizes the physical tortures that Chinese women have endured. Furthermore, the personal appropriation and recreation of myth is a long-standing literary tradition. After winning all the battles that her parents and her village have required, Fa Mulan's last battle is against a foe that has been Maxine's own personal bane. When the fat baron attempts, ironically, "to appeal to her man to man" and repeats the misogynist sayings Kingston hates, "Girls are maggots in the rice," and "It is more profitable to raise geese than daughters," (43) Fa Mulan/Maxine first slashes his face and then with one stroke of her sword strikes off his head. She then frees the women he has kept locked up "like pheasants that have been raised in the dark for soft meat" and whose feet have been bound so that they cannot run away. These women, it is rumored, later became a witch amazon army, killing men and boys and bringing up girl babies to avenge the many years of victimization they had endured.

The identification of Maxine with Fa Mulan, implied in the incident with the fat baron, is made explicit at the end of the chapter:

> The swordswoman and I are not so dissimilar. May my people understand the resemblance soon so that I can return to them. What we have in common are the words at our backs. The ideographs for *revenge* are "report a crime" and "report to five families." The reporting is the vengeance—not the beheading, not the gutting, but the words. And I have so many words—"chink" words and "gook" words too—that they do not fit on my skin. (53)

Finally, Kingston reveals that the real nature of her interest in Fa Mulan is literary and symbolic, rather than literal. Kingston sees herself as a woman warrior with grievances carved on her back—grievances against a sexist legacy from the Chinese culture and against a racist legacy from the dominant society. Returning to the etymological roots of the word "revenge" in Chinese, she justifies her method of fighting back: reporting is the revenge. In writing wrongs, she is doing her part to right them. Following the trail blazed by Edith Eaton at the beginning of the century, Kingston's pen is her sword, injustice is the wrong she hopes to right by writing about it.

The injustice that is the target of Kingston's revenge is the domination or repression of one person by another, the denial of an individual's full worth. The sexist sayings that her own parents quoted infuriated the young Maxine. Yet, in repeating all these hated sayings, Kingston forces her people and her readers to see them afresh. Her hope is that the Chinese will no longer continue to pass on, automatically and unthinkingly, a misogynist legacy but will realize the injustice of it and the pain it inflicts on young women. And she hopes that the censure of non-Chinese will assist in humiliating the Chinese into abandoning such maxims.

Racism is found in the examples of two former employers—one of whom offended Maxine by calling a paint color "nigger yellow" and the other who chose a particular restaurant because it was being picketed by CORE and the NAACP—by the derogatory slang names "chink" and "gook" given to Asians in the United States and by "those who can deny my family food and work" (49). Racism is blatant in the laws that Kingston records in the central chapter of her *China Men*. To cite only a few: in 1854, Chan Young was denied citizenship on the grounds of race (only "free whites" and, in 1870, "African aliens" could become naturalized American citizens); in 1878, only Chinese had to pay queue, pole, and laundry taxes, and fishing and shellfish taxes because they had brought nets from China and were catching more shrimp, abalone, and lobster than white fishermen; "no 'Chinese or Mongolian or Indian' could testify in court 'either for or against a white man'"; in 1893, "the U.S. Supreme Court ruled that Congress had the right to expel members of a race who 'continue to be aliens, having taken no steps toward becoming citizens, and incapable of becoming such under the naturalization laws.' This [circular reasoning] applied only to Chinese; no other race or nationality was excluded from applying for citizenship"; in 1924, any American who married a Chinese lost his/her citizenship.

The citing of the laws, without comment, smack in the middle of Kingston's account of the quiet heroism of the Chinese men whose back-breaking labor over several generations helped to build this nation, speaks eloquently for the injustice and the wrong done these men. Her book is her way of righting the past wrongs of the dominant society. *China Men*, the result of Kingston's research and her imagination, gives voice to the men who died swinging from baskets over rock cliffs blasting tunnels through the Sierra Nevada mountains for the railroad; to the men carving a sugar plantation out of the resistant tropical forest of the Sandalwood Mountains, who, because they were silenced by the foreman's whip, "dug an ear into the world" as an outlet for their bottled-up speech; to her father, silent, except for his occasional torrent of curses, and unwilling to speak the stories of his past. These men have been silenced by the hardness of their lot, and by the hardness of the reception they have had in the United States as documented in "The Laws."

The first chapter, about the man who came upon the Land of Women[6] and who was forced to undergo all the tortures that women undergo for beauty's sake, is emblematic of the emasculation of Chinese men in America. The belittling of their dignity, their relegation either to the work of beasts of burden (hauling, hacking, digging) or to "women's work" (cooking and laundry), and the denial of basic rights of citizenship are the equivalent of the tortures Chinese women have endured for the traditional notion of beauty enforced if not always by, at least, for Chinese men. Kingston is sly in slipping her own feminist protest in while protesting racism on behalf of the men, by equating the suffering Chinese men have endured at the hands of whites to the suffering Chinese men have inflicted on their women. In a sense, she is saying to Chinese American men, from the very start of the book that she has devoted to them, "The suffering you have endured is no worse than the suffering you have inflicted. Let us all be more considerate in our treatment of one another."

A third type of denial of an individual's worth, a tyranny of a powerful individual over a weaker one, is that of parent over child. This is a delicate and controversial point, for obviously older and more experienced parents have the right to command and children the duty to obey. "Honor thy father and thy mother" is one of the Mosaic Ten Commandments and respect for one's elders one of the most basic tenets of Chinese culture. Yet, Kingston's books, particularly *The Woman Warrior*, are full of daring and forbidden tirades against the parents, anger against the father for his misogynist curses and anger against the mother for cutting her daughter's frenum, that thin muscle attaching the tongue to the lower jaw. Kingston's breaking of this taboo makes her Chinese readers particularly uncomfortable; the very fact that she tackles this subject so frankly shows how American she is.

Kingston devotes a great deal of space to the discussion of the cutting of her frenum, which, like so many other things her mother told her, she is not sure is factual or fictional. Though her mother claimed a good intention in committing this act, it is nonetheless a terrifying aggression, an act of violence and repression, for it made Maxine mute in school and gave her a "pressed duck's voice." The cutting of the frenum, taken symbolically, is the silencing that Maxine experienced as a Chinese American girl being "prepared" by well-intentioned parents for the larger world. However, theirs is a poor preparation, for it is totally centered in Old World Chinese ways, as though the daughter were growing up in China rather than the United States. Though born in the United States, Maxine is sent to kindergarten not knowing a word of English, little different from an F.O.B. (fresh off the boat); she is made fearful of the "outsiders," the "barbarians," the "ghosts" all around her. At the same time, she is told to avoid the fate of her No Name aunt, for if she breaks the villagers' sexual taboos she will be denied an existence, silenced forever. Though her mother observes the letter of the law, the customs of the Old World, she does not bother to explain their spirit to Maxine. She leaves her daughter confused and frustrated. When Maxine wants to confess the list of 200 things she has saved up so that her mother can know who she is "and to stop the pain in my throat," to find her voice, her mother doesn't want to listen and tells her to stop, to keep silent. When Maxine breaks loose and the torrent comes forth in spite of her mother's silencing, she finds that her items are no longer her own "sins" that she needs to confess but the "sins" against her that her parents are guilty of: they have not cherished or encouraged her, they have made her feel unwanted, stupid, ugly. Maxine is taken aback when her mother finally explains, "That's what we're supposed to say. That's what Chinese say. We like to say the opposite." Just when Maxine had found her voice in letting out pent-up anger, her mother again undercuts her by removing the reason for the anger. Only by getting away from the uncomfortable parental nest is Maxine able to find herself. Places away from home are ghost-free, and she doesn't catch colds or use her hospitalization insurance. But her mother tries to manipulate her with guilt into coming for visits more often and complains that she promises to come but doesn't. Maxine's response is, "I shut my teeth together, vocal cords cut, they hurt so. I would not speak words to give her pain. All her children gnash their teeth" (101).

The tyrants, the enemies, now established, the battles must be fought. In *Woman Warrior*, Kingston describes her own verbal protest as ineffectual when face-to-face with the 'two offensive employers: "'I don't like that word,' I had to say in my bad, small-person's voice that makes no impact" (48) and "'I refuse to type these invitations,' I whispered, voice unreliable" (49). As a child, when she heard the sexist sayings she hated, her response was to throw a tantrum: "I would thrash on the floor and scream so hard I couldn't talk. I couldn't stop" (46). This behavior was counterproductive since it seemed to testify that the fault was in her—she was demonstrably a problem child. In the "battle" against her parents, the only honorable recourse was retreat or escape until time healed the wounds, strengthened her power and weakened theirs. Exasperation, consideration, love, resentment, and anger are all enmeshed in this parent–child relationship, which is finally resolved by the mother's giving the daughter permission to stay away; to prove her love, she lets her daughter go. And for her part, the daughter realizes, at last and from a distance, that she and her mother have much, after all, in common: both are dragon women, born in the year of the dragon, and both are story-tellers.

Though Kingston's are stories of frustration, bitterness, and suffering, to a large extent, the texts she shapes out of her material are triumphant works of art. Their poetry is transcendent, their passion ennobling, their imagination breathtaking. The critical accolades she has received in the United States, the National Book Critics' Circle Award, her designation as a "Living Treasure of Hawaii" by Honolulu Buddhists, and the favorable notice given her in the Peoples' Republic of China would indicate that she has accomplished the goal she thought impossible: "conquered and united both North America and Asia." Like many of the writers in this study, her writing is not focused exclusively on women but she gives equal attention and space to the men. Among our writers, Kingston is probably the one most consciously and outspokenly feminist, and yet her sympathies are large. She may protest misogynist tendencies in her ancestral culture but she also protests racist tendencies in the dominant culture. Injustice is wrong whatever its source and one is duty-bound to right/write it.

Maxine Hong Kingston is the latest to fight the battles of racism and sexism, and Edith Eaton the first. In Eaton's day, racism was much more open, virulent, and widespread. From the nation's president and members of Congress to the ordinary men and women on the streets, the notion was prevalent that the Chinese were unassimilable heathens, "loathsome in their habits . . . and vile in their morals." Eaton's battle was against the attitude expressed forthrightly by a Montana journalist in 1873: "We don't mind hearing of a Chinaman being killed now and then, but it has been coming too thick of late . . . soon there will be a scarcity of Chinese cheap labor in the country . . . Don't kill them unless they deserve it, but when they do—why kill 'em lots."[7] Foremost in these sentiments is the economic motive; when the Chinese (Africans or Mexicans) are profitable to Caucasian Americans (as cheap labor), they are tolerable; when perceived to be taking away jobs from white workers, Chinese and other minorities are intolerable. Since they are less than human, they are expendable. In story after story, Edith Eaton showed the Chinese as lovable, honorable, brave, long-suffering, sometimes gullible and foolish, but always human. In story after story, she fought against discrimination and prejudice, but at her death the battle was far from won.

During the period of World War II, the young Lin Tai-yi took up the banner of China within the United States and was bold enough to scold Americans for allowing what is profitable to have precedence over what is right. At the tender age of 12, from her own initial experiences in this country, she had the astuteness to recognize that Americans had a curious, detached view of the Chinese: "It seems to me that they take these Chinese not as human beings but just as something strange and curious to know."[8] Five years later, though her extraordinary novel *War Tide* was written in English and published in the United States for an English-reading public, Lin Tai-yi nonetheless protested vigorously the gulf between the idealism of American rhetoric and the cynicism of American business: the United States proclaimed China as an ally while simultaneously selling raw materials to China's enemy.

To drive home her point, Lin Tai-yi first described the effect of Japanese bombs, using the example of one Chinese city:

> The planes dived down and let go of their deadly ammunition, and in a while Kiukiang was in flames, and the fumes and the black bitter smoke covered the city like a blanket . . . And underneath that blanket countless beings choked and died . . . and houses fell with loud sounds as they slumped, or else they chuckled with the devils as they burned, and the flames shot through a layer of black smoke and rose into the sky, and lit the heavens ablaze, and the chilled clouds melted, and the sun pierced through to see and laughed as it saw Kiukiang burn, burn, burn! And the drumming of the planes softened and died down, and left Kiukiang not far from hell itself. (120)

Lin Tai-yi's intense feeling for her people's suffering is conveyed in the breathless style of stringing together seemingly endless numbers of compound clauses, as though there is no limit to the devastation, nor time enough to tell it all. Her imagery is expressionistic in the hyperbolic effect of earthly ruin rising all the way to the heavens, melting the clouds and provoking the cynical laughter of the sun, and in the comparison of the bombed Kiukiang to hell itself (120).

With this shocking picture before her reader's eyes, Lin Tai-yi—17 years old, clear-sighted, and outspoken—boldly lays the blame of this destruction on "modern man, civilized man, scientific man" (euphemisms for Western man) and more pointedly on racism and greed:

> "I'll tell you why I look sad, Mother!" Lo-Yin said. "Wipe the dust off your skin, for did you ever hear of the inferior yellow race, or white superiority, or race prejudice, or empire or trade relations or petty politics, Mother? Did you know of oil? Don't you know oil makes good trade, good profit? Ha! Ha, weak China, polite China, bully the four hundred million people, for they have no feelings, their skins are yellow, how can they feel the difference between life and death, or love of mother and son? Scrap iron, Mother, iron waste, iron—they can be turned into profit. Profit, Mother, profit—don't you know that's the most important thing in the world . . . Don't you know, Mother, that the white man rules and governs by divine right? Heaven sent the Japs to us, but they forgot, white men must make a profit. Burn, burn! . . . Mother, have you forgotten? Blood, Chinese blood is yellow, it is not red. Oh no! But it is good enough to sacrifice to fill the bellies of the red-blooded with gold and silver! So sing out the praises of democracy and equality, but who will pay for all these lives and this torture? (121)

Her anger, scathing irony, and bitterness erupt here as molten lava from a volcano. Like Edith Eaton, her pride in her own ancestry intensifies her resentment over the scorn in which her people are held by the whites whose empires were built at the expense of the darker-skinned peoples of the world. Her moral indignation knows no bounds when faced with the egregious example of greed and profiteering in the selling of oil and scrap iron by the United States to Japan during the war. The Montana journalist's sentiments are echoed in her bitterly ironic sentence about Chinese blood being yellow and the yellow-blooded being just good enough to fill the coffers of the red-blooded. Finally, that Americans can boast of an idealistic tradition of democracy and equality at the same time as they contribute to the death of thousands of Chinese is an inconsistency she cannot let pass. She must express her outrage, and in this passage out it comes, unrestrained and unadulterated. No polite, soft-spoken, modest lotus blossom of a young girl do we find here but an ardent patriot whose indignation sets the page ablaze.

Though racism is no longer as blatant as in the past and though Civil Rights laws have been passed promising equality to every American citizen, few living in the United States even today can be colorblind. As W. E. B. Du Bois wrote in 1903, "The problem of the twentieth century is the problem of the color-line",[9] and we are, today, still living in the twentieth century. The color barrier exists even in the inaccurate term "peoples of color," which lines up "pure whites" on one side of the barrier and all other people on the other side. The drawing of a line in this fashion has created a large community of "others" brought together by their history and experience of rejection by the dominant group. Thus, it is to be expected that sympathy for African Americans and a sense of community with other minorities is to be found in the books of many of our Chinese American women writers. We have cited previously the passage from Helena Kuo's novel *Westward to Chungking* about the American's dislike for the Negro, of their lumping Chinese in the same category, and of the college-educated Chinese who could not find any work except as a waiter. And we have discussed Mai-mai Sze's empathy with the woman snubbed by two white women at a luncheon counter in Wellesley, Massachusetts, and of Sze's sisterly comment to this woman, "We're cause people whether we like it or not."

Though we have discussed Virginia Lee's *The House That Tai Ming Built* as a nostalgic evocation of the Chinese landscape and Chinese cultural glories, it is primarily a novel making a gentle protest against racism. The plot centers around the Romeo–Juliet romance of a young couple—the man is Caucasian and the woman Chinese American, the fourth generation in the United States—who defy both their families for love of each other. When the couple apply for a marriage license, however, they find that the state possesses the power their parents did not when the clerk tells them: "In the State of California the Civil Code provides that all marriages of white persons with Negroes, Mongolians, members of the Malay race, or mulattoes are illegal and void. It also provides that no license may be issued authorizing any such marriages."[10] Though not vigorously outspoken like Lin Tai-yi, Lee makes the miscegenation law the climax of her novel; such highlighting is ample proof of the protest the author intended. For Lee, no hyperbole, nor even editorial comment, is necessary; merely to show the law in action in a concrete case makes the injustice plain. The state's miscegenation law and the war together create the environment for tragedy; they are the agents of fate against which the individual is helpless. The young man dies in the war, and the young woman returns to the embrace of her Chinese family.

2. WRITING SEXISM

Though the battle for racial equality was the primary one for Edith Eaton, a secondary one was certainly the battle for sexual equality. A confirmed belief in the strength, courage, and independence of working women is evident in much of Edith Eaton's writing, and several stories place the bond of friendship between women above all other ties. In one story, "A Chinese Lily," a character named Sin Far gives up her life for her friend, a crippled young woman. In another, "The Heart's Desire," though father, mother, wealth, and tasty foods are offered a young unhappy princess, imprisoned in a gilded cage in the middle of an island, only another little girl, a sister, can make her happy. In "The Inferior Woman" Eaton elevates the working woman who has had to pull herself up through her own efforts above the wealthy woman who has had everything given her. In "What About the Cat?" a princess asks all her attendants where her cat is when she has it up her own sleeve all along. In her autobiographical essay, "Leaves From the Mental Portfolio of an Eurasian," Edith Eaton reveals that she (though she writes of herself in the third person) once gave in to family pressures and allowed herself to be engaged to be married simply "because the world is so cruel and sneering to a single woman—and for no other reason." Later, when she decides to break the engagement, she writes in her journal, "Joy, oh, joy! I'm free once more. Never more shall I be untrue to my own heart. Never again will I allow any one to 'hound' or 'sneer' me into matrimony" (132). Throughout her life, Edith Eaton was swimming against the current. She chose to embrace her Chinese heritage when her facial features showed no trace of it and at a time when the Chinese were under vigorous attack throughout the land. She decided to remain a single woman when all society, including her own mother and sisters, regarded spinsters as pitiable or queer creatures. She bravely followed the dictum, "To thine own self be true."

Winnifred Eaton, particularly in her later novels, also took up the cause of women. Personally a high-spirited and independent woman, she was bound to reach the conclusion, after researching Japanese culture for her "Japanese" novels, that women in Japan were much oppressed. Her novels gradually show this awareness in glimmers, and most explicitly in *The Honorable Miss Moonlight*, in which she touches upon the ills of the Japanese geisha system, the easy divorces available to men, and the trap of prostitution as the only livelihood available to a former geisha dishonored by divorce. This novel is a romance, like her others, and therefore unpleasant matters are not given the close focus that a naturalistic novelist would give them, but that these themes come up at all in this genre is remarkable. In her last novel, *Cattle*, closer to home and published under her own name, Winnifred Eaton Reeve presented the injustice done an orphan girl who was purchased, like cattle, at auction and later raped by her "owner," the cattle baron. Being treated little better than beasts of burden was usually the fate reserved for women of color in this society. "Women wasn't nothing but cattle," declared one ex-slave explaining how it was that the slave woman's reproductive capacity was the topic of casual conversation in the parlors and dining rooms of the antebellum South.[11] Ruthanne Lum McCunn's *Thousand Pieces of Gold* recounts the actual story of a Chinese woman in nineteenth-century San Francisco who was put naked on the auction block and sold like a slave or a prize cow.[12] The fact that Nettie Day is white yet treated like women of color demonstrates, in this case, at least, that sexual oppression is stronger than racial allegiance. Though *Cattle* ends with two conventional, happy marriages, throughout most of the book Nettie Day is assisted in her struggle against the cattle baron by an older single woman; and the two women together are shown, ultimately, to be as strong and more clever than the brutal man.

The banner of women's rights was carried on in the next generation by Helena Kuo, who began her first book, *Peach Path*, with these defiant, proud words adapting I Corinthians 13: "When I was a child, I spake as a child, I understood as a child, I thought as a child: but when I became a man, I put away childish things."

> This is a woman's book, written by a woman for women. To misquote St. Paul, and thus take revenge on the numerous well-meaning but unworthy translators of Confucius, when I became a woman I thought as a woman, I spoke as a woman, and I understand as a woman. So I write as a woman.[13]

With her emphasis on her female perspective in the audacious acts of thinking, speaking, understanding, and writing, she counteracts Confucius' infamous dictim about the hsiao ren, "little people," or women: "The aim of female education is perfect submission, not cultivation and development of the mind." *Peach Path* interweaves the maxims and legend from Kuo's old world, with individual, fresh reactions to her new world. The book expresses a divided state of mind: pride in the traditions of a homeland now looked back upon with nostalgia and progressiveness almost to the point of aggressiveness on the subject of injustice toward women. Kuo's pride in her country of birth is tempered by the misogyny that has been traditionally a part of Chinese culture and that she freely acknowledges: "The first awakening to the fact that I was a girl gave me an entirely different outlook on life. In China, though women have contributed much to the political, social and literary culture of the state, they have been ill-treated since the dawn of history" (49). She lays the blame for this ill-treatment of women squarely on the shoulders of the men: "The Chinese men in history and, sometimes, now have a habit of blaming women for their downfall . . . and they have always likened a beautiful woman to a snake or a cunning fox" (109).

Kuo attributes much of what she is today to her anger at the injustice of Chinese men toward women, and to Ban Tso's Three Obediences and Four Virtues, a code of behavior for women that has been a "yoke which has lain upon our frail shoulders ever since" the first century A.D. However, not only does Kuo attack Chinese tradition for its treatment of women, but she roots out sexism in the Judeo-Christian tradition in which she was also reared. Specifically, she questions the story of the Garden of Eden and argues that the precedence it gives to the male is the consequence of male authorship. She speculates that it is even more likely that " . . . woman was first in the world, and that the birth of man followed by natural process. Woman, however, has carried the burden of a stigma ever since man invented the legend of the serpent to cover his own perfidy." As if such an attack were not enough, Kuo adds a contemporary note: "There is a deeper significance in the skirt than merely being a covering for a woman's legs, which are so much better to look at, aesthetically, than those of the male. Our skirts were made for man to hide behind, and he does it most systematically" (6–7).

Kuo is an original and daring feminist in hoping for a time when women offenders will be tried by juries composed entirely of women, for "men are [either] too sympathetic or completely incapable of understanding a woman's viewpoint" (126). She believes in breaking the boundaries that separate men and women's spheres and that have traditionally excluded women from decision-making public posts and suggests that "feminine opinion and assistance can be as important in a war cabinet as in a local government scheme" (103). She voices feminist concerns in this exhortation to women: " . . . you must learn to employ your mind to its fullest extent. The day when you have nothing more than a reproductive body is over, except in a few backward countries. You are beginning to live" (104). Motherhood should not be a woman's only goal: "A woman has the right to make an achievement of her life. Why leave all your hope in life on a small child?" (178).

On the other hand, she believes, not totally consistently, that motherhood is an essential role for women: "I wish I could think that the woman who has never had a child could be entirely happy" (184). For women who cannot find suitable mates, however, she radically advocates single parenthood and adoption: "But if the fathers are not evident or willing, are we ourselves to fall from the tree of life unproductive and wrinkled because we have been denied fertilisation?" (184). The word "wrinkled" conjures up negative notions of spinsterhood, but, to give Kuo her proper due, she advocated single parent-hood approximately three decades before it became tolerated. In the Western world, Kuo was appalled to see cats and dogs pampered while orphans languished in institutions. Had she the power, she would legislate an act making adoption compulsory for all, even for unmarried people, for "they still have to be good parents responsible for the care and well being of a child before they can have a dog" (185). Many of Helena Kuo's ideas were fresh and startling in their boldness and unconventionality. Though she takes some courageous shots at both Chinese and Western patriarchy, the position she reverts back to in this 1939 book, so as not to cut herself entirely out of society, is a compromise somewhere in the middle: "I am a feminist as well as being feminine. I believe, paradoxically enough, that a woman's place is in her home, and I support her right to earn money to make and maintain that home if circumstances are such that her labor is needed for doing so" (5).

3. WRITING COLONIALISM

The writer with the most passionate and lifelong dedication to righting wrongs on an international scale, with the most number of causes to which she has given her energies and devoted her pen and even her fortune (for she is an extremely popular writer), is indisputably Han Suyin. The cause of peoples of color against discrimination and exploitation by whites; the cause of Eurasians against discrimination by both Asians and whites; of coolie laborers looked down on by arrogant aristocrats; of colonized against colonizer; of China against a hostile West; of those open to changing, multiple truths against fanatics certain of their exclusive and absolute hold on a single truth—all these are causes that Han Suyin has fought throughout her life and in her numerous books. The point she makes against sexism and racism on the international scale, in terms of the struggle of Third World nations against First World exploitation and domination, is completely applicable to racial minority groups within the United States, for the status of minorities in America in relation to the dominant group almost exactly parallels that of the Third World in relation to the First. Han Suyin's causes are but extensions of the causes within the United States, and, thus, to study her international causes is to shed light on our domestic ones.

Han Suyin's aristocratic Belgian mother accused her of having "nostalgie de la boue"[14] (nostalgia for mud) when she, as a child, brought home wounded hedgehogs or flogged beggars and ricksha pullers. Han Suyin empathized with the underdog, the victim, because she felt she herself was one. Being Eurasian, she has said, was the greatest obstacle in her life, "being unaccepted by both sides, being trivialized all the time and having to prove myself, and having to work three, four times as hard at everything I tried. But it didn't matter, because since they gave me the habit of working for everything, I never rely on anyone except myself—for everything." When Han Suyin was growing up in 1920s China, she often heard herself referred to as a "dirty half-caste"; both Chinese and Europeans believed Eurasians to be the offspring of promiscuity and thus tainted, innately and inevitably promiscuous themselves. At age 14, Han Suyin set herself a goal, "to make of what everybody looks down on—a glory."[15] And to a large extent, she has.

Within China, the racial dominance of the Europeans was most egregiously manifested in the insulting sign posted on the gate to the riverside park in Shanghai: "No Chinese or dogs allowed." Han Suyin's own father, an engineer trained in Belgium, earned only half the salary of less-well-educated Europeans, simply because of his race, and this was in China, his own country. With such a background, Han Suyin was led, naturally, to sympathize with Third World struggles toward nationalism against First World imperialism and interference. In her novel about the futile British attempt to stay the spread of Asian nationalism in Singapore, . . . and the Rain my Drink (1956),

Han Suyin's disdain for the British officer in charge of "resettling" thousands of Chinese on swampy land inside barbed wire fences is evident in her pithy description of this loyal servant of the British empire:

> Tommy Uxbridge had been a captain in the Indian Army and a major in Palestine, where he had acquired a bad knee and a slight limp. He was forty-three, childless, fond of dogs, and his wife had left him years ago for an American. He had served the Empire in its outposts before the Asian Revolution had become respectable, and his notion of the world, like Mont Blanc, consisted of a white top and a submissive yellow-brown-black base. In Malaya, he was not yet an anachronism.[16]

The author's tone is light and ironic; she deftly paints this man's portrait with a few bold strokes, equating his fondness for dogs with his wife's desertion, and making very clear the distance between his own opinion of himself and hers of him. In the Mont Blanc image, Han Suyin seems almost to be describing a dessert—a chocolate/butterscotch pudding topped with whipped cream. The light, clever surface tone of this piece of indirect discourse, reflecting as it does Uxbridge's view of the world, contrasts greatly with the weight of its underlying contempt.

In a powerful passage from the second volume of her autobiography, *A Mortal Flower*, Han Suyin links racism and sexism in drawing an analogy between colonialism and rape. The passage analyzes Joseph Hers, her father's employer on the Belgian railroad construction company in China:

> Like so many Europeans in China, Joseph Hers began to "love" China, a fierce, dominating, anxious, all conquering possessiveness, characteristic of the warped, twisted, and altogether vicious relationship miscalled "love" between the dominating and the suppressed, the powerful and the weak; the spoiler and the cheated. Like many foreigners, he expressed this "love" in sensual imagery; to all of them China was the WOMAN, the all-enveloping, soft, weak woman, who actually welcomed rape, welcomed being invaded. "Don't worry, China is feminine, she has always ended by absorbing all her conquerors," was their favourite explanation . . . Though Hers knew the cruelties inflicted upon China, this sexual explanation, equating the violation of China to the defloration a woman undergoes in marriage enhanced in them a feeling of superiority: The Great White Male seeding in the weak, moaning, submissive coloured female. And in this he was typical of nearly all the Europeans in China who declared the Chinese "forever unable to rule themselves, because they are weak, devious, volatile, timid." (216–17)

The analogy between colonization and sexual victimization is a startling and accurate one. Racial superiority is not only linked to but justified by sexual superiority; as men are stronger than women so some nations are stronger than other nations. In the opinion of the strong, any superiority, in and of itself, justifies dominance and even oppression "for the other person's (or nation's) own good" because one's superiority is not only physical but mental and moral as well. Thus, conscience is quieted because no harm is being done. Han Suyin's outrage against this doubly offensive attitude—offensive to her as a woman and as a Chinese—is evident in the violence of her images and the unsuppressed anger of her tone.

Not only is colonization a political, racial, and physical force but a cultural and intellectual usurpation as well. When the colonizer gains control of a nation's educational system, the young people of the colonized country are bereft of their own cultural heritage and brainwashed, in a sense, into the notion of the superiority of the colonizer's culture.[17] In Han Suyin's novel *The Four Faces*, Ahmed Fouad, a writer from Pakistan at a Third World writers conference near the ruins of Angkor Wat, speaks vehemently of the misguided young Pakistanis who have been educated in British-controlled schools:

> Whenever talk about writing comes up, the English literature B.A.'s are on the defensive, jumping in with "self-expression above all" and they only know English literature; they don't know a thing about how their own people live. They can't even read their own language. They're true colonial. They talk about their writing reflecting the writer's personality first, and the only personality they have is that of their lecturers in the English Literature Department, whoever happens to be in charge. Well-meaning people, no doubt, but unacquainted with Asian literature, they produce bad pseudo-writers.[18]

The discussion at this Third World Writer's Conference centers on the question of a writer's purpose: Does one remain apolitical and neutral in the fray between Communism and Capitalism? Does one write to express oneself or one's people? Does one aim for universality or is one bound to one's own time and place? The strongest answer comes from Ahmed Fouad (very likely Han Suyin's mouthpiece), who argues that writers cannot remain neutral, cannot be concerned only with "self-expression" as something separate from their time and place; they must be grounded in their culture and committed to speaking for their people:

> Trying to say something, not only within our own dimension, but with all our various consciousnesses aware of belonging to a culture, a national spirit, a sensation of being the spokesman for ideas, the demands of a people, are just as important a part of the self as the self-expression we were arguing about. Multiplicity is the writer's self. It can't be faked, or simplified . . .
> Those writers who refuse to understand, who bolster themselves up with the narrowness of their selves against the large movements of history, are compelled to a perpetual fleeing from the real, the vital issues of the day, or to describing an ever narrowing scope of individual appetites. That way lies impotence and oblivion. (112, 114)

For such an international figure, it is intriguing that the quality that stands out above all in Han Suyin's writing is her "consciousness of a national spirit." But her definition of "national" is not a narrow one. From the outset, she has expressed an awareness of the "large movements of history" and given voice to a multiplicity of selves and concerns. Though her first book, *Destination Chungking* (1942), focused on the story of her courtship and marriage to an officer in the Kuomintang army, it ends with an apostrophe to the Chinese coolie that is prophetic of the Communist victory and unusually sympathetic for one of her class and upbringing:

> We are not the important ones in China, we who ride in sedan chairs, while you bend to lift, to carry us. The officials, the bureaucrats, the would-be intellectuals—without you we are nothing . . . The important one is you, coolie . . . you who toil and fight and die dumbly, scarcely asking to know why. The significance of your gesture, coolie, when you raise your finger to trace the words on the wall . . . it shows me that something curious is awake in you, is beginning to ask questions. It is a gesture of profound meaning, and I who watch am suddenly happy and confident of the future, because I see you, in the mist of dawn, lift your finger to read . . . [19]

Even her most famous novel, *A Many Splendored Thing*, made popular by the Hollywood film version, is much more than a tragic love story. It is the story of a Eurasian vacillating between her two worlds. On the one hand, there is China, just over the hills of Kowloon, land of her father, her birth, her childhood and young adulthood. She knows and loves its people, language, customs, sights, and smells and fervently wants to return with her newly acquired medical skills to serve her people; to take part in the Revolution, in the rebuilding of China, to dedicate herself to something greater than herself, for she agrees with her friend François, "Il faut dire aux hommes pourquoi ils doivent se faire tuer" (You have to tell men why they must kill themselves. Editor's translation).[20] On the other hand, there is the comfort, beauty, pleasantness, and tranquility of upper-class life in the capitalist world of her mother, where individualism is encouraged, personal talent rewarded, and private, forbidden love deliciously possible. The Western world is tempting but its self-centeredness is soul-starving; in China she could readily feed her soul but she could also as readily lose her life, for her background was far from proletarian. Han Suyin could see clearly and was justifiably wary of the fanaticism of the new revolutionary government:

> Religious emotion; Faith in Man. Like all new-roused faiths, intolerant and fanatical. Come to clothe the poor, feed the hungry, do justice to the downtrodden. With its zealots, its saints, its soldiers. Rousing the lovely things in the soul of man: ardor, craving for purity, single-mindedness and self-abnegation. But also overreaching itself, working itself up into frenzies of hatred for those that did not conform; denouncing and suspecting heretics everywhere, imposing terror in the name of justice, and forgetting mercy; on and on, driven to purification by death, public execution and Holy War; nothing that other revolutions and other religions had not done, on a bigger or a smaller scale; inescapable, the pattern it would follow. (221)

Though Han Suyin after 1965 was to throw herself entirely into the "large movements of history" by giving up her medical practice to write and to lecture all over the United States against the Viet Nam war and in favor of the reforms accomplished by the People's Republic of China, this early clear-sighted criticism of the excesses of revolutionary zeal would not change. It remained underground during the years when she produced books lauding the Chinese Communist Party and its leader, and when the political leader-ship was more open and tolerant it surfaced again, decades later, in her novel, *Till Morning Comes*. In the 1960s and 1970s, she published three volumes of autobiography: *The Crippled Tree* (1965), *A Mortal Flower* (1966), and *Bird-less Summer* (1968), her answer, perhaps, to the autobiographies the Chinese government was then requiring of all its bourgeoisie; a prophecy, *China in the Year 2001* (1967); and a two-volume book devoted to the life of Mao Zedung and the Chinese Revolution: *The Morning Deluge* (1972) and *Wind in the Tower* (1976). As though she had taken Ahmed Fouad's words to heart, Han Suyin decided she could not remain neutral and committed herself anew to China, becoming in these books China's spokesperson in the anti-Communist West, explaining how China had become Communist and what the Chinese Communists had accomplished. Though some Western histo-rians thought her uncritical and partisan, they all envied her freedom to travel in and out of China and her access to its leaders, most notably Chou Enlai. Now that the United States is no longer in its hysterical anti-Communist mode, Han Suyin's books of this period deserve a rereading and reevalua-tion.

Despite her patriotic stance, in 1982 when Han Suyin published another novel, the revolutionary fanaticism she had criticized in *A Many Splendored Thing* emerges again as part of her picture of China, and this fanaticism is responsible for the tragic fate of her protagonist Jen Yong. In *Till Morning Comes*, history and politics become embodied in the fictional characters whose lives are controlled by the "large movements of history" in which they are actors: victims and heroes. Stephanie Ryder, an American journalist, daughter of a Texas oil magnate, is in China in 1941 to cover the war. She meets and falls in love with Jen Yong, a Chinese surgeon working for the Revolution. They marry, and the vicissitudes of their life together reflect the political upheavals of the decades between 1941 and 1971, in both China and the United States.

Not in biological fact, but in a psychological and cultural sense, both Stephanie and Jen are Eurasians, for their lives, their values, their interests, and, of course, their children are a blend of Euro-America and Asia. Coming from different races and nationalities, they have both had to stretch outside of themselves to love and understand the other. The cost of this stretching is high, for at one point, during the Cultural Revolution when America was being vociferously denounced, and both her husband and son were suffering on her account, Stephanie, then an outcast in China,

> wept for her own fragmentation; and the tears burnt her to clearness. She would never be whole, in the sense of those who are whole because they have only that narrow space of living which never queries itself and carries no ambiguity. These happy men have not ventured on long explorations in other men's minds, gone into different worlds of thought and being, and come back, like Marco Polo, to bear tales that no one would believe. (397)

Stretching one's understanding into other cultures and ways of being brings excitement and growth to the exploring individual, but its cost is a loss of wholeness and the sense of total belonging. Stephanie's Chinese marriage not only causes problems for her family in China but it creates problems for her back in the United States as well. She is out of step with her own people, for at that moment, in the McCarthy era when she returns to Texas to escape an anti-Western purge then in progress in China and to bear her second child in peace, she finds Americans also in a fearful and reactionary condition. As the wife of a Chinese, she is automatically suspect as a Communist sympathizer if not an actual Communist; her personal effects are confiscated at the airport, she is interrogated for hours on end, and afterwards repeatedly harassed by FBI agents who hope to find evidence against her. In China, as an advocate of American surgical methods at a time when Russia was China's strongest ally and America the enemy, Jen Yong is labelled a "counterrevolutionary" and sent into exile to a hardship post. Thus, nonpartisan Han Suyin draws a striking parallel between the fanaticism of the McCarthy era in the United States and the fanaticism of various purges in Communist China. She shows the narrowness of those who cannot see beyond their own obsessions, both Chinese and Americans; those who feel threatened by what they cannot understand. She quotes the words of Senator Fulbright:

> When our perceptions fail to keep pace with events, when we refuse to believe something because it displeases us or frightens us, or is simply startlingly unfamiliar, then the gap between fact and perception becomes a chasm. And action becomes irrelevant and irrational. (455)

Stephanie and Jen are both victimized by the irrelevant and irrational actions of those who are unable or unwilling to accept a multiplicity of ways because they can only see one way: their own. This kind of myopia, Han Suyin demonstrates in *Till Morning Comes*, is not limited to any one people or time.

Though Jen dies, a martyr, Stephanie prospers. Heir to her father's millions, she discovers that she possesses her father's talent for putting money to good use,

a special talent made up of shrewdness, audacity, a gambler's instinct, a necessary illogic, a never-slumbering alertness . . . The realization that brains were
purchasable; swiftness in judging brainpower, original thought, and snapping it
up. Taking risks cooly, letting down failures gently. This had created Space Time
Research Inc., STRINC, founded on Heston's idea, carried out by his daughter
Stephanie . . . She was a warrior. Fierce, treacherous, vicious board battles left
her unscarred. (455)

The audacity of trying to research, to know and thus to control space and
time, has a satiric edge. Stephanie is the epitome of American derring-do,
boldness that verges on megalomania, and fittingly she is from Texas, the
state where everything is larger than life. But as a woman warrior, she is
endowed with heroic dimensions making everything possible for her. "'She's
filthy rich, she's filthy mean,' they said of her. A female Howard Hughes. She
was hated, because she was a woman, and she beat men at their own games
of greed and money" (456). We can imagine Han Suyin smiling at this wish-
fulfilling creation of hers, a woman who outmans men and achieves the
materialist American dream on a scale large enough to affect international
politics. In Stephanie Ryder, Han Suyin has created the modern-day American woman warrior, who "beat the men at their own games of greed and
money" and who also has, what is important to Han Suyin and this study, a
between-world consciousness.

When Stephanie returns to China after 20 years, bringing together for the
first time her American-born daughter with her Chinese-born son, she is
restored to wholeness by remembered love for Jen Yong and her immediate
love for both her children. She finds a cause, a purpose for her energy and
her fortune that is totally satisfying:

A whole new world to make. And she could help. She would not wither, her
heart mummified, her mind amassing wealth with pointless energy. There was
so much to be done, so much. And she was committed, involved, as never
before. Not only the memory of the dead, but even more so by the living. (500)

Stephanie Ryder epitomizes the successful resolution of the between-world
dilemma. She is not "neither here nor there"; she is both here and there and
able to travel frequently back and forth between the two points. Her American upbringing and her American father's fortune ground her in the United
States while the memory of a loving husband and her own two children
ground her in China. Stephanie makes the most of her position as a bridge.
From experience she realizes that controlling money and making it multiply
alone had not been a sufficient reason for living, but devoting it to a cause, to
the service of a people who need it, is. The last paragraph of *Till Morning
Comes* suggests that Stephanie Ryder will bring the fruits of her American
harvest to the table of a Chinese need, and in this whole-hearted commitment to a worthy cause Stephanie will find her reward.[21]

4. CONCLUSION

The between-world condition is a duality that is characteristic of all people in a minority position. Many scholars have noted it and have given it various names in a variety of contexts. Between worlds is the "divided consciousness" that W. E. B. Du Bois in 1903 noted as characteristic of blacks in America, "this sense of always looking at one's self through the eyes of others, of measuring one's soul by the tape of a world that looks on in amused contempt and pity."[22] It is Mary Helen Washington's "divided self, woman split in two (which is closely akin to double consciousness) . . . found in literature by women, white and Black."[23] It is Elaine Showalter's "double-voiced discourse" that "always embodies the social, literary, and cultural heritages of both the muted [female] and the dominant [male]."[24] It is Gerda Lerner's observation that "women live a duality—as members of the general [male] culture and as partakers of women's culture," which she recognizes as a paradox, for "women are subordinate, yet central; victimized, yet active."[25]

The between-world complexity of Chinese women in America is indeed a paradox, for the women themselves are simultaneously subordinate and central, victimized and heroic and active. The very condition itself carries both negative and positive charges. On the one hand, being between worlds can be interpreted to mean occupying the space or gulf between two banks; one is thus in a state of suspension, accepted by neither side and therefore truly belonging nowhere. As we have seen, Edith Eaton, in the concluding lines of her autobiographical essay, hoped with characteristic modesty that by giving her right hand to the Occidentals and her left to the Orientals she herself, "the insignificant connecting link," would not be pulled apart. On the other hand, viewed from a different perspective, being between worlds may be considered as having footholds on both banks and therefore belonging to two worlds at once. One does not have less; one has more. When those who are entirely on one bank wish to cross the gulf, the person between worlds is in the indispensible position of being a bridge. Of course, being a bridge has its drawbacks; Han Suyin realized that, "If one is a bridge, one must expect to be stepped on." However, on the positive side, bridging an impassable gulf or river is a service not many are able to render. Thus, the factors—one's Chinese face and heritage, for example—that created a sense of alienation in one world are the very factors that enable one to perform the act of bridging; disadvantages are turned into advantages; by alchemy, dross transmutes into gold. What the black poet Nikki Giovanni has said of black women applies equally to Chinese American women: "But our alienation is our great strength. Our strength is that we are not comfortable any place; therefore, we're comfortable *every place*. We can go any place on earth and find a way to be comfortable" (Tate, *Black Women Writers At Work*, 70). Or as Maxine in *The Woman Warrior* comforts her mother over the loss of the family property in China:

> We belong to the planet now, Mama. Doesn't it make sense to you that if we're no longer attached to one piece of land, we belong to the planet? Wherever we happen to be standing, why, that spot belongs to us as much as any other spot. (*Woman Warrior*, 107)

The characteristics that literary theoretician Mikhail Bakhtin identified as central to the novel in general—"polyglossia" and the "dialogic imagination" or multiple voices in dialogue, multiple attitudes toward an experience—are, in particular, literally characteristic of our authors. When one is not totally absorbed within a culture, Bakhtin noted, as when one is conversant in different languages, one is enabled to see those cultures or languages from the outside and thus to see them more whole than can the people imprisoned within a single language or perspective:

> Only polyglossia fully frees consciousness from the tyranny of its own language and its own myth of language . . . Moreover, in the process of literary creation, languages interanimate each other and objectify precisely that side of one's own [and of the other's] language that pertains to its world view, its inner form, the axiologically accentuated system inherent in it.[26]

When one is interested in seeing the whole, then the marginal or between-world position becomes the advantageous one, for only from the outside can one best see the true nature of the inside. Thus, we find here an instance of what critic Jonathan Culler in another context called "a deconstructionist hierarchical inversion":

> This concentration on the apparently marginal puts the logic of supplementarity to work as an interpretive strategy; what has been relegated to the margins or set aside by previous interpreters may be important for those reasons that led it to be set aside.[27]

We return again to the paradox of the peripheral becoming central, of victim becoming victor.

Joan Didion, in an essay "Why I Write," has characterized the writing as an "aggressive, even a hostile act." But it is also an act of self-exploration, sometimes self-artifice, at other times self-denial or self-delusion, oftentimes self-celebration and, certainly, always, self-offering. In the very act of writing itself, all the women in this study have used their strongest talent and most powerful tool: words. Anne Ford, the protagonist of Han Suyin's *The Mountain is Young*, confiding to her journal, undoubtedly expressed the delight and hope in writing shared by all:

> And now I who have not written a line I wanted to write for nearly three years, suddenly I am writing for pleasure again, for myself, a diary to record myself. I

have become a little stiff, unused to communicate with myself, to talk to me, and yet I want, I must do it now, I want to grope and find the me again that I had lost, and put it on paper while it slips away from me as I am writing it down. Hurry hurry, suddenly I want to watch me live, I want to know, I want . . . for nothing is real, nothing is true, nothing happens, until it has been observed and noted and put down in words like bells, ringing the changes of love and hate, beauty and happiness and misery. Without words, how much of us really does exist? Perhaps all living is thus only echo, prolongation of sound into symbol, when the original, the primal fault, the stroke which began the lovely sound, is no more . . . For with names, with words is the world as we know it called out of empty air. In words written in dust and upon the worm and upon the stars, can they all claim the same immortality, immortality, a reverberation . . . an echo, echo. (40–1)

The women writers of this study have looked within and written out of themselves, and writing out of themselves, they have written for others. Without their words, these experiences and emotions would have no existence, no reality. What they have all proclaimed has been a most fundamental message, one that should be the birthright of all, a message that seems self-evident and even unnecessary to iterate: the affirmation of self in opposition to all forms of domination and negation.

That so many women of Chinese ancestry in America have found their voices and written what was on their minds and in their hearts in opposition to all constraints demonstrates their courage. That their texts are as finely crafted as they are shows these women to be artists. That their line extends back into the nineteenth century gives their cause a tradition and a history. That these women of Chinese ancestry are but a small part of a growing contemporary wave including African American women, Italian women, Latina women, American Indian women whose writings are being collected and published, edited by such people as Helen Barolini, Alicia Partnoy, Diana Velez, Juanita Ramos, Mayumi Tsutakawa, and Shirley Geok-lin Lim[28] demonstrates the urgency of their need to voice themselves. That their message—I am here and I am worthy—needs to be proclaimed over and over, from one generation to the next, by one group after another,[29] shows the extent that things are still awry and need righting/writing. And those in the best position to understand what is awry and in need of righting/writing are those in between worlds.

Notes

PREFACE

[1]Alice Walker, *In Search of Our Mothers' Gardens: Womanist Prose* (New York: Harcourt Brace Jovanovich, 1983) 4.

[2]Alice Walker, "Finding Celie's Voice," *Ms.* December 1985: 96.

[3]See Barbara Herrnstein Smith, "Contingencies of Value," *Critiqal Inquiry* 10 (1983): 1–35.

[4]Jane Tompkins, *Sensational Designs* (New York: Oxford UP, 1985) 126.

CHAPTER ONE

[1]Joan Didion, "Why I Write," in *The Writer on Her Work*, Ed. Janet Sternburg (New York: W. W. Norton, 1980) 17.

[2]Han Suyin, foreword, *Destination Chungking*, 1942 (London: Mayflower, 1970) 8.

[3]I am indebted to Lucinda Pearl Boggs, PhD, author of *Chinese Womanhood* (Cincinnati: Jennings and Graham, 1913, 17–20), for singling out this poem and the second one quoted later in my text. But after consulting the literal translation by Bernhard Karlgren, *The Book of Odes* (Stockholm: Museum of Far Eastern Antiquities, 1950, 130–31), I found Arthur Waley's translation, *The Book of Songs* (New York: Grove, 1960, 1937, 282–84), preferable because it is closer to the original. However, Dr. Boggs' translation of the second poem had such a lively convincing voice that I have quoted from Boggs in the second instance. Another English translation of the ancient Chinese classic is by James Legge, DD LLD, *The Book of Poetry* New York: Paragon Book Reprint Corp., 1967; first edition published in Shanghai, China, n.d.).

[4]Julia Kristeva, *About Chinese Women*, trans. Anita Barrows (1974; New York: Urizen, 1977), 75.

[5]Lucinda Pearl Boggs, *Chinese Womanhood* (Cincinnati: Jennings and Graham, 1) 1913, 97.

[6]John K. Fairbank, *China: The People's Middle Kingdom and the U.S.A.* (Cambridge: Belknap Press of Harvard UP, 1967 1) 21.

[7]All three Confucian quotes were found in Kristeva's *About Chinese Women* 76. Kristeva was citing Robert van Gulik, *La Vie Sexuelle dans La Chine Ancienne* (Paris: Gallimard, 1971).

[8]For the story of Ban Tso, the reputed author of the Three Obediences and Four Virtues, I am indebted to Helena Kuo, *Peach Path* (London: Methuen, 1940), 10–14.

[9]M. T. F. (Mae T. Franking), *My Chinese Marriage* (New York: Duffield and Co., 1921) 152–54. The narrator, an American woman, married a Chinese and lived nearly a decade in China.

About widows in twentieth-century China, she says: "In the Chinese family, the widow who does not remarry received honor and veneration second only to the mother-in-law. With age, she acquires added authority" (153). According to the copy in the collection of the Library of Congress, this book was ghostwritten by Katherine Ann Porter.

[10]Wang Chia-yu, *Loves and Lives of Chinese Emperors*, trans. and adapted T. C. T'ang (Taipei: Mei Ya, 1972) 26.

[11]Helena Kuo, *Peach Path* 136.

[12]M. T. F., *My Chinese Marriage* 84.

[13]My two sources disagree as to the dates of Empress Wu. C. P. Fitzgerald in *China: A Short Cultural History* (1935; London: Cresset, 1954) says, on page 297, that Empress Wu died in 705 at "the great age of eighty one" which would put her birth at 624. Julia Kristeva gives her dates as 642–703.

[14]Helena Kuo, *Peach Path* 10–14.

[15]Roxane Witke, "Woman as Politician in China of the 1920's" in *Women in China*, ed. Marilyn B. Young, Michigan Papers in Chinese Studies No. 15 (Ann Arbor: U Michigan, 1973) 34–36.

[16]Julia Kristeva, *About Chinese Women* 103.

[17]Roxane Witke, "Mao Tse-tung, Women and Suicide," in *Women in China* 14.

[18]Janet Weitzner Salaff and Judith Merkel, "Women and Revolution: The Lessons of the Soviet Union and China," in *Women in China* 164.

[19]Soong Ching-ling, "Women's Liberation," reprinted from *Peking Review* 11 Feb. 1972, in *Women in China* 203.

[20]Judy Yung, *Chinese Women of America* (Seattle: U Washington P, 1986) 17.

[21]Yung 14.

[22]Lucie Cheng Hirata, "Chinese Immigrant Women in 19th Century California," in *Women of America: A History*, ed. Carol Ruth Berkin and Mary Beth Norton (Boston: Houghton Mifflin, 1979) 225.

[23]Kenneth Clark, introduction, *The Nature of Prejudice*, by Gordon Willard Allport, 25th Anniversary ed. (London: Addison-Wesley, 1979) 191.

[24]See Saundra Saperstein and Elsa Walsh, "A Journey from Glory to Grave," a front-page story about the Tran family (Madame Nhu's parents) in *The Washington Post* 19 Oct. 1987: A1, 8–9. On page A8, column two, referring to Madame Nhu, the wife of President Diem's brother, the authors write: "She styled herself as the first lady to the bachelor president, but her saber-tongued comments won her another name: the "Dragon Lady."

[25]"Chinese Woman Begins a Crusade Against Social Conditions in Her Country," *San Francisco Chronicle* 8 Nov. 1902: 7. I am indebted to Judy Yung for this article.

[26]See Judy Yung, "Unbinding the Feet, Unbinding Their Lives: Chinese Immigrant Women in San Francisco, 1902–1931," a paper presented at the Sixth National Asian American Studies Conference, Hunter College, NYC, June 1989.

[27]Lucie Cheng Hirata, "Chinese Immigrant Women in Nineteenth Century California," in *Women of America, A History* 226–7.

[28]Victor G. and Brett de Bary Nee, *Longtime Californ': A Documentary Study of an American Chinatown* (New York: Pantheon, 1972) asterisked footnote on 149.

[29]The story of Precious Jade included in "Golden Mountains" and "Precious Jade" takes up 228 pages of Monfoon Leong's 303-page collection inappropriately entitled, *Number One Son* (San Francisco: East/West Publishing Company, 1975). Had Mr. Leong not been killed in an automobile accident in 1964 (at age 48), one feels certain that Precious Jade would have been a novel. In its present condition, it already possesses the steeped atmosphere and character development of a novel.

[30]Ruthanne Lum McCunn, *Thousand Pieces of Gold* (San Francisco: Design Enterprises of San Francisco, 1981).

31Mai-mai Sze, *Echo of a Cry, a Story Which Began in China* (New York: Harcourt, Brace, 1945) 165.

32See Williamson B. C. Chang, "M. Butterfly: Passivity, Deviousness and the Invisibility of the Asian-American Male," a paper delivered at the Asian American Studies Conference at Hunter College, NYC, June 1989. Professor Chang justifiably complains that this "dyad" totally leaves out the Asian American male.

33For the entire poem, see number 165 in *The Complete Poems of Emily Dickinson*, ed. Thomas H. Johnson (Boston: Little, Brown, 1960) 77.

34DeVeaux is quoted by Claudia Tate in her introduction to *Black Women Writers at Work* (New York: Continuum, 1983) xxiii.

35Elaine Showalter, "Feminist Criticism in the Wilderness," *Critical Inquiry* 8.2 (1981): 185.

36In Joy Kogawa's exquisite novel *Obasan*, Aunt Emily, the indefatiguable protester of Japanese–Canadian relocation, is called a "word warrior." *Obasan* (Markham, Ontario: Penguin, 1981) 32.

37A. T. Steele, *The American People and China* (New York: McGraw Hill, 1966) 14.

38Steele 17.

CHAPTER TWO

1I am indebted to Mr. L. Charles Laferrière, grandson of Agnes Eaton, the fourth daughter of Grace and Edward Eaton, for the correction of Edith's birth year. He has graciously supplied the photographs of Edith Eaton at her desk and of her tombstone on which the correct year is carved. Edith Eaton's birth year, cited as 1867 in her *New York Times* obituary is apparently incorrect.

2The *Who's Who in New York City and State* of 1909 has a listing for Winnifred Eaton Babcock, citing her birth year as 1879; however, Professor Paul G. Rooney, Winnifred's grandson, in a letter to me dated 9 September 1981, wrote that she could not have been born in 1879 since a brother, Hubert Eaton, was born in that year. Professor Rooney believes that Winnifred was born two years earlier and explains that she changed her birth year because "she was trying to hide from her second husband (Francis F. Reeve) the fact that she was somewhat older than he." Monsieur Laferrière has recently discovered the christening record for Lillie Winnifred Eaton giving her birthdate as August 21, 1875.

3See Jack Chen, *The Chinese of America*. (San Francisco: Harper & Row, 1980) 6–11.

4Diane Mei Lin Mark and Ginger Chih, *A Place Called Chinese America* (Dubuque: Kendall Hunt, 1982) 6.

5For many of the specific facts about the Chinese work on the railroad and in agriculture, and for Dennis Kearney and the Exclusion Act, I am indebted to Jack Chen, *The Chinese of America*. Kearney's slogans appear on page 141.

6For this and other anti-Chinese ordinances see Diane Mei Lin Mark and Ginger Chih, *A Place Called Chinese America* 29–44.

7Henry Pratt Fairchild, *Immigration. A World Movement and Its American Significance.* (New York: Macmillan, 1913, 1925) 102–3.

8Roy Garis, *Immigration Restriction: A Study of the Opposition to and Regulation of Immigration into the U.S.* (New York: Macmillan, 1928) 291–92.

9See Betty Lee Sung, *Mountain of Gold. The Story of the Chinese in America.* (New York: MacMillan, 1967); Roy L. Garis, *Immigration Restriction*, cited above; and Stanford Lyman, "Strangers in the City: the Chinese in the Urban Frontier" in *Roots: An Asian American Reader*, ed. Amy Tachiki, Eddie Wong, Franklin Odo with Buck Wong (Los Angeles: UCLA Asian American Studies Center, 1971) 151–87.

10Sui Sin Far, "Leaves from the Mental Portfolio of an Eurasian," *The Independent*, 21 Jan. 1909: 127. Hereafter referred to as "Leaves."

11Winnifred's grandson, Professor Paul Rooney, thinks that the invention of Nagasaki as

Winnifred's birthplace and a Japanese noblewoman for their mother was the work of Bertrand Babcock, Winnifred's first husband and literary agent. Letter to me from Paul G. Rooney, dated 29 Sept. 1981, 2.

12I'm always struck by the similarities in minority women's experiences. Kristin Hunter, in an interview with Claudia Tate, admired her people's pliancy and resilience: "I marvel at the many ways we, as black people, bend but do not break in order to survive." *Black Women Writers at Work*, (New York: Continuum, 1983) 84.

13For many of the facts about the family, I am indebted to correspondence with descendents of the Edward Eaton family, particularly Paul G. Rooney, Professor of Mathematics at the University of Toronto and grandson of Winnifred Eaton; Eileen V. Lewis, great grand-niece to the Eaton sisters; and Florence Winkelman, daughter of Edith and Winnifred's sister May. Professor Rooney and Ms. Lewis have been particularly generous in providing me with family "lore," photographs, and documents.

14*Marion, the Story of an Artist's Model* by Herself and the Author of *Me* (New York: W. J. Watt and Co. 1916) 42. In this book, Edith is called Ada, but she is clearly identified as the eldest sister.

15For information about the Canadian beginnings of Edith Eaton's career and for her obituary in the *Montreal Star*, I am indebted to Professor James Doyle of Wilfrid Laurier University, Waterloo, Ontario. Professor Doyle has done extensive research on the life and work of Walter Blackburn Harte (1866–1899), writer, editor, and short-lived husband of Edith's sister, Grace.

16Professor Sam E. Solberg, formerly of the Asian American Studies Department, University of Washington, has done research on the firms Edith Eaton worked for and the rooming houses where she lived during her decade in Seattle, from 1900 to approximately 1910. This information may be found in his "Addendum: Edith Eaton, 4-16-76," appended to his "Bibliographic Note. Edith Maud Eaton (Sui Sin Far) " dated "April 7, 1976 being the sixty-second anniversary of the day of her death," a typed manuscript.

17Linda Popp Di Biase, "*Mrs. Spring Fragrance* and Seattle's Springtime," *The Weekly* 10–16 Sept. 1986: 24–26.

18Sui Sin Far, "Chinese Workmen in America." *The Independent* 3 July 1913: 56–58.

19In his letter to me dated 31 August 1989, L. Charles Leferrière enclosed a copy of the baptismal record from the American Presbyterian Church in Montreal listing three daughters: "Christiana Mary . . . , May Darling (?) . . . and . . . Lillie Winnifred born August twenty-first in Montreal eighteen hundred and seventy-five, daughters of Edward Eaton of Hochelaga Province of Quebec, clerk (?), and of Grace his wife were baptized January twenty eight in Montreal eighteen hundred and seventy six."

20For this information and other specific family information, I am indebted to Winnifred Eaton's grandson Professor Paul G. Rooney of the University of Toronto.

21H. Phillipson Laing and A. R. Lee, *Interpersonal Perception* (London: Tavistock Publications, 1966) 5–6 quoted in Elizabeth W. Bruss, *Autobiographical Acts: the Changing Situation of a Literary Genre*, (Baltimore and London: Johns Hopkins UP, 1976) 13.

22Nina Baym, *Woman's Fiction, A Guide to Novels By and About Women in America 1820–1870.* (Ithaca: Cornell UP, 1978) 22.

23Jean Starobinski, "The Style of Autobiography" in *Autobiography: Essays Theoretical and Critical*, ed. James Olney, (Princeton: Princeton UP, 1980) 82.

24Houston A. Baker, Jr., "To Move without Moving: Creativity and Commerce in Ralph Ellison's Trueblood Episode," in *Black Literature and Literary Theory*, ed. Henry Louis Gates, Jr. (New York: Methuen, 1984) 244.

25Roger Rosenblatt, "Black Autobiography: Life as the Death Weapon" in Olney, *Autobiography* 171.

26"Literary Notes," *The Independent*, 73 15 Aug. 1912: 388.

27"A New Note in Fiction," *New York Times*, 7 July 1912: 405.

28Florence Howe, Afterword, *Portraits of Chinese Women in Revolution*, by Agnes Smedley (Old Westbury: Feminist, 1976) 180.

29Carole McAlpine Watson, *The Novels of Black American Women, 1891–1965*. (Westport: Greenwood, 1985) 9–11.

30Sui Sin Far, "The Inferior Woman," in *Mrs. Spring Fragrance* 35–6.

31For readers who find this story masochistic, may we remind them of the words of Jesus of Nazareth, "Greater love hath no man than this, that a man lay down his life for his friends" (John 15:13). Further, according to Beongcheon Yu in *The Great Circle: American Writers and the Orient*, "the sacrifice of self for others is the highest possible morality from any religious point of view, Christian or pagan" (Detroit: Wayne State UP, 1983, 120). Another explanation comes from the feminist critic Jane Tompkins who writes of the death of little Eva from *Uncle Tom's Cabin*:

> . . . in the system of belief that undergirds Stowe's enterprise, dying is the supreme form of heroism. In *Uncle Tom's Cabin*, death is the equivalent not of defeat but of victory; it brings an access of power, not a loss of it; it is not only the crowning achievement of life, it is life . . .
> Stories like the death of little Eva are compelling for the same reason that the story of Christ's death is compelling: they enact a philosophy, as much political as religious, in which the pure and powerless die to save the powerful and corrupt, and thereby show themselves more powerful than those they save. *Sensational Designs*. 127–28

32See Vladimir Propp, *Morphology of the Folktale*, trans. by Laurence Scott (Austin: U Texas P, 1968) for a full analysis of the structure underlying folk tales. I am indebted to his morphology for this discussion of the structure of Onoto Watanna's novels.

33Janice Radway, *Reading the Romance: Women, Patriarchy, and Popular Literature*. (Chapel Hill: U North Carolina P, 1984, 213).

34W. D. Howells, "A Psychological Counter-Current in Recent Fiction," *North American Review* 173 (1901: 881). In contrast to Howells' actual words, Winnifred Eaton is quoted as remembering that Howells had called her "a star of the first magnitude in the literary heavens." This quote is taken from a typed transcript of an article, presumably from a Calgary newspaper, with the headline, "Onoto Watanna, Famous in Literary World, Resides in Calgary to Write," by Elizabeth Bailey Price, no date, sent to me by Eileen V. Lewis, granddaughter of Florence Eaton Lewis, another of the Eaton sisters.

35"A Round-up of Story Books," *New York Times Book Review* 14 Jan. 1911: 16.

36Thomas E. Swann and Katsuhiko Takeda, *Essays on Japanese Literature* (Tokyo: Waseda-Daigaku-Shuppanbu, 1969) 52–53.

37Onoto Watanna, *The Diary of Delia: Being a Veracious Chronicle of the Kitchen with Some Side-lights on the Parlour* (New York: Doubleday, Page & Co., 1907) 6–7, 10.

38In J. D. Logan and Donald G. French, *Highways of Canadian Literature: A Synoptic Introduction to the Literary History of Canada (English) from 1760 to 1924*. (Toronto: McClelland and Stewart, 1924), *Cattle* is described as part of the "New Realism" in Canadian fiction, a reaction against the "romance with its insufficiency of motivation and its lack of fidelity to real life." Logan and French, however, read the book from a masculinist perspective, calling it an "almost brutally realistic presentation of a man whose sole aim in life was the acquirement of cattle—as a form of wealth—whose whole outlook on life was measured in terms of cattle" (313). In fact, the book is very decidedly focused on the young woman, Nettie Day, showing first how she is victimized and then how she fights back against abusive male power embodied in Bull Langden.

CHAPTER THREE

1I am indebted to the work of Karen Huck, University of Utah, whose paper, "Seeing Japanese: The Constitution of the Enemy Other in *Life* Magazine, 1937–1942," delivered at the American Studies Convention, New York, November 1987, directed me to the 22 December

1941 issue of *Life* magazine in which the article "How to Tell the Japs from the Chinese" appeared on pages 81–2.

[2]John Kobler, *Luce: His Time, Life, and Fortune* (Garden City: Doubleday, 1968) 108.

[3]John Gunther, *Inside Asia* (New York: Harper & Brothers, 1939) 106.

[4]John Gunther 239.

[5]Gunther 247 and Sulia Chan, "CAMJ Intended to Set the Historical Record Straight," in *Chinese American Forum* 3.4 (1988): 20–21.

[6]Though Anor Lin is the name used on the books published when she was a child, Ms. Lin has adopted the literary name given her by her father, and prefers to be known as Lin Tai-yi.

[7]The experience of World War II was so intense that decades later books were still written about it. *Sold For Silver, An Autobiography* (Cleveland: World Publishing, 1958) by Janet Lim is a fascinating account of a life filled with sensational incident, but as a resident of Singapore she falls somewhat outside the boundaries of this study.

[8]Delia Davin, "Women in the Liberated Areas," in *Women in China*, ed. Marilyn B. Young (Ann Arbor: U Michigan, 1973) 79.

[9]Adet Lin quoted by Lin Yutang, introduction, *Girl Rebel: The Autobiography of Hsieh Pingying*, with extracts from her new war diaries, trans. Adet and Anor Lin (1940; Da Capo, 1975), xviii.

[10]*Sao-ke Alfred Sze. Reminiscences of his Early Years*, as told to Anming Fu, trans. Amy C. Wu, preface Stanley K. Hornbeck, introduction Hu Shih (Washington, DC, 1962).

[11]Helena Kuo, "American Women are Different," *American Mercury* 54 (1942): 731.

[12]Helena Kuo, *I've Come a Long Way* (New York: Appleton Century, 1942) 277.

[13]Han Suyin, *A Mortal Flower* (New York: G. P. Putnam, 1965) 356.

[14]Richie Maybon, "Modern Youth in 'Ancient China,'" *Saturday Review of Literature* 1 Jan. 1944: 20.

[15]Lin Tai-yi, *War Tide* (New York: John Day, 1943) 2.

[16]Mary Ross, *Weekly Book Review* 14 Nov. 1943: 5.

[17]Pearl Buck, introduction, *Our Family*, by Adet and Anor Lin (New York: John Day, 1939) viii.

[18]Richard McLaughlin, "The Life Wish," rev. of *Silent Children*, by Mai Mai Sze, *The Saturday Review of Books* (17 April 1948): 38.

[19]Maria Yen, *The Umbrella Garden: A Picture of Student Life in Red China*, adapted from the Chinese by Maria Yen with Richard M. McCarthy (New York: MacMillan, 1954) 217.

[20]Sansan, *Eighth Moon*, as told to Bette Lord (New York: Harper & Row, 1964) 4.

[21]Yuan-tsung Chen, *The Dragon's Village* (New York: Pantheon, 1980) 134.

[22]Han Suyin, *My House Has Two Doors* (New York: G. P. Putnam's Sons, 1980) 365.

[23]Preston Schoyer, "The Smell of a Hidden World," *Saturday Review* 21 May 1955: 18.

[24]C. T. Hsia, *A History of Modern Chinese Fiction*, 2nd ed. (New Haven: Yale UP, 1971) 389.

[25]Shueh Ching-i, *Chang Ai-ling de Shao Shou Yi Shu* (The Art of Chang Ai-ling's Fiction) (Taipei: Kuo Tai Ying Shu Gwan, 1973) 27–31.

[26]Frank Chin, Jeffery Paul Chan, Lawson Fusao Inada, Shawn Hsu Wong, ed. *Aiiieeeee! An Anthology of Asian-American Writers* (Washington, DC: Howard UP, 1974) xxiii.

[27]The servant's names in *Spring Moon*, in contrast, are colloquial and condescending: Fatso, Dummy, No Stop. These translations do have the virtue of conveying social hierarchy and values.

CHAPTER FOUR

[1]W. E. B. Du Bois, *The Souls of Black Folk* (1903; New York: Signet, 1982) 45.

[2]Notes and comments from Diana Chang in response to a first draft of my article about her, "Writer in the Hyphenated Condition: Diana Chang," 16 Sept. 1980.

[3]Frank Chin et al. in the introduction to *Aiiieeeee!* claim "That the cultural superiority of the

Chinese served white supremacy by keeping Chinese in their place in the work of Jade Snow Wong and Virginia Lee" (xxiii). Though granting that fewer "formal modes" were available to Wong writing in the 1940s than Kingston in the 1970s, nonetheless, Patricia Lin Blinde finds Jade Snow Wong's work limited by virtue of its outdated "sense of a totalized and thus stable world" In "The Icicle in the Desert: Perspective and Form in the Works of Two Chinese-American Women Writers" (MELUS 6 (1979): 57), Elaine Kim found the "sparks of inner life . . . submerged in Fifth Chinese Daughter" and takes Jade Snow Wong to task for defining her Chinese identity by "whatever was most exotic, interesting, and non-threatening to the white society that was her reference point." See Kim's Asian American Literature (Philadelphia: Temple UP, 1982) 66.

4Maxine Hong Kingston in a letter to me dated 28 April 1988.

5Patricia Lin Blinde, "The Icicle in the Desert: Perspective and Form in the Works of Two Chinese-American Women Writers," MELUS 6.3 (1979): 59.

6Kathleen Loh Swee Yin and Kristoffer F. Paulson, in "The Divided Voice of Chinese-American Narration: Jade Snow Wong's Fifth Chinese Daughter" (MELUS 9.1 (1982)), find a precedence for the use of the third person in an autobiography in Henry Adams' The Education of Henry Adams, explaining, "In their third person autobiographies both Adams and Wong treat themselves as fictional characters, submerging the individual ego, the 'I,' within the influences of the forces which surround them." They object to what they see as Patricia Lin Blinde's unjustly negative appraisal of Wong's work.

7Maxine Hong Kingston in an interview with Kay Bonetti, American Audio Prose Library (Columbia, MO), June 1986.

8Kingston had initially intended to publish her book as a novel but her editors decided that autobiography was the more appropriate classification and one that would sell better.

9Lowell Chun-Hoon, "Jade Snow Wong and the Fate of Chinese American Identity," Amerasia Journal 1 (1971): 128.

10Jade Snow Wong, No Chinese Stranger (New York: Harper & Row, 1975) 17.

11For a fine exposition of the theme of the silencing of women's voices in the work of Maxine Hong Kingston and Alice Walker, see King-Kok Cheung, "'Don't Tell': Imposed Silences in The Color Purple and The Woman Warrior," PMLA 103.2 (1988): 162–74.

12Susan Brownmiller, "Susan Brownmiller Talks With Maxine Hong Kingston, author of The Woman Warrior," Mademoiselle March 1977: 148.

13Jane Kramer, "On Being Chinese in China and America," rev. of The Woman Warrior, New Times Book Review 7 Nov. 1976: 1.

14Sara Blackburn, "Notes of a Chinese Daughter," Ms. January 1977: 39.

15John Leonard, "Books of the Times: China Men," New York Times 3 June 1980. C9.

16Susan Kepner, "The Amazing Adventures of Amy Tan," Focus (KQED-Public Television Magazine) 36.5 (1989): 59.

17One thinks immediately of Henry James' Portrait of a Lady, Gustave Flaubert's Madame Bovary, Leo Tolstoy's Anna Karenina, Theodore Dreiser's Sister Carrie, Stephan Crane's Maggie, A Girl of the Streets, and Daniel Defoe's Moll Flanders. But beyond these, we find only brilliant portraits of women as parts of larger stories, such as Chaucer's Wife of Bath, Shakespeare's Cleopatra and Portia, or we have texts with a woman's name as a title but actually focused on a man's devotion or obsession with that woman, like Dumas' La Dame Aux Camelias. An entire book written by a man focused primarily on a woman is, proportional to their entire output, relatively rare.

In fact, in his preface to Portrait of a Lady, James quite explicitly states the difficulty of making a young woman the central subject of a novel. Though young women figure largely in many works of literature, and he names "Romeo and Juliet," "Middlemarch," and other George Eliot novels, James concludes: "They are typical, none the less, of a class difficult, in the individual case, to make a centre of interest; so difficult in fact that many an expert painter, as for instance Dickens and Walter Scott, as for instance even, in the main, so subtle a hand as that of R. L. Stevenson, has preferred to leave the task unattempted." Challenged, James deliberately sets himself this task: "Place the centre of the subject in the young woman's own consciousness," I said to myself, "and you get as interesting and as beautiful a difficulty as you could wish" (10). The main difficulty for James, however, was not the crossing of the gender barrier but the limitations of action available to a young woman of the nineteenth century, or, in his words, of finding enough "to make an ado about" (9) in "her little concerns" (11).

Nor have gender-crossing women writers in the Euro-American tradition been numerous. Apart from George Eliot's *Daniel Deronda*, Mary Shelley's *Frankenstein*, and Virginia Woolf's *Orlando* (which crosses the gender barrier a number of times), other examples do not stand readily forth.

[18]Joanna Russ and other contemporary feminist writers too have complained about the continued difficulty of writing about heroines as opposed to heros; what have girls been allowed to do but fall in love, get married, and have children? See Joanna Russ, *How to Suppress Women's Writing* (Austin: U Texas, 1983).

[19]*Flowers in the Mirror* was translated into English by another author in this study, Lin Tai-yi, and published in 1965 by the University of California Press. Kingston modifies her source as she did in conflating the legends of Hua Mulan (the woman warrior) and Yueh Fei (the male general whose parents carved characters on his back). In the original version, it is Merchant Lin, Tang Ao's brother-in-law, who lands in the Country of Women, not Tang Ao, as Kingston has it. But the name of the male visitor is hardly a significant detail; what he must endure there is what really matters and this Kingston does not change.

[20]See Linda Ching Sledge, "Maxine Hong Kingston's *China Men*: The Family Historian as Epic Poet," *MELUS* 7.4 (1980): 3–22.

[21]See Leslie Rabine's fine article, "No Lost Paradise: Social Gender and Symbolic Gender in the Writings of Maxine Hong Kingston," *Signs* 12.3 (1987): 471–92.

[22]A passage from Trinh T. Minh-ha's *Woman, Native, Other: Writing Postcoloniality and Feminism* (Bloomington and Indianapolis: Indiana UP, 1989) sheds additional light on this mirror image phenomenon. She writes,

> Writing necessarily refers to writing. The image is that of a mirror capturing only the reflections of other mirrors. When i say "I see myself seeing myself," I/i am not alluding to the illusory relation of subject to subject (or object) but to the play of mirrors that defers to infinity the real subject and subverts the notion of an original "I." A writing *for* the people, *by* the people, and *from* the people is, literally, a multipolar reflecting reflection that remains free from the conditions of subjectivity and objectivity and yet reveals them both. I write to show myself showing people who show me my own showing.

[23]See Dorothy Ritsuko McDonald, introduction, *The Chickencoop Chinaman and The Year of the Dragon: Two Plays by Frank Chin*, by Frank Chin, (Seattle: U Washington P, 1981) xiv, xv.

[24]Wu Ch'eng-en, *Monkey*, trans. Arthur Waley (1942; London: Penguin, 1961) 7.

[25]See Dorothy Ritsuko McDonald's introduction to the two Chin plays, xi.

[26]For example, Chin wrote in the introduction to *Aiiieeeee!* (1974): "The white stereotype of the acceptable and unacceptable Asian is utterly without manhood. Good or bad, the stereotypical Asian is nothing as a man. At worst, the Asian-American is contemptible because he is womanly, effeminate, devoid of all the traditionally masculine qualities of originality, daring, physical courage, and creativity" (xxx). Ironically, Chin castigates writers like Jade Snow Wong, Virginia Lee, and Betty Lee Sung for being servants of "white supremacy" but does not see that he himself has totally imbibed white stereotypes of masculinity.

CHAPTER FIVE

[1]See Germaine Greer, *The Obstacle Race: The Fortune of Women Painters and Their Works* (New York: Farrar Straus Giroux, 1979) 172.

[2]Mrs. N. F. Mossell, *The Work of the Afro-American Woman*, 2nd ed. (1894; Philadelphia: George S. Ferguson, 1908), 20. In addition to Deborah Gannet, Mrs. Mossell, journalist and educator, in this historic volume draws up an inspiring list of Afro-American women of accomplishment in a wide variety of fields only three decades after the Emancipation Proclamation.

[3]William Frederick Mayers, *Chinese Reader's Manual: A Handbook of Biography, History, Mythology, and General Literary References* (Shanghai: Presbyterian Mission Press, 1924) 170.

[4]Ch'en Hui-wen ed. *Selected Chinese Poems*. (Taipei: Hua-lien Publishing Co., 1968, 47–51).

[5]Nancy Milton, "A Response to 'Women and Revolution'," in *Women in China*, ed. Marilyn B. Young (Ann Arbor: U Michigan, 1973) 191. Another essay in this collection tells of a modern-day Fa Mulan: Ku'o Chiang-ch'ing, whose story appears in Chapter 1.

[6]The story of the visit of Tang Ao to the Country of Women is taken from an early nineteenth-century novel, *Flowers in the Mirror*, by Lu Ju-chen, translated by one of the authors in this study, Lin Tai-yi (Berkeley and Los Angeles: U California P, 1965). This novel has been described as a combination of *Grimm's Fairy Tales, Gulliver's Travels, Aesop's Fables, The Odyssey*, and *Alice in Wonderland*. In the original, however, it is Merchant Lin, Tang Ao's brother-in-law and travelling companion, who is caught and painfully fashioned into a beautiful woman before being rescued by Tang Ao. See chapter 13 of *Flowers in the Mirror* 107–14. This is but another example of Kingston's adaptation of Chinese myth and materials for her own purposes.

[7]Quoted by Stanford Lyman, "Strangers in the City: the Chinese in the Urban Frontier," in *Roots: An Asian American Reader*, ed. Amy Tachiki, Eddie Wong, Franklin Odo, and Buck Wong (Los Angeles: UCLA Asian American Studies Center, 1971) 165. Lyman reports that these anti-Chinese sentiments appeared in the *Mountanian* 27 March 1873 and were quoted in Larry Barsness, *Gold Camp: Alder Gulch and Virginia City, Montana* (New York: Hastings House, 1962) 239.

[8]Adet and Anor Lin, *Our Family* (New York: John Day, 1939) 104.

[9]W. E. B. Du Bois, *The Souls of Black Folk* (1903, New York: New American Library, 1982) 54.

[10]Virginia Lee, *The House That Tai Ming Built* (New York: Macmillan, 1963), 204. Before 1901, there were laws in California forbidding marriage between blacks and whites, but in 1901, Asians were added to the list of races whites were not allowed to marry. This law stayed in effect in California until 1948.

[11]Quoted by Deborah Gray White, *Ar'n't I a Woman? Female Slaves in the Plantation South* (New York: W. W. Norton, 1985) 31.

[12]Ruthanne Lum McCunn, *Thousand Pieces of Gold*, a biographical novel. (San Francisco: Design Enterprises of San Francisco, 1981).

[13]Helena Kuo, *Peach Path* 1.

[14]Han Suyin *A Mortal Flower* (New York: G. P. Putnam's Sons, 1965) 342.

[15]From my interview with Han Suyin in Beekman Place, New York City, 20 February 1985.

[16]Han Suyin, . . . *and the Rain my Drink* (Boston: Little, Brown, 1956) 112.

[17]For interesting essays on cultural colonization within the United States see particularly Leslie Silko's "Language and Literature from a Pueblo Indian Perspective," in *English Literature: Opening Up the Canon*, ed. Leslie A. Fiedler and Houston A. Baker, Jr. (Baltimore: Johns Hopkins, 1981) 54–72.

[18]Han Suyin, *The Four Faces* (New York: G. P. Putnam, 1963), 10.

[19]Han Suyin, *Destination Chungking* (1942; London: Mayflower, 1970), 252. Sixteen years

earlier, Andre Malraux had also noted the awakening of the Chinese coolie: "Coolies are learning that they exist, just that they exist . . . The French and Russian revolutions were powerful because they gave every man his own share of the world; but this revolution is giving every man his own life. And no Western power can stop that" *The Conquerors*, translated by Stephen Becker (New York: Holt, Rinehart and Winston, 1976; original French edition copyright 1928) 10. I do not know if Han Suyin was influenced by Malraux, but since French was her mother's tongue she certainly could have read *Les Conquérants*. On the other hand, she may have been writing from firsthand observation about a fact verifiable by any perceptive observer.

[20]Han Suyin, *A Many Splendored Thing* (Boston: Little, Brown, 1952) 296.

[21]Like her own fictional character, Han Suyin herself has committed half of her income to assist in the modernization of China through a trust fund for scientific exchange between China and the West. Established in 1986, her fund provides one fellowship per year either to a Chinese for travel and study abroad in an area useful to China (flood control, agricultural technology, etc.) or to a Westerner with such knowledge to visit and study in China. Thus, not only has Han Suyin devoted her pen to the cause she has espoused, but, more importantly, as the popular saying goes, "She has put her money where her mouth is."

[22]W. E. B. Du Bois, *The Souls of Black Folk* (1903; New York: New American Library, Signet Classics, 1982) 45.

[23]Mary Helen Washington, "Teaching *Black-Eyed Susans* : An Approach to the Study of Black Women Writers," in *All the Women Are White, All the Blacks Are Men, But Some of Us Are Brave*, ed. Gloria T. Hull, Patricia Bell Scott, and Barbara Smith (Old Westbury: Feminist, 1982) 209.

[24]Elaine Showalter, "Feminist Criticism in the Wilderness," *Critical Inquiry* 8.2 (1982): 201.

[25]Gerda Lerner, *The Majority Finds Its Past* (New York: Oxford UP 1979, 1981) 52.

[26]Mikhail M. Bakhtin, "From the Prehistory of Novelistic Discourse," in *The Dialogic Imagination*, ed. Michael Holquist, trans. Caryl Emerson and Michael Holquist (Austin: U Texas P, 1981) 61, 62.

[27]See Jonathan Culler, *On Deconstruction* (Ithaca: Cornell UP, 1982) 140.

[28]See Helen Barolini's introduction to *The Dream Book: An Anthology of Writings by Italian-American Women* (New York, Schocken 1985) for similar expressions of resentment over the repressions that Italian American women have suffered within their own tradition as well as their alienation from Anglo-American traditions. Collections of minority women's writing seem of late to be mushrooming; to name a few, see Diana Velez, *Reclaiming Medusa: Short Stories by Contemporary Puerto Rican Women* (San Francisco: Spinsters/Aunt Lute, 1988); Juanita Ramos, *Compañeras: Latina Lesbians (An Anthology)* (New York: Latina Women's Educational Resources, 1987); Alicia Partnoy, *You Can't Drown the Fire: Latin American Women Writing in Exile* (Pittsburgh: Cleis, 1988); Shirley Geok-lin Lim and Mayumi Tsutakawa, *The Forbidden Stitch* (Corvallis: Calyx, 1988); Asian Women United, *Without Ceremony* (New York: Ikon, 1988) and Asian Women United of California *Making Waves* (Boston: Beacon, 1989).

[29]Black feminist scholars years ago discovered that it is "an act of political courage" to study and thereby place value on the history and accomplishments of black women:

> Merely to use the term "Black women's studies" is an act charged with political significance. At the very least, the combining of these words to name a discipline means taking the stance that Black women exist—and exist positively—a stance that is in direct opposition to most of what passes for culture and thought on the North American continent. To use the term and to act on it in a white-male world is an act of political courage. Gloria Hull et al., *But Some of Us Are Brave: Black Women's Studies* xvii.

Bibliography

This is an annotated bibliography of women writers of Chinese Ancestry who have published books of prose in the United States. The authors are listed in alphabetical order; each author's books are in chronological order. Most of the authors have Western first names or, like Nien Cheng, have reordered their names to conform to the Western style; these authors have therefore been listed in the usual bibliographic fashion: last name, comma, first name. Some authors, however, have retained the Chinese customary word order of "last" or family name first, then given name (Han Suyin, Liang Yen, Lin Tai-yi, Tan Yun, for example). In these cases, their names have remained unchanged since the "last" name already comes first. Sui Sin Far and Chuang Hua are unique cases. Sui should be a last name, but since Edith Eaton referred to herself in her autobiographical essay as Miss Far we will follow her lead. Since Chuang Hua is the author's given name, and she does not wish her family name made known, we have followed the Western tradition and listed her under H.

REFERENCES

Chang, Diana

Frontiers of Love (New York: Random House, 1956). Fiction. Three Eurasians search for their identity in the International Sector of Shanghai at the end of World War II.

A Woman of Thirty (New York: Random House, 1959). Fiction. Witty, intelligent, resilient Emily Merrick develops self-reliance after an unhappy marriage, a divorce, and an affair with a married man.

A Passion for Life (New York: Random House, 1961). Fiction. After much anguish, Barbara and Geoffrey Owens decide to keep her baby, the result of a rape.

The Only Game in Town (New York: Signet, 1963). Fiction. A farcical love story between a Caucasian Peace Corps volunteer and a Communist Chinese dancer.

Eye to Eye (New York: Harper & Row, 1974). Fiction. Artist George Safford, a husband and father, falls blindly and hopelessly in love with a Jewish writer, sees a psychiatrist about his problems, and makes a surprising discovery.

A Perfect Love (New York: Jove, 1978). Fiction. Frustrated in her marriage, Alice Mayhew has a passionate affair with a charming but married younger man.

Chang, Eileen

The Rice Sprout Song (New York: Scribners, 1955). Fiction. Model farmer, Gold Root, and his wife, Moon Scent, pressed beyond endurance, lead a revolt in which peasants storm the granary storing grain they have grown but kept from them by Communist officials even during a famine.

The Naked Earth (Hong Kong: Union, 1956). Fiction. The story of Liu Ch'uen's progressive disillusionment with the work he is required to perform for the Chinese Communist Party.

The Rouge of the North (London: Cassell, 1967). Fiction. Yindi is married off to a blind, opium-addicted son of a wealthy family. She patiently plays the subservient role of daughter-in-law until it becomes her turn to tyrannize over a daughter-in-law and to ensnare her son into opium.

Chao, Evelina G.

Gates of Grace (New York: Warner, 1985). Fiction. Leaving Canton on the last ship before the Communists arrive, Mei-yu Wong hopes to find a free new life in the United States only to discover herself the pawn of unscrupulous power-wielders in New York's Chinatown.

Chen, Su Hua Ling

Ancient Melodies (London: Hogarth, 1953; New York: Universe, 1988). Autobiography. Charming memoirs of upper-class family life in early twentieth-century China written and illustrated by the tenth daughter of a mayor of Beijing. Dedicated to Virginia Woolf and Vita Sackville West, who encouraged the author.

Chen, Yuan-tsung

The Dragon's Village (New York: Pantheon, 1980). Fiction. Seventeen-year-old Ling-ling goes to work for the Revolution in a land distribution enterprise in a remote northwestern Chinese village and finds her idealism severely tested.

Cheng, Nien

Life and Death in Shanghai (New York: Grove, 1986). Autobiography. A courageous woman's seven-year struggle for survival and dignity while imprisoned and harrassed during the Cultural Revolution.

Chennault, Anna

A Thousand Springs; The Biography of a Marriage (New York: Paul S. Eriksson, 1962). Autobiography. Journalist wife of Claire Lee Chennault, the famous World War II Air Force major-general and founder of the Flying Tigers, recounts their meeting, courtship, and marriage.

The Education of Anna (New York: Times, 1980). Autobiography. Anna Chan Chennault or Chan Sheng-mai, political hostess in Washington and adviser to presidents, tells her life story. Much overlapping with earlier book.

Chi, Yuan-lin

A Shadow of Spring (New York: Vantage, 1975). Fiction. Uneven in style but a moving story of an extramarital affair between a Chinese woman living in Denmark and a Danish spy once married to another Chinese woman.

Chun, Jinsie K. S.
I Am Heaven (Philadelphia: Macrae Smith, 1973). Fiction. Biographical novel about the brilliant rapacious career of Chao, the seventh-century woman who rose from lady-in-waiting to Empress of China, Wu Tse-tien, ruling for 38 years during a period of peace and prosperity.

Far, Sui Sin (pseudonym, Edith Maud Eaton)
Mrs. Spring Fragrance (Chicago: A. C. McClurg, 1912). The first collection of short stories about Chinese American life at the turn of the century by a Chinese Eurasian. Eaton protests racial discrimination and shows the Chinese in a sympathetic light.

Han Suyin (pseudonym, Rosalie Chou)
Destination Chungking (London: Jonathan Cape, 1942). Fiction. Autobiographical novel of the courtship and marriage of the author with Tang Pao-huang, an officer in the Kuomintang army amidst the upheaval of World War II.

A Many Splendored Thing (Boston: Little, Brown, 1952). Autobiographical novel of a tragic love story between a Eurasian doctor and an English journalist set in Hong Kong.

. . . and the Rain my Drink (Boston: Little, Brown, 1956). Fiction. Malaya in the throes of freeing itself from British colonial rule with Asians and Europeans all caught in a tangle of intrigue, terrorism, and chaos.

The Mountain is Young (New York: Putnam, 1958). Fiction. A beautiful English writer falls in love with an Indian engineer in Nepal, leaving her self-righteous retired civil servant husband for the mystical/physical "modern incarnation of the Lord Krishna."

Two Loves (New York: Putnam, 1962). Fiction. Two novellas in one volume: "Cast But One Shadow" and "Winter Love." In the former, two Frenchmen come to a Cambodian village searching for the sister of one of them whom they both loved, but one killed. The latter is a tale of lesbian love between two students at a science college in London.

The Four Faces (New York: Putnam, 1963). Fiction. During a writer's conference held at Angkor Wat, Cambodia, a murder occurs.

The Crippled Tree (New York: Putnam, 1965). Nonfiction. The brilliant first volume of Han Suyin's autobiography intertwining her parent's history with the history of China in the late nineteenth and early twentieth centuries.

A Mortal Flower (New York: Putnam, 1966). Nonfiction. China's history and Han Suyin's personal story from 1928–1938 with brief biographies and evaluations of Chiang Kai-shek, a misguided man who "pursued a humbug of personal grandeur" and Mao Tse-tung, the true nationalist and patriot. She tells of her first job, her first lover, her studies at Yenching University and the Université Libre de Bruxelles.

China in the Year 2001 (New York: Basic, 1967). Nonfiction. A discussion of agriculture, industry, trade, and population in China as well as an examination of Mao Tse-tung's thought and foreign policies.

Birdless Summer (New York: Putnam, 1968). Nonfiction. Volume three of her autobiography, covering the years 1938–1949, presenting the marriage with Tang Pao-huang in a totally different light than in *Destination Chungking*.

The Morning Deluge: Mao Tse-tung and the Chinese Revolution. 1893–1954 (Boston: Little, Brown, 1972). Nonfiction. First volume of the biography of Mao from early school years to leadership of China, thoroughly researched and presented from a perspective of great admiration.

Wind in the Tower: Mao Tse-tung and the Chinese Revolution. 1954–1975 (Boston: Little, Brown, 1976). Nonfiction. Mao's accomplishments further extolled.

Llasa, the Open City: A Journey to Tibet (New York: Putnam, 1977). Nonfiction. Advances made by Tibetans since the Communist victory.

My House Has Two Doors (New York: Putnam, 1980). Nonfiction. The final volume of her autobiography, from 1949 until the present, with an emphasis on the world leaders she has known, including China's foremost men.

Till Morning Comes (New York: Bantam, 1982). Fiction. Stephanie Ryder, a Texan and journalist, covers China during World War II and falls in love with Jen Yong, a Chinese surgeon. Their marriage is torn apart by the political upheavals of various Chinese purges and by US fear and hatred of Communism.

The Enchantress (New York: Bantam, 1985). Fiction. A pair of twins, Bea and Colin Duriez, leave eighteenth-century Switzerland on a journey to China and Ayuthia, the ancient capital of the Thais, bringing their separate knowledges: Bea's ancient Celtic mysticism and Colin's mechanical inventiveness.

Hua, Chuang

Crossings (New York: Dial, 1968; Boston: Northeastern UP, 1986). Fiction. An experimental fragmented narrative, mixing dream, memory, and metaphor, to recreate the life, anxieties, and loves of a much-travelled Chinese American woman.

Joe, Jeanne

Pieces of a Childhood (San Francisco: East/West, 1982). Nonfiction. Sketches of a single-parent childhood in Chicago's Chinatown.

Kingston, Maxine Hong

A Woman Warrior, Memoirs of a Girlhood Among Ghosts (New York: Alfred Knopf, 1976). Nonfiction. A brilliant collage of myth, memory, fantasy, and fact on growing up female and Chinese American in a family dominated by a strong-willed mother.

China Men (New York: Alfred A. Knopf, 1980). Nonfiction. The experiences of Chinese men in the United States, recreated from history and embellished by imagination, from the mid-nineteenth century until the present.

Tripmaster Monkey: His Fake Book (New York: Knopf, 1989). Fiction. Wittman Ah Sing, a Chinese American Berkeley graduate and would-be writer, loses his job in a department store, marries a girl he meets at a party, looks for his grandmother, and puts on a play. Full of puns and verbal pyrotechnics.

Koo, Hui-lan

Hui-lan Koo: An Autobiography As told to Mary Van Rensselaer Thayer (New York: Dial, 1943). Nonfiction. The story of a fabulous, aristocratic girlhood in Java and marriage to Ambassador Wellington Koo.

Kuo, Helena (or Kuo Chin ch'iu)

Peach Path (London: Methuen, 1940). Nonfiction. Collection of essays from a feminist perspective about women in China, past and present, and Chinese culture.

I've Come a Long Way (New York: D. Appleton-Century, 1942). Kuo's autobiography tracing her origins from a well-to-do family in Macao, through her education to her emigration to Europe and the United States.

Westward to Chungking (New York: D. Appleton-Century, 1944). Novel about a

Chinese family's struggle, sacrifice, and heroism during the Japanese invasion of China.

Giants of China (New York: E. P. Dutton, 1944). Nonfiction. An introduction to eleven heroes and heroines of China from Huang Ti, the first emperor, to Madame Chiang Kaishek. Written for young people.

The Quest for Love of Lao Lee. Lau Shaw, trans. Kuo (New York: Reynal & Hitchcock, 1948). Fiction. A satiric account of a romantic minor official from the country disillusioned by the backbiting pettiness of the big city folk in Beijing.

The Drum Singers Lau Shaw, trans. Kuo (New York: Harcourt, Brace, 1952). Fiction. The effect of war and social prejudice on a family of troubadors in Chungking.

Dong Kingman's Watercolors (New York: Watson and Guptil, 1981). Nonfiction. Commentary on Kingman's paintings.

Lee, Virginia

The House That Tai Ming Built (New York: Macmillan, 1963). Fiction. Bo Lin, a third-generation Chinese American, born and reared in San Francisco's Chinatown, falls in love with a Caucasian, but discovers that their marriage is forbidden by law.

Liang Yen (pseudonym for Margaret Yang Briggs)

Daughter of the Khans (New York: W. W. Norton, 1955). Autobiography of a Khan or Mongol, an ethnic minority in China, expressing a sense of alienation from the Han, or "mainstream" Chinese. Born in Beijing, Liang Yen's life is eventful as she travels throughout China, to Rangoon, Burma, and finally the United States and marriage to a Caucasian.

Lim, Janet

Sold For Silver (London: Book Club; Cleveland: World, 1958). Nonfiction. Eventful autobiography of a young Chinese girl sold as an indentured servant who uses her wits to ward off her master's advances, escapes from a Japanese prison camp during World War II, and survives a shipwreck.

Lin, Alice P.

Grandmother Had No Name (San Francisco: China, 1988). Nonfiction. Memoir of life in China, Taiwan, and the United States with a special emphasis on women.

Lin, Hazel Ai Chun

The Physicians (New York: John Day, 1951). Fiction. Hsiao-chen's birth causes her mother's death, her father's retreat, and her grandfather's estrangement. Excelling in Western medicine, she gains the respect of her grandfather, who is a great Chinese physician.

The Moon Vow (New York: Pageant, 1958). Fiction. A woman doctor works indefatigably on the case of a young bride who cannot consummate her marriage because of a vow to a secret lesbian society. Set in China.

House of Orchids (New York: Citadel, 1960). Fiction. A beautiful girl from a destitute family is sold to a house of prostitution and falls in love with a student.

Rachel Weeping for Her Children Uncomforted (Boston: Branden, 1976). Fiction. A Chinese medical student turns down a marriage proposal from a childhood friend, has an unfortunate affair with a Caucasian surgeon old enough to be her father, undergoes an abortion, and suffers a nervous breakdown.

Weeping May Tarry, My Long Night with Cancer (Boston: Branden, 1980). Nonfiction. A brief, moving diary of the author's emotional and psychological battle with cancer.

Lin Tai-yi (also Anor Lin or Lin Wu-shuang) (See Tan Yun for books coauthored with her sisters.)

War Tide (New York: John Day, 1943). Fiction. The effect of the Japanese atrocities on the Tai family and how their resourceful daughter, Lo-Yin, rises to the crisis. A brilliant first novel.

The Golden Coin (New York: John Day, 1946). Fiction. Wen Lang, a man of science and reason, marries Sha, a young woman from the Shanghai slums, whose vitality, intuition, and idealism culminate in the belief that their son has special lucky powers. Wen Lang works to prove her wrong and destroys both wife and son. Set in China during World War II.

The Eavesdropper (Cleveland: World, 1959). Fiction. Su-tung feels that the events of his life are not under his control as he moves back and forth between the United States and a China at war, as he falls in love with his brother's wife and marries a woman he doesn't love, as he eavesdrops on life and puts it into novels.

The Lilacs Overgrown (Cleveland: World, 1960). Fiction. Sima, the elder sister, marries a poor man who is revealed to be heartless, and Ahua weds a wealthy man, who is immature and useless. Set in the late 1940s China.

Kampoon Street (Cleveland: World, 1964). Fiction. Extreme poverty limits the opportunities open to the Tsoi family of Hong Kong—widow, daughter, son—and forces them into less-than-fastidious moral choices.

Flowers in the Mirror. Li Ju-chen, trans. Lin Tai-yi. (Berkeley and Los Angeles: U California P, 1965). Fiction. Tang Ao and his brother-in-law, Merchant Lin, travel to strange lands whose customs satirize human foibles. Akin to *Gulliver's Travels* combined with *Alice in Wonderland*.

Lord, Bette Bao

Eighth Moon (New York: Harper & Row, 1964). Nonfiction. Sansan describes her girlhood in Communist China and her reunion with her family after 17 years.

Spring Moon (New York: Harper & Row, 1981). Fiction. An epic novel of the vicissitudes of the House of Chang from the Ching Dynasty until 1972 with emphasis on Spring Moon, who survives marriage, motherhood, love affairs, and revolutions to become the family matriarch.

McCunn, Ruthanne Lum

Chinese American Portraits, Personal Histories 1828–1988 (San Francisco: Chronicle Books, 1988). Nonfiction. In-depth stories of selected, representative Chinese Americans complete with rare, interesting photographs.

An Illustrated History of the Chinese in America (San Francisco: Design Enterprises, 1979). A concise introduction to Chinese American history in pictures.

Thousand Pieces of Gold (San Francisco: Design Enterprises, 1981). Biographical novel of the life of Lalu Nathoy (1853–1933), abducted by bandits in China, sold into prostitution and shipped to San Francisco, purchased as a saloon hall girl in Oregon, who finally becomes a respected homesteader on the River of No Return, Idaho.

Sole Survivor (San Francisco' Design Enterprises, 1985). Recreation of the true-life story of Poon Lim, who held the Guiness World Record for survival at sea. Shipwrecked by a German submarine, Poon Lim used his ingenuity to survive 133 days on a wooden raft in the Atlantic.

Sze, Mai-mai

China (Cleveland: Western Reserve UP, 1944). Nonfiction.

Echo of a Cry. A Story Which Began in China (New York: Harcourt, Brace, 1945). Nonfiction. A thoughtful, humorous, poignant account of the childhood and young adulthood of a Chinese diplomat's daughter in China, England, and the United States. Illustrated by the author.

Silent Children (New York: Harcourt, Brace, 1948). Fiction. A band of homeless children in the aftermath of a war survive by stealing from the city across the river.

The Tao of Painting. A Study of the Ritual Disposition of Chinese Painting (New York: Pantheon, 1946). Nonfiction. A two-volume, fully illustrated study of Chinese painting.

Tan Yun (pseudonym for Adet Lin)

Our Family (New York: John Day, 1939). Written jointly, at age 16, with sisters Anor, 13, and Meimei, 8. The daughters of Lin Yutang paint amusing pictures of their famous father, their mother, themselves, their daily activities in the United States and abroad, and their memories of China.

Girl Rebel. The Autobiography of Hsieh Pingying with Extracts from Her New War Diaries (New York: John Day, 1940), trans. Adet and Anor Lin. Nonfiction.

Dawn Over Chungking (New York: John Day, 1941). Nonfiction. Coauthored with sisters Anor and Meimei. Teenagers' poignant response to firsthand experience of Japanese bombings during a return visit to China.

Flame from the Rock (New York: John Day, 1943). Fiction. Lively upper-class Kuanpo Shen falls in love with Wang Tsai, a taciturn peasant soldier, impressed into giving her blood when she was wounded in an air raid.

The Milky Way and Other Chinese Folk Tales (New York: Harcourt, Brace, 1961). Fiction. Traditional Chinese tales translated and retold for American readers.

Tan, Amy

The Joy Luck Club (New York: G. P. Putnam's Sons, 1989). Fiction. Interlaced first-person stories of four Chinese immigrant mothers and their American-born daughters, exploring the tensions, tragedies, jealousies, and love they share.

Telemaque, Eleanor Wong

It's Crazy to Stay Chinese in Minnesota (Nashville: Thomas Nelson, 1978). Fiction. A 17-year-old Chinese American girl, daughter of a restauranteur in a small town in Minnesota, struggles to find her own identity.

Watanna, Onoto (pseudonym for Winnifred Eaton Babcock Reeve)

Miss Nume of Japan: a Japanese-American Romance (Chicago: Rand, McNally, 1899). Fiction. Two couples, one American, one Japanese, cross paths and exchange partners. The Japanese man commits suicide; the Japanese woman marries a Caucasian.

A Japanese Nightingale (New York: Harper, 1901). Fiction. An American visiting Japan marries a beautiful Eurasian singer-dancer, who continually asks him for money and periodically disappears.

The Wooing of Wisteria (New York: Harper, 1902). Fiction. Lady Wisteria, from a socially outcast family, falls in love with the Prince of Mori, son of her father's enemy.

The Heart of Hyacinth (New York: Harper, 1903). Fiction. An English girl, reared by a Japanese woman, is claimed by her long-lost father but chooses to marry the Eurasian son of her adoptive mother.

Daughters of Nijo (New York: Macmillan, 1904). Fiction. The illegitimate daughter of the Prince of Nijo, restless and bored with her country village life, exchanges places with her look-alike half-sister in the palace.

The Love of Azalea (New York: Dodd, Mead, 1904). Fiction. A cruel stepmother chases young Azalea into the arms of an American missionary. After marriage, he is recalled home; she remains in Japan, undergoing tremendous suffering before they are reunited.

A Japanese Blossom (New York: Harper, 1906). Fiction. All the children in a Japanese family must adjust when their father marries an American woman with two children of her own. The 1905 war takes the father's life.

The Diary of Delia: Being a Veracious Chronicle of the Kitchen with Some Side-lights on the Parlour (New York: Page & Co., 1907). Fiction. Delia O'Malley, general housekeeper for the Wooley family, confides to her diary in Irish American dialect all her woes, her mistress' tempestuous love story, and her own clever way of finding out which of her two suitors really loves her, rather than her money.

Tama (New York: Harper, 1910). Fiction. An American professor in Japan, intrigued by reports of a fox spirit shunned and feared by villagers, captures her and discovers a beautiful, blind Eurasian orphan, living by her wits. He arranges an operation to restore her sight and marries her.

The Honorable Miss Moonlight (New York: Harper, 1912). Fiction. Against his mother's wishes, Lord Gonji loves and marries a beautiful geisha. Because she does not conceive after a year, he is forced to divorce her and remarry. Ironically, the second wife remains barren while the discarded wife bears his son and is restored to her place at his side.

Me, a Book of Remembrance (New York: Century, 1915). Fictionalized autobiography. Nora Ascough leaves home at age 17 with 10 dollars, a trusting nature, and high literary hopes. She works as a reporter in Jamaica, as a stenographer in a Chicago stockyard, accepts three proposals of marriage while loving a married playboy, and has her first novel accepted for publication in New York.

Marion: a Story of an Artist's Model by Herself and the Author of Me (New York: W. J. Watt, 1916). Nonfiction. The story of Winnifred's sister Sara's struggles to make a living as a painter and a model in Boston and New York.

Sunny-san (New York: George H. Doran, 1922). Fiction. A mistreated Japanese-Eurasian girl, a tightrope walker, "adopted" by a group of American boys in Japan comes to the United States years later to hold them to their promise to take care of her.

Cattle (London: Hutchinson, 1923; New York: W. J. Watt, 1924). Fiction. Nettie Day, purchased and raped by Bull Langdon, regains her dignity with the help of an independent woman and wins the man she loves.

His Royal Nibs (New York: W. J. Watt, 1925). Fiction. A seemingly bumbling English greenhorn attaching himself to P. D. McPherson's Albertan ranch turns out to be a painter and a hero and wins the hand of Hilda McPherson.

Waung-ling, Betty Siao-meng

Days of Joy (New York: Carlton, 1975). Nonfiction. Memoirs of the well-educated daughter of a well-to-do Shanghai family, of her marriage and life in Singapore, Australia, Nigeria, and Florida with her hotel-manager, restauranteur husband and four children.

Wei, Katherine and Terry Quinn

Second Daughter, Growing Up in China 1930–1949 (Boston: Little, Brown, 1984). Nonfiction. Memoir of difficult family relations, particularly mother–daughter tensions in an upper-class Westernized family in China.

Wong, Jade Snow

Fifth Chinese Daughter (New York: Harper & Row, 1945). Nonfiction. Jade Snow Wong recounts her childhood and upbringing in Chinatown, San Francisco, with very strict, traditional parents. She works her way through college and establishes her own ceramic studio.

No Chinese Stranger (New York: Harper & Row, 1975). Nonfiction. Jade Snow's life continued: marriage, children, and travel to Asia under the auspices of the US government.

Wong, Su-ling and Earl Herbert Cressy

Daughter of Confucius (New York: Farrar Strauss, 1952). Autobiography of the daughter of a wealthy Chinese family.

Yen, Maria

The Umbrella Garden (New York: Macmillan, 1954). Nonfiction. Student life under the new Communist rule becomes extremely regimented and oppressively supervised.

Index

About the Author

Born in Beijing, China, Amy Ling came to the United States at age six with her parents and younger brother. She attended American schools from first grade through a Ph.D. in comparative literature, but was rarely assigned a book by a woman and never by a writer of color. After completing her dissertation on the painter in the fiction of William Thackeray, Emile Zola and Henry James, she decided to complete her education by researching, reading, and writing about the work of ethnic minority American writers and of women. *Between Worlds: Women Writers of Chinese Ancestry* is the fruit of nearly a decade of her efforts to search for her "literary roots" in this country.

After working briefly as reservations agent for Air Canada and as a bilingual secretary in Paris, France, she began a career in teaching. She taught English in the Department of Foreign Languages and Literatures at Chengkung University in Tainan, Taiwan; writing and literature in the SEEK Program at the City College of New York and Brooklyn College; and Ethnic American literature and Women Writers at Rutgers and Georgetown Universities. In 1984, she published a chapbook of her poems and paintings, *Chinamerican Reflections*. In 1989–90 she was a Rockefeller Fellow in the Humanities at the Asian/American Center at Queens College of the City University of New York, working on her next project, a biography of the Eaton sisters, the first Asian American writers of fiction.

She makes her home in Washington, D.C. with her husband Gelston Hinds, Jr., a public administrator, their son Arthur, age 8, and daughter Catherine, 5.